The Essence of Therapy

In this book, Mo Mandić explores the very phenomenon of therapy, based on the fundamental question of being human, in order that therapy itself might be better understood in the light of this.

Psychotherapy, historically understood as a theory and practice that has emerged and developed over the past 120 years, has made few attempts to explore what it is that most fundamentally constitutes therapy from an experiential perspective. This book offers a language in which readers can understand the way that therapy unfolds, how it 'happens' and what gives it its essential character. It discusses the key elements of this form of caring for and towards the human being that distinguishes it from psychology, psychiatry, anthropology and social care. The book is presented in 14 main sections, each exploring a central feature that constitutes the essence of therapy. Concrete examples are also included where appropriate, in order to illustrate and emphasise the practical relevance and importance of another way of thinking both about and within therapy.

The book's contents will be accessible to new and experienced therapists, trainees and students who wish to engage in a more primordial understanding of therapy.

Mo Mandić, PhD, is a visiting lecturer at Regent's University London, School of Psychotherapy and Psychology and at the New School of Psychotherapy and Counselling.

'Mo Mandić's *The Essence of Therapy* is a breath of fresh air in the polluted atmosphere of current university courses for psychiatrists, psychologists, clinical counsellors and other "helpers". Therapy is a practical science, Aristotle wrote, like ethics and politics: no theory, no technique, no blueprint. To quote R. D. Laing, "Psychotherapy must remain an obstinate attempt of two people to arrive at a recovery of the wholeness of being human through the relationship between them". To do no harm, we all need to engage with this book'.

Andrew Feldmár, *author and a therapist for over 50 years, Vancouver, Canada*

'Mo Mandić has written a thoughtful, highly original and deeply reflective book, inviting readers into a profound engagement with Martin Heidegger's later philosophy and its implications for therapy in the present age. Mandić challenges therapeutic conventions, encouraging practitioners to move beyond rigid theories and attend instead to *Ereignis*, to the disclosive event of being itself. Both demanding and rewarding, the book is an essential read for existential psychotherapists and those willing to question the foundations of their own self-understanding'.

Kevin Aho, *Professor of Philosophy, Florida Gulf Coast University, USA*

The Essence of Therapy

Heideggerian Deliberations on Being Human

Mo Mandić

Routledge
Taylor & Francis Group
LONDON AND NEW YORK

Designed cover image: Mint Images © Getty Images

First published 2027
by Routledge
4 Park Square, Milton Park, Abingdon, Oxon OX14 4RN

and by Routledge
605 Third Avenue, New York, NY 10158

Routledge is an imprint of the Taylor & Francis Group, an informa business

British Library Cataloguing-in-Publication Data
A catalogue record for this book is available from the British Library

ISBN: 978-1-041-07077-1 (hbk)
ISBN: 978-1-041-07075-7 (pbk)
ISBN: 978-1-003-63869-8 (ebk)

DOI: 10.4324/9781003638698

Typeset in Times New Roman
by KnowledgeWorks Global Ltd.

For Teo

Contents

Acknowledgements

Certain moments tend to present themselves as opportunities to pursue one's interests in ways that could neither have ever been imagined nor foreseen. The unexpected invitation of my colleague, Dr Alfred Denker, then Director of the Martin Heidegger Archive in Messkirch, Germany, to pay an extended visit to Messkirch castle, gave me complete access to the Heidegger archives preserved there, over the period of my month-long stay, from 10th December 2023 to 10th January 2024. It was at that time that I was heavily immersed in reading and being challenged by Heidegger's later lectures and texts, all of which came some years after his renowned work, *Being and Time*. Living in rooms looking directly out onto St Martin's Church and Heidegger's family home was a form of inspiration for me, insofar as I was, at the same time, able to forego the many routines that usually structured my days, and to simply set more time aside for thinking, or rather, let thinking happen. This book can be said to be a contribution towards what opened and revealed itself.

Students over the years have immeasurably enriched my world in the light of my continued efforts to make further sense of therapy. It is they who have continually reminded me that an openness to questioning is the basis of any approach that considers itself to be therapeutic in any way. May they continue to bestow me with this gift, for which I am deeply grateful.

Family and friends have always been the mainstay and support for me throughout all my challenges and sojourns in the course of writing this book. This is now my chance to thank them all and to say how much I appreciate their being there for me when it all really matters.

Lastly, many thanks to the editorial team at Routledge, namely, Alice Maher, Pragati Sharma and Uma Maheswari for helping to bring the text to a more presentable standard.

Introduction

This book draws centrally on the voluminous writings of Martin Heidegger, a German philosopher, who lived from 1889 to 1976. He was born in Messkirch, a small town in Southern Germany. Initially, Heidegger was destined for the priesthood, but then changed his mind, devoting himself instead to studying philosophy at Freiburg University. His reading of a book given by the rector of the secondary school that he attended as a student determined his lifelong project of addressing the question of being, or what it is for anything to simply *be*.

Heidegger's extensive writings, presented to us through lecture notes, transcripts, essays, personal reflections and narrativized conversations, challenge us to extend our thinking beyond the ideas we encounter in his rich and complex text, *Being and Time*. It is this work that is most commonly introduced as the main source and reference for discussing Heidegger's ideas with students and trainees pursuing a more phenomenological and existential orientation. But as Heidegger himself later remarked, this text did not manage to free itself from the very issues that he was attempting to overturn, transcend or dismantle. Should this be construed as a failure of sorts, however, it is only a failure on *our* part to see what Heidegger had been attempting to do, as becomes clearer when we read the later lectures and essays. For him, to think was to follow a certain path, rather than to settle upon a final answer. This is clearly reflected in his inscription at the beginning of his collected writings, 'ways, not works'.

It is Heidegger's later contributions that have been of particular interest to me, given that they extend his thinking in important ways when considered in relation to therapy and human existence. However, it is these very texts that also pose particular difficulties in both understanding and making accessible to therapists the thoughts that are being expressed, let alone conveying their relevance and significance to the world of therapy today. Anyone who picks up a later essay, for example, will have the experience of being able to follow the first few pages, which set out a more familiar way of thinking about the topic being addressed, but then be confronted with a wall of seeming impenetrability in understanding what then follows. There are good reasons for this, and I urge readers who find themselves in this position to persist with the challenge of continually questioning what is being attempted. Heidegger was in the privileged position of being able to draw on the history of Western thinking

DOI: 10.4324/9781003638698-1

over the past 2500 years in order to see something about the whole trajectory of our understanding of ourselves, but that has at the same time taken us away from ourselves, or at least been deflected away from a return to the rich insights already articulated by the early Greek thinkers, particularly, Anaximander, Heraclitus, Parmenides and Empedocles.

Why This Book?

Over the years, I have come to appreciate the occasional settings and discussions that moved me towards a questioning of the very ideas that various therapeutic approaches embraced as distinct orientations of their own. But not only this. It was the attempt to question the fundamental basis of therapy itself, to try to reach beyond the theories and schools that have become almost second-nature to our understanding of it as a practice. What is it that makes therapy what it is? To address this question by responding to it with yet another theory or 'answer' is to misunderstand the question, and to therefore deviate from what is being asked.

In this book, I try to stay with what is simply given in the happening of therapy, rather than attempting to provide an account of how therapy is done. Many introductory texts on counselling and psychotherapy will typically lay out the nature of therapy by attending to its various enumerated or identified attributes, providing an explication of its workings, as well as offering evidence that supports its effectiveness (see Lykou, 2025 and McLeod, 2025, for example). The *givenness* of what presents itself as therapy, however, is prior to any such conceptual or theoretically-oriented way of thinking about therapy that ultimately attempts to map a correspondence between concepts and theories onto therapy itself, rather than letting therapy 'speak for itself'. Hearing it in its speaking presents us with a much more difficult and onerous task than resorting to any theory. It is therefore incumbent on us to listen closely to what emerges, whilst acknowledging that such an attempt will always be open to further thinking and clarification.

To take some terms that Heidegger himself introduces in *Being and Time*, we can track the way in which we stray from what is given and then move into something more conceptual and fixed. The most basic sense of being-with or being in a with-world, for example, *precedes* our current understanding of ourselves as autonomous, separate, isolated or individual beings. From the basic sense of the phenomenon of being-with, one might be tempted towards thinking in terms of, 'relation', such that the 'being' in being-with has now slipped out of the picture, leaving us with a noun that is inclined more towards a Cartesian understanding. From 'relation', we might then think in terms of 'relationship', and that then takes us to a rather familiar term in most therapeutic approaches, which is 'inter-subjectivity'. Or we can think of 'being in the truth', so to speak, or 'true-ing', as I put it, which is the fundamental sense of existing and disclosing ourselves as we are in our very way of being. By contrast, we are accustomed to think rather more abstractly about truth as a correspondence relation between what we might say or think about something, someone or a situation, and the actual thing, person or situation itself. For example, 'John is walking towards me' is a true statement insofar as it correctly corresponds to John's *actual* walking towards me.

Who Are We?

It is perhaps a seeming irrelevance to therapists to underline the fact that we are historical beings. This is something that we already assume, tend to forget or take for granted, but we do so at our peril. Why? Because it leads to a metaphysical understanding of truth, of being human and of a meaningful existence, which our current age and understanding of what it is to be human assumes is the highest, truest and *only* possible understanding. We think historiographically, rather than historically, in other words. When we think historically, we open ourselves to the fact that our current technological age does <u>not</u> reflect the *final* understanding of what it is to be as anything, including being human. To acknowledge this opens us to a way of relating to ourselves and our age differently. This is also pertinent to the domain of therapy, where an overwhelming resistance to confronting itself, and asking deeper questions about the tenets upon which it rests, persists to this day. When we relate to therapy itself as historical, we open it to questioning and further understanding, rather than as something that conforms to a more technological and time-independent understanding.

Posing the question of who we are is to reflect on who we have become, and are becoming. Very sketchily, and amateurishly on my part here, we can quickly present an account of how such change has taken hold in relation to ourselves. For example, with the advent of industrialisation, our world moved away from a more agrarian society and community into one that introduced machinery, processes, production and the organisation of labour to convert such raw materials as steel and coal into usable sources of energy. This allowed for a transformation of economies on an enormous scale, as well as political and societal changes that impacted on the ways in which we came to relate to ourselves. In other words, we were drawn into other forms of existence that were new and unfamiliar to us.

Industrialisation and industrialised society, over time, became deeply embedded in our world, such that it brought us to shape our lives around the kinds of activities that we chose to pursue. Our world became structured in a way that provided us with possibilities, but only those possibilities that were available within the pre-existing social, economic and cultural framework that had already established itself, and into which we were already thrown. This resonates for us in how we now find ourselves today, as we live through an age of information that brings with it its own considerable challenges, both for us and our world, as it undergoes rapid and radical reconfigurations and transformations.

Our Modern age has valorised the idea of autonomy and maturity as central to our understanding of ourselves. This has mostly been promoted through the kinds of work that we pursue, projects that absorb us and meaningful worlds that we embrace. At certain times, however, we welcome the time and space to reflect on and consider ways of thinking about who we are, and how we have articulated and grounded ourselves in established styles of certain practices over the course of our own lives. Such a possibility to reflect, and to express ourselves through thoughts and feelings, is to address the issue of our being in a way that we rarely, if ever, find occasion to experience in our lives. Most of the time, we coast along in the every-day, that is, the social and cultural practices that carry us along in our existence, but moments do arise for many of us where certain disruptions and breakdowns open us to glimpse the tensions that we experience between, on the one hand, belonging with and being amongst others, and, on the other, being ourselves. Our political, economic, social and cultural age's emphasis on autonomy and being individuated as citizens and voters also impacts on how we relate to others and ourselves, particularly in the case of difficulties that can sometimes manifest for us.

Metaphysics

Much of what is covered in the book refers to metaphysics. This is a term that should not overwhelm us. Our understanding of therapy is framed in terms of metaphysics, which means that it is fundamentally representational in character. In being representational, it is founded upon a dualist picture of the human being. This dualism says that we are made of two basic kinds of 'stuff': the mental, and the material (or extended). We might refer to each as two wholly different kinds of substance, but this suggests something physical and spatial, which is not applicable to the domain of the mental. The dualism here is a fixed and atemporal understanding of ourselves, and so is meta-physical – beyond (*meta*) what is apprehensible (physical) – thereby making a universal claim about what is *ultimately* true about us. In other words, no 'higher' truth is possible than the truth that is presented to us in metaphysics.

Therapy adheres to theory, or some other abstract set of ideas, as the basis for matching or corresponding aspects of theory to the client's presented issues and experience. When a client talks about the anxiety of working with their boss, for example, a metaphysical interpretation links the experience with a theory about father-son relationships, or draws on the idea of human 'dysregulation' to account for some lack, deficiency or deviation from what is considered as being 'regulated'. Another way of putting it is that there is a tendency in therapy to experience its effectiveness and semblance of power through the use and application of abstract concepts that reside in the world of the supersensible, to use a Platonic idea. The supersensible lies beyond the world in which we live, so to speak, which is the sensible world, or world of the senses. On this picture, then, any attempt to understand the human from 'inside' the world is riven with imperfection and thereby invalidated. In this way, a metaphysically-oriented therapy succumbs to an understanding of itself as a system, and attempts to systematise and structure its approach such that it establishes itself as a school of thought or orientation.

According to our accustomed Western way of thinking, *being* and *becoming* have become separated, mainly through the contributions of Plato and Aristotle (Capobianco, 2021:462). The metaphysical tradition that developed from them has understood the *being* of anything as timeless, universal, replete and real, whilst becoming was something incomplete and therefore lacking in being. In other words, to be is to endure in its presence, and thereby is real – or 'really' real. Becoming was only 'on the way', so to speak, and therefore time-bound, provisional and unreliable. Heidegger's project, by contrast, has been to encompass both being and becoming as one.

Essence

The usual way in which we think of 'essence' when we ask about the essence of something, and in this case, of therapy, is to reflect on what it is that defines it, and identifies certain necessary and sufficient conditions for it to be the very thing that it is in the first place. One way of doing this is to contrast therapy with what it is *not*, in order to expose the differences that then somehow determine it with certainty. So, to continue with the example of therapy, we might say that it is not coaching, or nursing, or psychiatry. As we do so, we illuminate the differences that underline the difference. In a more positivistic way, we might claim that the essence of something is to describe its function or purpose. On a more mundane level, then, the essence of the scissors is to cut, cut through, separate. Of course, they may have many other uses, such as their being used as a paperweight, or a weapon of sorts. But this, and I take it that we all agree, is not the true essence of the scissors.

By contrast, I am interested in pursuing a different sense of 'essence' here, which is the way in which something moves, unfolds and happens in its temporal character. A German 19th century philosopher, Georg F. W. Hegel, pursued this approach using a method of *dialectically* unfolding a concept, until its resolution could be brought out through a process of moving between one position (or 'thesis', as he called it), then to its 'antithesis', since it addressed the limitations of the prior position by providing an opposing position, and finally to the 'synthesis' of the two, but with both positions incorporated as necessary to the final resolved position in this process. In the case of therapy, its essence can only be brought out if its temporally unfolding character is illuminated in some way, rather than approached from an understanding of essence as static, permanent, cross-cultural, atemporal and unchanging. For example, stating that therapy is a way of supporting a person to alleviate their unease or suffering or sense of disorientation in no way captures how it manifests and takes its course when 'therapy-ing'.

The idea of an essence of therapy really follows the kind of language that Heidegger himself used in pursuing a question or topic, as is evident in the titles of certain essays and writings that he developed and revised over time. However, in his essay, *On The Essence of Truth* (2011), he thinks of essence in a verbal sense of an unfolding coming-to-be. The question of the essence is addressed in relation to many topics and themes that we encounter in his work. In each case, he subjects the phenomenon to an extended questioning and thinking, and finally comes to unveil what was hidden but was in need of uncovering. What he unveils is the *essence* of the thing or entity under enquiry. To provide a number of examples here, Heidegger attends to the essence of truth, which he unveils as unconcealment (ἀλήθεια); the essence of ground, as the nothing that allows beings as a whole, in their totality, to appear; the essence of freedom, as the fundamental openness of existence, but that is dependent upon truth; the essence of poetry, which is the primordial way in which being discloses itself through language; the essence of our human way of being-there, which is existence; the essence of language, which is the 'showing' of ἀλήθεια; the essence of dwelling, which is the preserving of the fourfold as a onefold; the essence of *Ereignis* (a term that Heidegger uses, but that I will not expand on in this book), which is gathering, appropriation, adaptation; the essence of nothing, which is the nihilation of beings as a whole; and the essence of technology, which is enframing (*Gestell*). Most of these terms will be covered in the course of what follows in certain chapters.

The Structure of the Book

Each chapter presents conversations that are presented in 'dialogical' form, as they are called, in Plato's writings. The purpose of this is both to present ideas and perspectives in the movement of the conversation, but also to try to show how the participants engage each other, rather than staunchly maintaining and protecting their positions. At the outset of some of the dialogues, the participants show a degree of uncertainty as they enter the discussion, unsure of how to begin. As the conversations open themselves more, they are increasingly attuned to the mood, the precariousness of their openness and their being taken along by the topic, rather than steering it according to their own preferences. In some cases, I then follow the conversations with comments and elucidations on the ideas that the conversations present, but also introduce a larger perspective on the topic being addressed in the chapter as a whole.

In focusing on a particular element of therapy, each chapter makes frequent repetitions of points as well as important terms and ideas that are to be found elsewhere in the book. This is somewhat inevitable, but also necessary, if the question of the essence of therapy is to be properly addressed. The process of attending to one aspect of therapy opens us to the overlaps and enmeshments with others. To take an example, thinking itself is a questioning, and questioning is to converse with others, which means listening to the truth of what is being disclosed. As already mentioned, metaphysics also features in certain chapters, as does theory and a representational approach to the topic under enquiry.

In order to provide a sense of what each chapter addresses, I very briefly summarise them in order to orient the reader towards their contents. A difficulty that persists, however, and one that is irresolvable, is the attempt to place the chapters in some kind of logically sequential order, since the topics overlap and constitute a whole, rather than being separate from each other. In other words, each chapter is so interwoven with the others that it has been somewhat challenging to place them in some kind of satisfactory ordering. In that sense, I think it is very likely that reading certain chapters will involve a degree of a backwards and forwards, to-and-fro movement and cross-checking between different parts of the book. The chapter summaries are as follows.

Dis-close-ing is a term that reflects the fact that we are self-disclosive beings, that is, beings who disclose a world. This already suggests that we are familiar with what 'world' means. This is explicated using Heidegger's clarifications on this, in order to then reflect on the distinction between disclosedness and discoveredness, the relation of disclosedness to care, place and placedness, and finally, their relevance to therapy.

True-ing addresses our familiarity with the term, 'truth', in order to then distinguish it from a more basic and primordial sense of its unconcealing character. True-ing, in its dynamic sense, is explored through different 'levels' of what we mean by 'truth', in order to arrive at an understanding of truth as disclosing.

Gather-ing is a term that is important for Heidegger and emerges out of his thinking and reading of the early Greek thinkers. The chapter introduces other terms that are associated with gathering, including event-ing, letting, allowing and unifying unity. It is also addressed in its relation to conversation, but also considered in its bearing on phenomenological enquiry.

Converse-ing is central to therapy, and contrasted with 'dialogue'. Other thinkers' contributions on the meaning of conversation are also explicated, in order to then bring the chapter to a close with some thoughts and reflections on its bearing on therapy.

Listen-ing is a necessary feature of the therapeutic relationship. However, whilst everyday listening, or listening in other settings and contexts is well understood, I claim that therapeutic listening is very different in character. This is addressed by exploring the *act* of listening, as well as the ways that it attends to the client's way of being.

Question-ing is similarly a necessary aspect of therapy. This is brought out more by looking at other forms of questioning, and then turning our attention to the therapy setting in which it is understood more as a questing, opening up and enquiring.

Dwell-ing is then explored in relation to therapy and the client's experience of being at home, homelessness, being out of place, alienation, homecoming and dwelling in the world.

Think-ing is an aspect of therapy that is much neglected, except for certain therapeutic approaches that confine it to a cognitive understanding. Sections in this chapter elaborate on different ways of thinking, or a more philosophical approach that elucidates the various forms of thinking, and then considers thinking from a more existential perspective.

Care-ing is addressed in the chapter that follows. This is the very way in which human beings are 'structured' as the beings that they are. Different perspectives on care are offered, in order to then attend to Heidegger's approach to this. Some attention is given to care as it relates to the age in which we find ourselves, with a view to showing how therapy itself is essential if we are to preserve and safeguard the very meaning of being human.

Play-ing is a sorely neglected aspect of therapy, though it is prevalent in certain therapeutic approaches, such as child therapy and dramatherapy. Different understandings of play are considered, as well as elaborations on the role of play in the work of two major exponents of therapy.

Ungrounded Ground-ing is covered in a chapter that includes a discussion of the notion of ground, being grounded, the nothing, abyss and groundless ground. This is then all brought to a final section that addresses its relation to therapy.

Intuit-ing is a particularly overlooked topic when considered with respect to therapy. Some attention is given to unravelling this notion in order to get clearer on how we might understand it. Since there are questions that challenge the idea of intuition, these are addressed in relation to cognition and also bias. A separate section also looks at the relation of intuition to play, followed by comments on certain selected thinkers' stances on this term.

Clear-ing, a specific term introduced by Heidegger, attends to the way in which openness, or a space of possibilities, can become distorted or filled, such that metaphysics takes hold. Where this happens, we are placed along a path of eventual nihilism, because truth as unconcealment becomes reduced to something else, so that we lose the sense of living in the truth, so to speak.

Free-ing, as the final chapter, moves us towards an understanding of the essence of therapy, which is freedom. A conceptual understanding of freedom is first considered, followed by Heidegger's own account. This then moves on to a section that explores freedom and its challenges in our age, given the way that the essence of technology drives everything towards optimisation, resources, calculation, machination and acceleration.

As a final note, frequent references are made to Heidegger's *Being and Time* in some of the chapters that follow. In order to direct the reader to the relevant passages and terms from that work, I use the abbreviation 'BT', followed by the page number in the English edition.

Chapter 1

Dis-close-ing

Introduction

This chapter attends to a particular understanding of ourselves as *world-disclosers*. This is so basic and 'close' to us, existentially speaking, and also farthest from us in terms of our awareness. It is also difficult to understand if we start from our accustomed way of seeing ourselves as independent, detached beings who 'sit inside' an 'outside', external world. Such a picture of ourselves rests on, and is underpinned by, a philosophical position known as *realism*, namely, that our thought, speech, knowledge and experience is independent of an external reality that we call 'nature', or 'world' in its material, objective sense. As a direct challenge to this, an alternative picture of ourselves is our always already being enmeshed in a world. That is, our existence is only possible on the basis of there being a world at all, such that our being and the world are a *unitary* phenomenon. In other words, there is only the 'oneness' of existing-in-the-world. Given that we are worldly beings, we are always *disclosing* our world. In being world-disclosers, we can *discover* things around us, but only if there is something about our way of being, namely being human, that always already *discloses* a world in the first place. This is an important feature of being human for therapists to appreciate, as it addresses the very way in which we understand ourselves and our clients as existing beings. In attending to the idea of disclosedness, a clear distinction between 'discovering' and 'disclosing' needs to be made, which I will go on to clarify as we turn our attention to these terms.

Conversation on Dis-close-ing

Thinker: Based purely upon my own thoughts about what therapy offers, it's a way of helping people to overcome issues that they see as problems at a certain point in their lives.

Therapist: Well, yes, OK. I think that would be how I hear many people describe it. But I would try maybe to refine it a little more. It's basically a space that invites a process in which the client feels that they can open up.

DOI: 10.4324/9781003638698-2

Thinker: Yes, I see. An opening up.

Therapist: Which actually means much *more* than might initially appear, I think.

Thinker: Perhaps we can say that it's a *speaking* that opens up what is currently preoccupying them.

Therapist: Yes.

Thinker: But this is based on the fact that we are all *already* disclosing all the time. In other words, we are disclosers by dint of being human.

Therapist: You mean something more basic than opening up something or other, in terms of talking about it in the therapy session?

Thinker: Yes. I'm describing the way that we fundamentally *are* as human beings.

Therapist: That we're disclosive beings?

Thinker: Yes. The client is a world discloser. They disclose a world. But they are also *self*-disclosing in being disclosive beings, or world disclosers. And so we're fundamentally open beings.

Therapist: Let's go back a step. That sounds like a bit of an important distinction that you made there. I want to try and get clearer on this. The client might talk about things in the sessions, and that's their opening something up as they talk. But what if they open something that they had not previously opened up? They hear something new or different in what they are saying, in other words.

Thinker: In that sense, they are *dis-covering* or un-covering something. They hear something that they hadn't discovered before.

Therapist: There's still an uncovering there.

Thinker: Yes, but it's still in the explicitness of the conversation, if you see what I mean.

Therapist: So, why not call it 'disclosing' something, then? Why a discovering? You mentioned that the client is a discloser, didn't you? And where does disclosing end and discovering start?

Thinker: As I already mentioned, there is, as you say, a distinction that we need to be clear on so that we are sure we understand what is being named here. When the client, and all of us, for that matter, uncovers something, they see what they have uncovered, which is a discovering of something. That discovering can be of something in or about the world, or something that they discover about themselves. But in order to be able to discover things about the world and about oneself, I need to recognise something about the kind of being that I am. And that is that I am a disclosive being. I am not a thing, like the pen or the table. They don't have it imbued in their way of being that they are disclosive beings. Being disclosive is the condition for the possibility that we can claim to discover something or other.

Therapist: So, we have our way of being that is unlike anything else, and that is to be disclosive.

Thinker: Yes, it's so basic to us that we never really acknowledge this or notice it. Just as the fact that we are fundamentally finite beings. To stay with that for just a second, we disclose our finitude. When we acknowledge this feature of ourselves, that we are disclosive beings, that changes the way that therapists might approach their understanding of therapy and of their clients in their work.

Therapist: I'd be really interested to see how that might impact on therapeutic work with clients. I might be able to dig out something that I drafted some time ago in preparation for some students to look at and discuss as a group. But more on that later. Back to the idea that we're disclosive beings.

Thinker: Another term that we could use instead of disclosedness is that we are being 'there'. We are in a world, we find ourselves in a situation, we are there. I might ask someone, was my friend, Carlos, in the restaurant earlier? And the reply that might come is, yes, he was there. The 'there' is that we are always in the disclosing of being there. Insofar as I exist, what it means to exist is that I'm always already finding myself there, which we can then describe concretely as a place, somewhere or other.

Therapist: It's so basic, as you say, that we already understand it in our way of going about the world.

Thinker: Yes, very basic, but the overriding tendency is to not see this *because* it's so basic to us. It reflects our need to just describe how we are, rather than getting caught up in theories, abstractions and clever stories about our way of being, which, in fact, just take us away from the fundaments. If we are clear on our fundamental way of being, we aren't so tempted to go astray and get into metaphysical, that is, abstracted theoretical accounts of our way of being human.

Therapist: Yes, from what I have already understood, metaphysics already takes us as a mind and body, internal and external, feeling and thinking and various other dualisms that develop from that picture of ourselves.

Thinker: So, disclosedness is the way we humans exist. We exist insofar as we disclose. In disclosing, we exist. I'm trying to put it in as many ways as I can, but I'm just saying the same thing.

Therapist: OK. But insofar as we exist as disclosive beings, as you said, we disclose a world, and we disclose ourselves in our being, or existing. Is that where it ends?

Thinker: No, not at all. We can elaborate on this a little more.

Therapist: Please do.

Thinker: One way that we might disclose ourselves is when we experience a certain feeling of being unsettled by the way that we are living. We coast along, we're happy enough, everything is in its place. But we have this underlying question, is this how I want to live?

Therapist: The finger points back to ourselves, that's right.

Thinker: It's a moment of being explicit towards oneself in bringing out the question.

Therapist: So, that's a conversation with oneself, in a way. It's like a background hum that starts to emerge.

Thinker: Yes. The career that we happen to be in, the organisation that we work for, the projects and challenges that we pursue, they all gather themselves into something that is meaningful for us. And yet, at a certain point, there's something like a silent voice that is beckoning us, summoning us to open ourselves to the biggest question: is this really *me* owning me in my way of existing?

Therapist: Or, as is the case for many and for the most part, am I living my life in a way that just tries to fit in with the way that everyone else thinks and endorses as living a good, respectable, successful life?

Thinker: Yes, that's it. The voice is drawing us towards having to answer *to ourselves* whether we are being true to *our* existence or not. It's uniquely our own. It might well be that we get a sense that we've invested so much time and energy doing what we think is 'right', but right for whom? We really then start creeping towards an understanding of ourselves as mortal rather than eternal and immortal, like gods.

Therapist: That's all in the background though. There's rarely a moment in therapy, unless it comes up in very specific cases, where the client really understands this.

Thinker: They disclose themselves as mortal beings as they go out into the world and engage with others, and themselves, differently. They face the situations that they find themselves in rather than deflecting themselves away from them. They comport themselves mortally, if you like. As disclosive beings, we might add, they disclose themselves authentically. They find themselves in situations, and they deal with them not in some kind of formulaic way, but as if they encounter them for the very first time. That the situation is always treated as a 'one-off' rather than as a repetition of the same.

Therapist: What's important about that? 'As if for the very first time'?

Thinker: If they deal with a situation in a habitualised way, they're on auto-pilot. They take themselves *as* themselves out of the situation, or stand at a safe distance from it, and don't really open themselves to it. They take an inauthentic stance, in other words.

Therapist: So, I think it would help me if we both look at this fictionalised transcript that I put together before our meeting, of a client that I call 'Jasmine'. It seems to be appropriate to what we have been discussing, so it's timely. I'm drawing on a possible way that a client might present something, and how I imagine a conversation might go. I want to get some of your reactions to it, if that's OK.

Thinker: I'll try my best.

Therapist: OK, here goes. Remember, it's only a snippet of a whole session, but I've edited it in various ways so that it doesn't really truly convey the *real* time in which the conversation happens, and the way that both of them are being together. But that's the limitation of any transcript format. I'm just trying to illuminate some possible things that we can discuss.

Transcript

Jasmine: I'm feeling really confused at the moment. I have been single for three years. I own my own flat, have a secure career working free-lance as a consultant, but I'm just angry all the time. I can't see why, but I just know I am. I have friends. Both of my brothers are married with kids, and I get on well with them.

Therapist: You mentioned being confused and it's your anger that's confusing?

Jasmine: Yes. There is nothing to be angry about, is what I'm saying.

Therapist: It's more a mood?

Jasmine: Yes, like a cloud hanging over me. I just see myself getting into a rage about everything and everyone around me.

Therapist: Everything?

Jasmine: (Pause). I don't really have anything to be angry about. I wanted kids myself, but the guys I was in relationships with didn't work out, they were quite tempestuous and explosive.

Therapist: Your partners were explosive? Or the relationships? Or both?

Jasmine: The relationships. My friends are fine, though, I get on with them, but we're not close, really.

Therapist: Close in the sense of …

Jasmine: Well, I get a bit exercised and irritated by them at times, which ends up with me getting a bit heated in the conversations. When things quieten down, they've told me that I can be a bit unpredictable.

Therapist: What do you make of 'unpredictable' when you hear them saying that to you?

Jasmine: Not sure. (Long pause). I guess I'm prone to just launch into something and get really animated, especially if it's something they've said that I think is wrong. I just get annoyed, but I suppose it just comes out of nowhere for them and escalates quickly. (Pause).

Therapist: That 'unpredictable' and 'escalation': it only comes up with friends?

Jasmine: (Pause). I get angry with my parents at times too. I really upset them once, and I felt so bad afterwards.

Therapist: What was 'bad' about it, then, for you?

Jasmine: They're good people, you know? I mistreated them, verbally abused them when I shouldn't have. It wasn't right. (Pause). It brings me back to my feeling confused about why I'm so angry.

Therapist: And it's with people, right?

Jasmine: Yes, of course it is.

Therapist: I just wondered, as you didn't mention things, being angry with things at all.

Jasmine: Things do happen, and I get angry about them happening in the way that they do. But people get to me, I suppose. I've tried all kinds of ways of looking at this: going on retreats, courses, going to therapy, getting away for a while. Nothing changes.

Therapist: How have you engaged with these things?

Jasmine: How do you mean?

Therapist: How have you been when you've really got involved with these things?

Jasmine: I gave them all a go, stuck through them, and at the end – nothing. Nada. Zilch.

Therapist: What was it like as you were going through them?

Jasmine: Did what I was asked to do, went along with it, did and acted as I was instructed, but it didn't change things.

Therapist: You went along with these things …

Jasmine: Yes, I told you. Why do you say it like that?

Therapist: Like what?

Jasmine: Like that!

Therapist: What did you hear in what I said?

Jasmine: As if going along with things was … not enough. I did everything that I was meant to do, I wanted it to change things. But it didn't.

Therapist: I'm sure you did. I hear that. What I was wondering was *how* you were being in the doing of the 'going along with it'.

Jasmine: (Takes a long pause before speaking again). When I graduated out of college 14 years ago, I found a job in junior management with a large corporate financial services organisation. It was a buzz going straight into a new job, and also getting reasonably well-paid from the start. Career prospects looked good, the pension scheme was very generous and I just felt that I was on the ladder to building something of myself. It got tougher as time went on, and responsibilities started to mount as I got promoted and took on some of the more prestigious, high-value accounts. After a while, I fell into a relationship and things went really well. I was happy. We liked doing the same things, we had a good social circle of friends and we had enough money to get away on a frequent basis. Life was good. (Long pause). And now … as I think about it … (pause).

Therapist: How is it now?

Jasmine: It's different. I'm feeling I'm getting into a rut, but I can't admit it, because there is so much at stake. I want something to change.

Therapist: So, if you change some things, it will change how you are now?

Jasmine: I think so.

Therapist: And there isn't something that you can actually point to that you could change?

Jasmine: No. (Looks withdrawn and distant, as if not wanting to be here. A minute of silence follows). I want something more, but I don't know what that is. Or something different. My job. I have this picture of myself doing this job, being in finance for the rest of my working career. And I don't like it.

Thinker: This is a helpful way of going into the detail of what we were talking about and how it's being expressed in this piece that you've written. Let's take it bit by bit, shall we?

Therapist: Yes, though I also think we shouldn't lose sight of the whole at the same time.

Thinker: Very good point. The first thing is that the client is disclosing an all-encompassing disposition, mood, or an 'atmosphere' in which she lives. It's anger and irritation. She is naming and uncovering, or dis-covering it in saying that it's anger, but, really, she is *disclosing* something through her living in a mood or disposition of anger. She sees the world through these red-tinted glasses or lenses that colour the world as irritating, not giving her her due, not meeting her … I'm guessing all the possible things that the angry mood might be disclosing, but not speaking and discovering. Mood is a '*background*' disposition, in the sense that you can't observe and 'see' your mood. It's like the fish in water: try as much as you might to show the fish that it's a completely underwater life that it lives, you'll fail. So, your client here is seeing her anger in the moment, the present moment in which it manifests. But mood is always already how she finds herself. It already has been that way, it has a 'before the present moment' quality to it, because it was there all along before you notice it now, and now, and now … You're just catching hold of it now and *discovering* it as an angry feeling as you talk about it.

Therapist: I like the idea of the client's mood 'colouring' everything. What I'm sensing with the client is this: if I feel that something is holding me back, and I want to go forward, I'm in that tension. Because I don't really see or understand what's holding me back, I feel irritated, frustrated. But maybe I also don't know where I'm headed if I *do* free myself of whatever it is that's pulling me back. So, it feels really overwhelming.

Thinker: Yes, so mood is disclosing the client in that respect.

Therapist: And I think the transcript tries to stay with the anger. But at a certain point, the client gets a little angry or irritated with the therapist as well. There was an attempt to invite the client to reveal, uncover or discover something as she was in the experience, in the conversation, in the session.

Thinker: Yes, and that could have been a moment where the client further unveils something about her world. But for me, there is also something in that moment between therapist and client that is about *time*, or temporality, that is being disclosed. When I get irritated, for example, I'm in some way pointing towards time as not being more meaningful for me, or that time is being wasted, or that the other person isn't keeping up to speed with me, or being in sync with me. If we're out of sync, time gets disrupted. It's a kind of, 'catch up, will you?!' attitude. And that links to wanting to feel understood in some way.

Therapist: That certainly is a 'walking alongside' that I think reflects what happens in therapy. But only in terms of 'being alongside', not in 'understanding alongside', since that is an ongoing conversation about the client disclosing more and more of their world.

Thinker: In reading it, I also have the feeling of a certain tension between showing up in the world in a certain way, and the extent to which she feels a little disconnected from that, at odds with herself. Is this really me, she is asking herself.

Therapist: There's much more to say about this client and her disclosing herself in the therapy room, but maybe we can come back to it again in another conversation.

Disclosing and Discovering Worlds

In order to come to an understanding of disclosedness, we have already said that such disclosedness is the disclosing of a *world.* This is essential to existence in a way that simply cannot be said of non-human beings, such as tables, chairs, pencils and the various things and other entities that show up in the world. In the attempt to unravel this a little more, we first ask, what is a 'world' in the first place? We can think of this in four distinct ways, according to Heidegger (BT93). Attending to the world will allow us a way to understand what we mean by it in the way that it has been presented. To put this as plainly as possible, the four ways of understanding 'world' are:

1 The things contained within the world
2 The way of being of things in a world
3 The placedness of things within a world
4 Being-in-the-world

1 A first way to understand 'world' is the totality of all the things, beings, or entities that are in place, or are placed, in an enormous physical container, which we call the 'world'. Here we can think of the way that we tend to use the word to refer to our planet Earth as the natural world that is external to us and that we each occupy, or 'move inside', so to speak. We find any number of beings and entities, such as books, knives, cars and houses that are also explicitly identifiable objects within it. This is a realist understanding of world.
2 A second sense of 'world' is to think of it in terms of the way that we talk about the 'world of theatre', or the 'world of fashion'. This collects all the relevant beings that are within that particular world, so that it effectively says how they are being, rather than just thinking of them as objects, or things, as in the first sense. For example, in the world of theatre, the hall, amphitheatre, building, actors, the stage, the play, to name just a few of the many features, have their way of being, or their 'is-ing', only insofar as they fall within the world of theatre.

3 A third sense of 'world' is the place or site in which we live, whether it be our house, country, continent and so on. This refers to a geographical space that is strictly impersonal. We measure and express distances in terms of the location of things, and we frequently use mathematics and geometry to do this where greater precision and accuracy is warranted.
4 The fourth and last sense of 'world' is the way in which we ourselves *are* as humans, which is 'being-in-the-world'. This is not to see ourselves as objects of some kind, one item among numerous others in a container, as described in the first sense of 'world', nor as being 'placed' in a world, as in the third sense of 'world', but as wholly absorbed in dealing with situations in which we already find ourselves, being 'space-ish' in a way that is not found in tables and chairs, reckoning with the temporal aspects of our way of being, whilst at the same time, experiencing a certain overarching mood that 'colours' our world in some way or other, whether it be dark, grey, flat, uneven, glowing bright, or cold, for example.

Discovering and Disclosing

In the case of the second and fourth senses – that is, the worlds that show up, including the world of therapy, in the second meaning, and being-in-the-world in the fourth – they are not so much discovered *by* us, but disclosed *to* us. For the most part, when we attend to our worlds, we *discover* all the various things, items or entities that are to be encountered. But in order to discover any number of things, we are necessarily always already disclosing our world. We cannot be otherwise, because we are being-in-the-world. Our world and being-in-the-world are not explicit things that can somehow be objectified, as in the first and third senses of 'world', which is a world in which there are a totality of various things that we can see and grasp and hold, as well as point to as the particular place that is our home. In these instances, we discover what is there. As said already, but in another way, the condition for the possibility of discovering the world and its entities is that a world be disclosed in the first place, since, to repeat, to be human is to be a world-discloser. This is something that we cannot observe about ourselves, as if standing outside and apart from ourselves, as temporal beings. That would be to assume that the human being and disclosedness are separate entities that we can then just somehow glue together. To think in such a way assumes that disclosedness is a property that is attributed to us, and that it is something that could also be lost, much like losing our hearing or sight. Similarly, our talk about being-in-the-world means that our being cannot be somehow seen as being independent of the world: hence the hyphenation that emphasises this.

Disclosedness

Now that we have moved a little closer towards a sense of the distinction between discoveredness and disclosedness, how might we further our understanding of disclosedness itself? A way of putting this is to say that, insofar as we are worldly beings, our world 'lights up'. We usually grasp the idea of something lighting up when we enter into a completely pitch-dark space, and then a light being switched on. This, however, is not what we mean here by a lighting up of a world. The lighting up, or illumination, is always already and constantly switched on, such that we always discover something or other (even a dark space) *in* the illumination. This happens, then, because it is already 'built into' the way that we encounter the world, in its very constitution and as the constant 'being switched on' of the illumination. As well as this, the illumination is not something that we can see, but is simply reflected in our encountering things and entities in the world.

Another, and related term that we can use here in terms of the lighting up, is the 'clearing'. There is always an 'opening up', which is the basis for anything being discovered or apprehended. As a way of bringing this out as concretely as possible, we can think of the way in which someone is experiencing so much disorientation and confusion in their life at a certain point in time. They 'can't see the wood for the trees', to use a common English expression. They might describe it in terms of a numbness and darkness, that nothing is clear, or that there is no clarity. In fact, there is *nothing* to go on in order to get a handle on their experience. In order for there being something to engage with and to 'step into', that is, for particular things to show up *as* something, there has to be a lit-up 'region' in the first place in which the person can then address the issues that they are experiencing. The clearing lights up the space for a path that can then be taken. As a path is lit, one possibility might be to open this to further exploration by, for example, engaging in therapy. Taking a therapeutic orientation means to be heedful of what opens itself in the course of the conversations within the encounter. Therapy acts as a clearing, or disclosive space of possibilities in which clients can uncover what was veiled in its absence from view. An example might illustrate this a little more clearly. In working briefly as a therapist in a prison many years ago, a client reflected on his own resigned mood, and alighted upon the insight that, once released, he would return to a world of drugs and crime, because that world was already configured and set to continue in that same way for him. That is, friends, family, the living environment and the limited range of possibilities, meant that the client was resigned to falling back into way of life that reinforced itself through others' interactions with him. It was only on the basis of a clearing that the client could articulate this clearly for himself. It opened a space to disclose a world that then offered the client a new-found way to be open to other, unforeseen possibilities. It was only when he was able to understand the way in which his world was already pre-structured, and thereby destined to repeat itself out of the way that it had already been thus far, that he began to entertain and play with possibilities that reflected a different structure or understanding in terms of being-in-the-world.

Both disclosedness and the clearing are not something that human beings will, construct or actively bring about. Instead, it is by dint of the 'thereness', or the 'there' of being-*there* that is *already* disclosing and *is* the clearing, that is, the space or site in which the opening happens. By contrast, neither the table nor the chair discloses or 'clears'. In the course of therapy, then, the clearing cannot be somehow constructed, manufactured or created, as if it is possible to extricate oneself from one world and jump into another. Rather, as already reflected in the example given, the client's world is explored in its already being disclosed, so that understanding takes hold, and in understanding, possibilities become more apparent and manifest. At the same time, clients undergo a change in their all-encompassing disposition, or mood in how they experience their world, and this inclines them to project some such possibilities that their prior disposition had no possibility of illuminating within their world-horizon.

Disclosedness and Care

A further question that now emerges from this is, how is this constant illumination possible in the first place? The answer comes from the very core of our being, that being human is care. In existing, I am always already oriented towards the world, the world that I care 'about', structurally speaking, in terms of my directedness and openness towards it, but in a number of other ways as well. Given that care is the way in which human existence is most fundamentally structured, this is to be distinguished from our dispositional caring about something or other. At the same time, such expressions of care in *concrete* situations originate from this core of being human (that is, the care structure; this is covered in the later chapter on Care-ing). It is always already in or through being care that our being matters to us, is an issue for us, and is at stake in our existing for as long we are alive. In other words, I live for the sake of my being, that is, my existence, always already continually standing out in the 'there', in always being situated, and towards which I am always already disposed to care.

Emphasising the fact that our being human is care is important, because we tend to *explain* the way that we discover things in the world as an active turning of our gaze towards the things themselves, such that we experience sensations through receptors in the eye that are then transmitted via the optic nerve to the brain. But this says very little, if anything, about our human *existence*, since it offers a scientific, mechanistic account of the human being in terms of a biological process that relates to its functioning. If we venture to take a step beyond this mechanistic picture, the discovery of the various entities in the world, to remind ourselves again, is only ever possible because we are disclosive beings in the first place. As well as this, in the very disclosing of a world, it is *ourselves* who are being disclosed (as care), in our existence. We take this not as a piece of knowledge or set of facts that we attend to or even monitor closely. Rather, we are already 'there', disclosing and being disclosed, opening and being opened up, in the world. Such opening, or opening up, is wholly different to the sense of opening the fridge door, or opening a present. Rather, it is that we are always already 'there' in a world, that we are 'there'-ing beings. This is already given or 'thrown' to us, rather than enacted or willed in some way. Our placedness is integral to what it means to be human, to put it in another way. Being placed involves our having some kind of relation to place, and this is where care also comes into the picture.

Disclosed Placedness

Placedness is fundamental to Heidegger's thinking. This is reflected in his term, 'Dasein', translated as 'being-there', which names the kind of being that we are. The Da- in Dasein means 'there', that we are already there. Nothing of this is captured when we talk about a person, individual and even human being, since these terms omit any reference to the there, and its worldly character. Some have even misread this term. For example, when we consider Sartre's reading of Heidegger's term, Dasein, it is based on a classic misunderstanding that most people can quite easily find themselves making. Sartre renders it as 'the human reality' (*la réalité humaine*), which simply says that 'the human is'. Such an egregious error reflects something that Heidegger spent his life's work resisting, which is anthropocentrism. This is a position that places the human being at the centre of the world, such that everything is comprehensible in terms of ourselves. As a consequence, the 'there' is lost, by only being rendered as 'position'. Put in a different way, leaving the 'there' out of the picture of our being, our placedness is ignored or omitted from the account. In failing to recognise the 'there', we become isolated, self-encased beings who move around within a massive world container. If this might seem an odd notion to us, the idea of being 'there' is not new. We find it in written fragments left by the 6th and 5th centuries BC Greek thinker, Heraclitus of Ephesus. Although his aphorisms are exceedingly difficult to understand – no wonder he was known as 'the Obscure' – some of the fragments express the very same sense of humans as being disclosed by place.

Returning to Sartre once again, however, given that he fails to think the placedness of human being, or the Da, he distorts and effectively mischaracterises much of what he goes on to say in his thinking about our kind of being. In starting from 'the human reality', he mentions the necessity of action, to point to one example, but as he does so, he doesn't take into account the *continuity of place*. This is 'Da-ing', or 'there-ing'. If we ignore or inadvertently miss this we are guilty of misunderstanding ourselves, and we fall into positioning the human as being at the centre of our world, or as anthropocentric.

As therapists, in thinking about clients' worlds, we are not thinking purely in anthropocentric terms, but, rather, relationally, and in a radically different way to a Cartesian relationality, for example. In this sense, we act as custodians of being-there, and not only in the present, but also in relation to the future. In other words, we also care about the future of our relation to the earth, the sky and the enchantments that the world offers when we dwell and feel at home in the world. These are all in an interwoven relation to one another, grasped as a oneness. Being custodians of the future means that futurity is grounded in the present, because we preserve and 'shepherd', or act as guardians, of the 'there' and every other way of being. From a therapeutic perspective, it is only by reminding ourselves of the 'there' of our clients that we relate to them in an open way, that is, in their wholeness, rather than as subjects who are separate from the world. The danger that therapy faces is to ignore and forget this, and more worryingly, to forget that it has forgotten.

Disclosedness, Discoveredness and Therapy

Making these distinctions is important for therapy because our overriding tendency is to think of our world in terms of the subject-object distinction, such that everything is objectively and permanently present to us as experiencing subjects. This follows a metaphysical picture of our kind of being, and reduces us to independent, isolated beings that are explicable in other, more abstract terms.

The essence of disclosedness is the way in which our being is always a Da, that we are there-ing, and which fundamentally constitutes us. When therapists embrace this as the basis for our understanding of what it means to be human, and therefore that the client before them is Da-sein, or being-there, they encounter the being before them not as a self-encased entity in the world, but as a being that discloses their world. The therapist attends to the client's disclosed world through the conversations that open up and light up the way in which the client has made their world intelligible to themselves. This intelligibility is not, by any measure, a cognitive understanding, but rather is borne out by their very way of living and sustaining their worlds.

Working with clients means that therapists are attuned to the distinction between discoveredness and disclosedness, relating this to the therapeutic space as a site for the client to disclose and discover as they enter into discourse. This means that the therapist exercises patience, embracing a certain restraint in letting things be and letting them show themselves as they unfold. This points to the fact that disclosing is an un-concealing or truth-ing. For example, the table before me is unconcealed in its showing up as a table. In its manifest appearing, I am then able to speak of it, which is a dis-covering of it as the table when asserting that the table is brown, for example, and that it is in my living room. However, therapeutic conversations more generally provide a space in which the client discloses their world, such that moods, understanding and ways of reckoning with the world can be articulated and given greater sense and meaning through a hermeneutic process of questioning and thinking. In other words, walking along cleared paths.

Chapter 2

True-ing

Introduction

The idea of truth is indispensable to us in our daily lives, and for a variety of reasons. For one, it holds a certain pragmatic value for us. We listen to the weather forecaster, for example, inform us that 'today will be a wet day, with frequent showers and some sleet at times'. We take it as being true on a pragmatic level, given the trust and reliability that we generally invest in meteorologists, the technological tools and instruments that are available to them, and the high degree of predictability that they have consistently managed to show over time. Thinking of its relevance in another way, we take truth as an overarching coherence, gathering elements into a whole. In this sense, we typically say, 'I now have the whole picture', that is, all the pieces fit together, and now we see the truth of a situation, for example. We have been pointed towards a coherent totality that reflects truth. We also speak of truth in other ways, however. I might, for example, say that I am true to my partner in committing myself to our relationship in declaring my love for them, as I embrace our common visions, projects and plans for our years ahead. In yet another sense, I might say that, 'Pablo is a true friend to me'. We might also think of something being true when the carpenter uses a plane on a piece of wood until it is completely and perfectly level along its length. However, a more fundamental way of thinking of truth is in its existential sense, as we might commonly find when someone declares, 'I really *am* a mortal being'. Such an existential truth reflects a sense of owning up to ourselves who, what or how we are in terms of our human condition, rather than avoiding certain unpalatable truths about our existence. In line with this, we can draw on certain notions of authenticity and inauthenticity that name the ways in which we can either flee from or own up to what is true about us as human beings.

Conversation on True-ing

Therapist: I have been pondering on what we might mean by 'truth', and how it is relevant to therapy.

DOI: 10.4324/9781003638698-3

Thinker: I don't know, I'm not familiar with the world of therapy myself, but maybe the issue is around how we *usually* think of and understand truth itself. We can start there and then see what comes up.

Therapist: That would be helpful. I can start, then. I think of truth and what is true as being the opposite to what is false.

Thinker: That's certainly our understanding of truth in our Modern age.

Therapist: What do you mean by 'Modern'? The current trend or fashion in which we live?

Thinker: Well, more broadly and 'historically' than that. The Modern age came as a radical change or new configuration of thinking that came after the Mediaeval period, that is, the Middle Ages, where human existence was very much defined, shaped and understood through religion and its own way of understanding ourselves, others and the world at large.

Therapist: So, there was something radically new and different that came afterwards, called the 'Modern', in terms of the way in which we understood ourselves, and still *do*, to this day?

Thinker: Yes, that's right.

Therapist: So, how does that connect to truth as we understand it, then?

Thinker: The Modern way of thinking of truth is that it is a correspondence relation between something I say or think or believe, on the one hand, and whatever it is that I am saying or thinking about, on the other.

Therapist: So, if I say something like, 'the client is silent', that means that they actually have to show up as being silent in order for my claiming that to be true? On the other hand, if I say that they are silent, but in actual fact, they are talking, then what I say happens to be false?

Thinker: Yes. What you have just expressed is a representational account of truth. It says that one thing represents, or corresponds to, the other. And, if it's false, it means that that correspondence fails.

Therapist: So, what's wrong with that way of understanding truth? That makes sense to me.

Thinker: It's not wrong, it's correct. But what we see here is the way that the Modern approach looks for what is correct, and what is incorrect, and stops there. It doesn't get to what truth *essentially* is, how truth 'truths', how it unfolds in its temporal, 'live' sense. What we have so far identified is a static, frozen sense of truth, as if it's a mathematical equation. It's like an adequate matching of one thing with another, that 'this adequately captures that'.

Therapist: OK. So, that's a 'surface' level of truth, which is truth as communication?

Thinker: Yes, I suppose you can put it like that. It's speaking, uttering something, and then seeing if what has been spoken actually fits with the state of affairs, how things are in the world. This is truth as correctness.

Therapist: OK, so is that what science does? Looks at the world, or the natural world, and then makes statements about it through theories, experiments and the like, which end up as truth, because they can be repeatedly checked against the world for their correspondence?

Thinker: That's right, science is aiming for what is correct, and certain.

Therapist: It may be worth rehearsing the moves that science makes, just to be clear that therapy is not science. To say that therapy is science, surely, is to speak falsely, to go back to the true-false distinction. So, tell me more about how science works.

Thinker: In the Modern understanding, we are subjects who experience a world, nature, etc., that is outside of us, separate from us, that is, an objective world. We then say, well, to get to the world outside us, we put our senses to work in identifying and explaining whatever it is that we are exploring and trying to understand that is part of that external world. But to understand anything in that world, we have to break it up into small, manageable parts.

Therapist: But what if you and I are trying to explore something. I might then see one thing and you might see something else. What happens then? How can that be reliable? That won't get us to any truth, surely?!

Thinker: That's right. So that's where science comes in. Here we might also think of anything that comes under the description of science, such as psychology, biology, psychiatry, medicine and so on. Science says, we need a method so that we get to see what is there, independent of feelings, opinions, beliefs and suchlike that can distort our attempts to see things as they are when we observe them. Science says, follow a method, a rational approach that is logical and moves progressively from particular things to eventually the greatest possible observation of all those same particular things, until we can say with confidence that we see what they all have in common. We can then call that a 'hypothesis'. We keep testing and testing to see whether we identify some particular aspect or feature that collapses that hypothesis, and if our hypothesis holds up in the face of all that, it becomes a theory, as we call it.

Therapist: Give me an example. That's all still too abstract for my liking.

Thinker: OK. I'll take a very popular kind of example that has been traditionally used: let's take white swans. I keeping seeing white swans in Regent's Park, in central London, on my way to work. I observe those several white swans, and conjecture that all swans are white. If I'm approaching it scientifically, that is an unwarranted, unjustified claim, an enormous leap and one that doesn't follow a rational procedure. So, as a scientist, I approach this rationally, and I use scientific method. I travel all over the world and observe all the possible swans I encounter on my travels, keeping a record of how many swans I have observed, so that I eventually come to the conclusion that all swans are white. That's my hypothesis.

Therapist: And so you've taken this neutral, detached observer stance, so that you don't prejudice or bias what you have found?

Thinker: That's right. But note what is underlying all this. I am taking an empirical stance, which says that there is a world out there, separate from me, which I reach out to through my senses. So, I am committed to a dualistic stance: me, my mind, my senses, on one side, and on the other, the observable world of nature, that is not-me, we might say. Truth is established when I have arrived at a certain consistent pattern in all my observations of a certain object in the world, such that I can claim with certainty that this pattern is universal, true at all times and in all places, including cross-culturally.

Therapist: OK. So, truth can be understood in a certain way through this empirical approach?

Thinker: Yes. And it is grounded in a representational understanding of truth.

Therapist: But thinking of myself as working empirically as a therapist would be to think of myself as a scientist, which is certainly the complete opposite of how I think of myself. If anything, I think of myself as embracing a more 'artistically-oriented' temperament.

Thinker: Yes, I think that's right. So, the question now is, where do we go from the empiricist position, which has its own understanding of truth, to *another* way of thinking of truth?

Therapist: Well, I suppose the other possibility is that if we don't presume that the truth is 'out there', so to speak, that we don't think that we can find truth by just reading off the data of the world, another possibility is to say that it's all 'in here', in my mind, the contents of my brain.

Thinker: Yes. We could call that the rationalist move. Or as the French philosopher, Maurice Merleau-Ponty called it, the intellectualist position.

If we stick with 'mind', that might be a better way of talking about this because we're still holding to the dualism of what is 'inside' and 'outside' that we had started with when talking about the empirical.

Therapist: OK, that makes sense. As I see it, a therapeutic approach that is traditionally 'internally' focused is psychoanalysis. Whilst it addresses the patient's experiences, memories and so forth, psychoanalysis trains its attention on the workings of the mind, its systemic and dynamic character, in order to offer the patient a way of explaining and accounting for why it is that what manifests in their lives is troublesome, challenging, disturbing, and is reflected in human suffering.

Thinker: Yes, it doesn't discount what's out there, as such, it's just saying that the mental is the repository of what we make of whatever might be out there, so we need to stay with what's inside, in the mind. So, the 'inward' focus now takes it that truth is arrived at by applying psychoanalytic concepts to the patient's reflections and disclosures, taking it that their utterances are decipherable and explicable as representations of a deeper mental activity, that is, a kind of language of the mind that psychoanalysis is claiming to have articulated. Whatever kind of truth there is to be found is only possible through psychoanalytic language that provides an adequate relation or match between its concepts and the words expressed. Instead of going out into nature, this time it's the (patient's) mind that needs to be 'observed' sufficiently closely in order to arrive at such truths.

Therapist: But that's too 'in the head' for me. There's a concrete world, and I'm engaged in it.

Thinker: Well, that would be my view too. But there is at least one more move that we could make about a therapeutic approach.

Therapist: What's that? So let me review how I've understood it so far. The empirical, scientific approach to therapy would say, you need to start from the external world, and not have a distorted or unrealistic reading of the world, but one that is appropriate – correctly adjusted – to it. In effect, you need to calibrate your thoughts, feelings and behaviours so that they correspond to how the world actually *is*, in order to be 'well-adjusted'. The other approach – the rationalist position, as you called it – is saying, your mind is structured in a certain way so that it deals with the world out there according to the way in which that structure operates. My mind deletes what is painful, or represses it out of my awareness, so that I can deal with the world and others in a manageable way. I am replete with drives, complexes and defences, and they need to be brought out so that I can release myself somewhat from the way in which I am held hostage by them. I regain some semblance of mastery over what becomes manifest, because I gain knowledge of myself through what comes out of the analysis.

Thinker: Yes. But note that a psychoanalyst might say that what the analysis is doing is uncovering, revealing, discovering truth, or the truth that is deeper than the representational account of truth. That warrants a separate discussion of its own, which I will leave to one side. But let's keep going with my third proposed move that we can make that goes beyond the empirical and the rationalist positions.

Therapist: OK, so what's the third position?

Thinker: It's to see something patterned that takes what we experience as, at the same time, only being experienceable against a background. To put it crudely, the previous two positions take one side of the dualism. We have the objective position, in the case of the empiricist, and the subjective, in the case of the intellectualist or rationalist position. What we are now presented with is that whatever shows up always has a contextual background that is necessary for anything to show up at all. This is a Gestalt psychological approach, based on its work on perception, which says that we have to see this as a whole, that what we perceive, or the 'figure', always comes together with a background, or 'ground'. So, you can't really just speak in a way that separates them from each other.

Therapist: That sounds very compelling. It makes a lot of sense to me. A client is experiencing a disturbance in the ground, or in the figure, namely, what they perceive in their experience, and that unsettles the whole, the holistic picture. The harmony of the figure-ground becomes more fragile.

Thinker: Yes, according to this picture, all reality operates according to forms and structures. It is claiming a naturalistic picture of how reality works. In other words, it's saying, this is the more correct way to understand science. It's objective, naturalises the order of things and the natural order of things is that it's all objectively structured. The mistake that I think this makes is that, when it comes to being human, we don't just operate mechanically, or objectively, according to forms and structures. The Gestalt account also follows what we find in the empiricist and intellectualist positions, which is to think in terms of causality. That's what makes it hang together. But we're not beings that can be accounted for through causal explanation.

Therapist: But the whole of figure-ground still makes sense to me.

Thinker: The thing that the Gestalt account does is that it thinks objectivistically, as if there is no-one there experiencing something for themselves. It's like trying to describe something as if that's possible from an out-of-body experience. I think that these accounts can be challenged by the fact that humans have a point of view on the world, rather than a fixed position, that is, that we have a constantly changing perspective on what we are experiencing, rather than objectifying what we experience. That seems to me to capture how we exist. The three positions that I outlined are all metaphysical, in my view.

Therapist: We need to think of it more existentially?

Thinker: Exactly. And not existentiali*stically*, not falling into a metaphysics of the existential, which is existentia*lism*.

Therapist: I think I'd like a recapitulation again, as you've moved us on in terms of thinking about truth. That will hopefully give us a chance to build on what has been said so far.

Thinker: Yes, OK. And that would be a way of moving towards further understanding, I think.

Therapist: The empirical puts us into a relation to the world where we are observers that are detached from the world and we read off 'data' from the world in order to make claims about it, which we present as theories. But this doesn't get to a deeper sense of truth as we understand it in our experience. To just bring this here, because it has just popped into my head, we can sometimes say things like, 'I want to discover the truth about the situation', to have something actually revealed to me in a way that goes *beyond* straightforward representation, a correspondence fit, if I can put it like that.

Thinker: Yes, just communicating something isn't getting us to truth as we think of it in the deeper sense. We can say that it *is* truth as communication, though. The example you gave of wanting to get to the truth of things is a good one. I'll give another example of my own: 'John is walking away from me'. That simple kind of communication relies on someone or something – in this case, John – as the subject, and something being predicated of it, which is 'walking', or 'walking away'.

Therapist: That's the technical way of putting it, and more than I need, but thank you. Let's stick with wanting to find out the truth about something; in the example, then, that I want to get to the truth of John walking away from me, right?

Thinker: Yes. This is more basic than the communication notion of truth as correctness. The very fact of the revealing of John, and John walking, and walking away is the deeper level, which is the sense of truth as discoveredness. The revealing, or unconcealing of John acting in this way is already presupposed in our only then being able to put it into spoken words. John has to show up, and be revealed in his walking away, in order to only *then* communicate it as truth, but truth *as correctness*. It's reliant upon truth as discoveredness, the revealing aspect.

Therapist: I'm with you so far. Something just showing up is a deeper sense of truth. So, isn't that what speaking does? It is speaking the revealing, surely? Or am I getting confused?

Thinker: That level of truth as communication is not putting the revealing into words, but rather, the revealing is being covered up, concealed, we might say. It's not made explicit and spoken. But that's fine, that's how this works. Speaking is correct insofar as it is communicating, but it hasn't got the deeper understanding or level of truth as revealing.

Therapist: So what happens in a conversation? In a therapy conversation, for that matter?

Thinker: Well, that is where the sense of exploration and elaboration comes in. The client communicates and speaks, but in the speaking, so much still remains covered up. Someone might say in your therapy session, 'I feel really unhappy in my relationship', and that's true, but true in terms of being correct. But if they want to find out the *truth* about this, then they come to dis-cover what is not actually being spoken. What they eventually uncover, with time and exploration, is revealed truth – truth as *experienced* – which is then put into words and is spoken in the conversation.

Therapist: I think that's how the process of discovery, uncovering, revealing happens in therapy.

Thinker: But – and I wouldn't venture to tell you how to do that – it requires a real sensitivity to the language, and looking to avoid any attempt to match some of the therapist's theoretical concepts to what the client is actually communicating. That way would be to simply stay on the level of a correspondence idea of truth, truth as correctness.

Therapist: I suppose it feels more grounded if we approach it in *that* way, if that's the right word. In the hands of the therapist, it says, I know what I'm doing, because I have the knowledge and theory to make these correspondences. I can link theory to practice.

Thinker: You mention 'ground' here, which is a very important idea, and does relate to truth. We can cover that in another conversation and at another time, hopefully, but not at the moment.

Therapist: So, how would you see the conversation going when exploring something that the client has spoken about?

Thinker: I think it would involve a lot of listening, and listening for, among many other things, the phenomenon. What am I hearing? Am I hearing the phenomenon? Or do I see or hear it yet? Or do we need to explore further so that the client continues to speak about the issue? But it only happens in the process of ongoing elaboration through further and further description. The idea here is to go back to the things themselves in their concreteness, without drifting into abstraction and generality. I stay with the specificity of it, which means that I also stay with the context.

Therapist: Could we call that a method of enquiry?

Thinker: No! Not in the sense of 'method' as a logical set of steps, a procedure, an algorithmic movement that we follow to the letter. But if you mean 'method' as the Greeks meant it, which is just finding a 'way towards' something, then I am wholly agreeable to that. I would rather think of it as our embracing a certain 'spirit' of enquiry in the course of undertaking such explorations. If we follow a procedure, we stay in a very 'correctness'-oriented mode of investigation.

Therapist: So, based on what you have just described, what I am trying to do in working in that way is to stay at the level of the concrete, the particularity of the phenomenon, and stick to that. But that can be hard to do, and I can sometimes veer away from it and into something that is generalised, like a formula, into a general proposition or statement. That would be to fall back into 'correctness', correspondence and matching, the first level of truth that you mentioned earlier.

Thinker: Yes, it's not easy to stay at the level of description, and that's where curiosity and a certain attitude of questioning supports that. If you get back to the general, it's limited. Actually, let me put it more strongly: it's empty and misleading, because it keeps you and the client from seeing what is revealed by moving closer to understanding the truth of a situation.

Therapist: When I reflect on my work as a therapist, I now see how the uncovering, the dis-covering, unveiling is actually how the therapeutic process happens. It's like something emerging out of the conversation that has been illuminated through the process of enquiry. It's a little like an epiphany, a way in which something moves. But the more I try to put it into words, the less I'm able to do justice to it.

Thinker: That's the challenge, I agree. We usually try to make everything immediately explicit, present to us, nothing ever hidden. It goes back to what science is trying to do: let us see everything laid out before us.

Therapist: And I suppose the question is, to what end?

Thinker: Science is extremely important to us, but it doesn't think. It is after knowledge.

Therapist: So truth as knowledge?

Thinker: I think that's right. But it doesn't ask the deeper, more essential question, where are its limitations? We live in a world where science is seen as the sole means by which we can arrive at truth. That leaves out a lot, and it pushes us into a rapacious technological world, whilst excluding any other possible way of thinking about things. There's a real danger in that.

Therapist: From what you have just said, what has really struck me is the questioning that is always key. It's what makes us human. When I think of therapy, the danger, to use your word, is that we fall into only *one* way of thinking, that it needs to bring about an outcome, that it bases itself on a particular understanding of ourselves, that it has done all the thinking that it needs to do. The true danger is that it doesn't even notice that it isn't thinking. It serves up and replicates and elaborates on what it already claims to be true, whether in terms of theory, or a particular orientation that it holds to without questioning itself.

Thinker: Yes. But I think your use of the word 'thinking' is saying that we don't go to the deeper questioning that tries to get to the *essence* of therapy, rather than just saying something more technical about it. That is a pursuit of the truth unveiling itself in the course of the questioning.

Truth as Correspondence and Representation

When we speak of truth, we think in terms of its correctness and accuracy of an assertion or statement that is 'about' something. If the statement is inaccurate or incorrect, then it is deemed untrue, and when there is a correspondence between the statement and the very subject matter or state of affairs to which it refers, then it is true.

If I make a very simple reference and say, 'therapy', I am not predicating anything of therapy, as I would if I were to say, 'therapy is a process of attending to the deeper concerns of the individual'. In the act of predicating something, I attribute something or other to the subject to which I am referring, namely, therapy, which will happen to either be true or is false. I am making a statement that has the subject, 'therapy', correspond to 'a process of attending to the deeper concerns of the individual', that is, what is being predicated of therapy. There is a 'rightness of fit', we might say, when we make such claims to truth. Such a 'fit' is otherwise referred to in terms of a representational account of truth: a sentence or utterance accurately and correctly represents whatever it is referring to in the utterance. Whilst this has its place in our practical dealings in the world, it leaves us with certain questions that are not sufficiently addressed, or even considered.

To approach this from a different angle, we tend to think in terms of concepts. A concept is an idea that has entered our language through naming the idea, and thereby establishing it as being somehow indisputable, or bearing truth. When we take up an initial exploration of a phenomenon, or whatever it is that shows itself to us, we arrive at a point where we take hold of it and thereby determine it by fixing it into place, thus bestowing it with a certain status, namely, that of being a concept. Freud's own contributions, in a similar fashion, have introduced the unconscious as just one of many of the concepts that we find in the field of psychoanalysis, its use now even having extended into our casual everyday conversations. Similarly, 'empathy' has become a very familiar concept that is generally accepted in many therapeutic approaches, even though it was first introduced in the domain of aesthetic perception.

The import of thinking in terms of concepts is that, as soon as we put something into a conceptual form, we immediately close it down into the very way that we now continue to think of it. In the first instance, we name things; we give to them a word that will correspond to what it is that we are addressing. So, when I talk about friendship, I am presenting it as a concept that applies to two (or more) people. But, in itself, it says very little, if anything at all, apart from what we already take friendship to be. The word closes off an understanding of the experience that goes beyond or lies beneath the application of a concept, thereby arresting elaboration and exploration of the (character of the) particular relation between the friends in question. In doing so, we assume a position of claiming to already know what it is that we are pointing to, and no longer needing to attend to the experience.

Heidegger on Truth

Following Heidegger, when asking what truth is, we are looking to arrive at its *essence*, how truth unfolds, or 'sways', moves, we might say. The essence of true-ing, we can then add, is 'the way that something pursues its course' (Heidegger, 1954/1977:3). In other words, it is the unconcealed, or that which comes out of concealment. However, following Heidegger, and drawing on the work of Wrathall and Withy, we can identify three 'levels' of truth.

Truth in Speaking –

A first level of truth is truth's correctness or accuracy. This is based on our usual, everyday sense of truth, and is to speak truthfully when we say something that accurately accords with what it is referring to.

In naming something as we speak, we are speaking correctly about what is being spoken, which is what we take to be true. In a conversation, for example, truth is that which is being communicated and made manifest in the speaking about something that is present to us. 'The table is brown' is being communicated by one person to another, and the table's being brown supports and confirms that the person speaking is making a true utterance. It is only in the speaking something about the table that is communicating truth when it makes a correct statement about the table's brownness.

Truth as Discoveredness –

In order for the person to make the utterance about the table and its brownness, the table has to be unveiled as a table in the first place. Heidegger draws on the Greek term *phusis*, which is translated as 'nature', but actually has a dynamic, moving and temporal character to it. As he elaborates, it is an 'emerging' that 'becomes immediately clear to us through the emerging of the seeds sunken in the earth, the sprouting of shoots, the emerging of the blossom. Additionally, the spectacle of the emerging sun points to the essence of emerging' (Heidegger, 1994/2018:67). This is different to the commonly understood sense of an emerging chemical reaction between two liquids, because it draws on a scientific understanding that explains emerging in terms of a *natural* chemical process. By contrast, there is a *prior* emerging within which the liquids, the beakers and pipettes, for example, show themselves in the first place. This is what *phusis* means. The emerging, then, is truth in the sense of the dis-covering, or showing, of what is manifest.

Truth as Disclosing –

When we undergo certain experiences in which our world collapses, and our accustomed routines and practices no longer sustain and support us in our going about our everyday business, everything falls away. We no longer relate to any one thing or another. In this moment, we are world-less. However, such moments actually disclose a world to us in the first place, which is truth as unconcealment. It is only in the clearing, or the space of illumination, that this is unconcealed.

Whilst we understand this in terms of the light of the clearing that unconceals, or 'trues', it is also the case that the darkness of the night-sky unconceals the stars that twinkle and shine brightly, whilst the daylight, by contrast, conceals them. Heidegger sees truth and un-truth – unconcealment and concealment – as belonging together, rather than in terms of a binary opposition. Unconcealment and concealment are therefore to be understood as a kind of unity. This unity, however, is not a simple oneness, but a rich standing together as a *unifying* rather than static unity.

Reflections on True-ing

True-ing can be characterised in terms of its opposite, namely, 'false-ing', or what is false. At the same time, intentionally false-ing can be said to be a form of lying, which is a deception that already requires and presupposes a grasp of the truth.

But there might also be ways in which something is not true without it amounting to being false in the sense of its being deceitful and dissembling. For example, the Danish philosopher, Søren Kierkegaard, used various pseudonyms in authoring his numerous publications. In doing so, he was not considered an impostor, but simply conjuring up fictitious names as a literary distancing device, among other things. We also experience a kind of false-ing that is not deceitful when the client describes a situation that is incomplete as an account of what happened. The conversation between therapist and client takes a more phenomenological turn in exploring the intricacies of the event, such that previously absent details are now included in the account. Of course, various questions may arise as to the possible context for the client talking about their experience: whether there was a 'motivated forgetting', or the client had simply overlooked aspects of the situation, or had attempted to capture and convey the experience in very general and concise terms, rather than the minutiae of the event. None of this could necessarily be taken as being tantamount to deceit. When taking a phenomenological approach in a therapy session, the phenomenon under investigation is itself covered over and layered, and requires a measure of hermeneutic analysis to 'lay bare' what was initially only a semblance of its true appearance. All this is intended to show that un-truth is not the same as the false.

Heidegger thinks of concealment as more basic or primordial, and itself is what allows for this belonging together with the unconcealed. We tend to think in terms of binaries because we have already become absorbed in a way of thinking that reflects a representational understanding of the true, or truth. The more primordial sense of truth escapes a subject-object, representational understanding. In thinking of the false in an oppositional way to the true, the standard tendency is to avoid the false, or else attempt to completely erase it, because we have already deemed it to be 'negative', as Heidegger describes this (1982/1992:44). In a way, we also conceal by a form of self-deception that which is not false, although we might somehow try to 'falsify' it, as in the case of our own mortality. It lies concealed at the very heart of our being, and yet we might find ways to turn ourselves away from it in order to avoid unwanted anxiety and discomfort (Heidegger, 1982/1992:44).

The very way in which we are present to what unconceals itself, or to true-ing, reveals how we understand truth itself. Heidegger says that 'a scientist "attacks" something' (1982/1992:7). There are two German words that Heidegger is drawing on to bring out an important distinction here: Anfangen and Angreifen (1982/1992:7). These are commonly translated as 'to start' and 'to begin', in the case of the former, and 'to engage' or 'attack', in the case of the latter. However, Heidegger uses these terms differently, and in a way that are not easily translatable for us as ones who remain embedded in a Cartesian linguistic framework. He re-engages with these terms differently, because he is attempting to bring out the ways in which we relate to what unveils itself in its moment of unveiling. In Anfangen, there is a holding to what has been unconcealed, catching up to it and being there with it as it moves, so to speak. By contrast, in Angreifen, the scientist, for example, holds onto something, and holds it firmly, as if attacking it, so that it's <u>not</u> moving. In Anfangen, we can think of a game of tag, where I try to catch the other person, and even as I catch up to them, they continue to move. We also relate this word to Heidegger's term, 'seinlassen', a letting be, which is contrasted with mastery and control, as reflected in a scientific approach, and which does not let things be because it is preoccupied with the attempt to overcome, subdue and master them.

Therapy and True-ing

Therapy offers the client the possibility to be 'in' the truth, that is, to speak truthfully about themselves and their lives, whether from the perspective of their past, their present or future. This might open itself as a straightforward series of self-confessional reflections. Conversely, it could involve a gradual realisation over time that something that hadn't previously been given consideration and thought had now emerged in the light of certain exploratory paths that were taken over the course of therapy. Whichever course or path the therapy takes, it is continually engaged in the question of truth, in one way or another.

Therapy is not ultimately looking to arrive at a one-to-one correspondence between the concept and the thing or phenomenon that it is naming, although this is where therapy might start from. As the conversations move and open something in the attempt to arrive at a deeper understanding, certain assumptions are uncovered that can be put into question, whether because they obscure our ability to see the phenomenon clearly, or because such assumptions have been handed down to us over time and have distorted a truer picture of what we are trying to understand. This can be said to be true of many things, and a mutual exploration offers the possibility to uncover, un-conceal what lies deeper, in terms of the thing in question being understood in its essence.

Bibliography

Heidegger, M. (1954/1977). The Question Concerning Technology. In W. Lovitt (ed.). *The Question Concerning Technology and Other Essays*. New York: Harper & Row. pp.3–35.

Heidegger, M. *Parmenides*. (1982/1992). Trans. A. Schuwer & R. Rojcewicz. Indianapolis: Indiana University Press.

Heidegger, M. (1994/2018). *Heraclitus: The Inception of Occidental Thinking; Logic: Heraclitus's Doctrine of the* Logos. Trans. J.G. Assaiante & S. Montgomery Ewegen. London: Bloomsbury Academic.

Withy, K. (2022). *Heidegger on Being Self-Concealing*. Oxford: Oxford University Press.

Wrathall, M.A. (2011). *Heidegger and Unconcealment: Truth, Language, and History*. Cambridge: Cambridge University Press.

Chapter 3

Gather-ing

Introduction

The intention in this chapter is to bring out an understanding of gathering in its relation to therapy and the therapeutic relationship. At first glance, we might hear it as a term used to describe social or religious activities, whether that be of groups that attend mass demonstrations, or of a congregation at a church service, for example. On some occasions, it is also a summoning of others to, 'all gather round!' These are well-founded uses of the word. The focus here, however, is on bringing out the essence of gathering, or gather-*ing*, and its way of be-ing in the therapeutic space.

In finding ourselves with others in an unfamiliar setting, we are strangers to each other. We feel somewhat disconnected, having no background context or orientation to draw on to engage with one another, nor even a sense of how well-disposed we and others might be to being approached for initial contact. In that sense, we might easily recall the start of the first day at a new school, brought into a world that carries a sense of the uncertain and the unknown. Or we imagine standing in a crowded lift or elevator, gazing intently at the ceiling or floor lest we inadvertently make eye contact with others. These examples raise the question of the possible ways in which, with the passage of time, we are brought closer to each other, and more open to situations.

In what follows, attention is given to the way in which a situation gathers, or is gathered. The idea of gathering is an important aspect of the therapeutic relationship, but also the particular *way* in which it gathers. The moment or process of gathering can be otherwise rendered as an 'event', or an 'event-ing', where things, moments or people *come together* in some way, rather than being a reference to a planned, formal, organised and managed occasion that simply takes place over a certain stretch of time. In such cases, we tend to speak of an event purely as a calendarised fixture, rather than in terms of its dynamic character.

DOI: 10.4324/9781003638698-4

Conversation on Gather-ing

Trainee: I try to work with my clients in a way that brings about results.

Supervisor: You say 'results'?

Trainee: Yes. They come initially to resolve something, so that's what we agree to work on. I then try to get as clear as I can on what a successful therapy might look like.

Supervisor: 'Successful' in terms of meeting goals?

Trainee: Yes.

Supervisor: Does that already pre-frame the way that therapy is assumed to work, though?

Trainee: How do you mean?

Supervisor: Well, it suggests a uni-dimensional, 'from here to there' sense of fixing.

Trainee: But that's what the client has said that they want to work on.

Supervisor: So the way the client relates to the issue that brought them to therapy is that it can all be worked on in a linear, logical, progressive and optimal way. But that's not who we are, as human beings, or *how* we are who we are.

Trainee: That leaves me a bit stuck now. If the client wants to work on their relationship with their partner, then we can work on ways in which they can improve their communication skills, explore feelings that might come up and look at alternative ways that they can relate to their partner, say.

Supervisor: That all sounds very logical and rational. I suppose it hangs on the idea that we are, at bottom, rational beings. So, when we are irrational, or deviate from being more rational, we're not being what we fundamentally are.

Trainee: Yes, when you put it like that, it sounds right.

Therapist: OK. Let's try another way of thinking about this. When you hear the client and accept that that is where they start from, does it necessarily continue in that way?

Trainee: No. Other clients might start from a similar place, and then gradually settle in. They begin to see it differently.

Supervisor: How so?

Trainee: Over the course of a number of sessions, a closeness and familiarity develops between myself and my clients. We relate to each other in a more relaxed and open way.

Supervisor: So it becomes more attentive to the meandering of the process of opening, exploring, playing with something by turning it around and seeing the same thing but from different perspectives, and then something possibly showing itself as meaningful, or offering a meaning that is new, different or adds to the meaning that was already there, but now deepens the client's understanding in some way?

Trainee: Sometimes, not always.

Supervisor: What if you think about what is going on between you, in the hiddenness of what is nevertheless there, if you see what I mean? Something that you can't point to, 'thingify'?

Trainee: The relationship.

Supervisor: Yes, that's not explicitly present, but in its hiding, it is there. But just stay with the mood or atmosphere in the room for a moment as you both find yourselves in the sessions.

Trainee: Well, if I were to try to stay at the descriptive level, we become closer, we're not making something happen. We're open to how the conversation goes, and the client is talking about things that are personal, private.

Supervisor: And you walk along with them on that path?

Trainee: Yes, I'm trying to understand what it's like for them.

Supervisor: What about the space in the room? How would you describe it?

Trainee: You mean how big the room is? Whether it's comfortable?

Supervisor: Experientially, how do you experience the space?

Trainee: Well, we're sitting together, so we're close to each other. But, experientially, the client has a lot of space to talk and be open, it's 'roomy' in that way, yes. But also close, relationally speaking.

Supervisor: OK, so it 'makes room' for whatever the client talks about. That's the more existential sense that I was thinking about. You're existentially close to the client in terms of your relationship being close, say, and the client feeling they have a big space in which to open up and talk about whatever comes to mind for them.

Trainee: And when some clients talk about their world with others outside the therapy room, they might feel distant from them even though they've known them for years.

Supervisor: So, it's the experiential space that is important, but it isn't some kind of technique that makes it 'roomy', as you put it. Let me try to offer an example. I'm in a coffee shop somewhere, and the coffee I'm served is made to perfection. I start to read my paper, in this relaxed ambience. I find an interesting article to read, and as I immerse myself in it, I enjoy the fact that it's teaching me so much about the changes that are going on in the world. It's a quiet place, and I now feel very drawn to it. I feel free, relaxed, and the space is not just a 'location' of available space in which I can sit, drink coffee and read the paper. It's an 'open region'. It 'collects' me into the region or space. I am at one with it, or it's just a oneness. I don't separate it out and name all the things that are 'not me': that is, that the chair is not me, the table is not me, the coffee cup is not me, and so on. That way of looking at is to already invoke distance.

Trainee: So, you see it in terms of a wholeness, rather than lots of separate bits that then get put together in some way?

Supervisor: Yes, there is an openness, and in the openness, something is happening. The openness holds things and brings them together. The barista comes and removes my empty coffee cup, so some things are no longer there, but the openness still remains, because it's active, it keeps holding things together in its oneness.

Trainee: And what's making the openness stay open?

Supervisor: It's not about 'making' something happen. Rather, it throws itself open so that we can abide in it. We are ourselves opened, and at the same time opened to things. It's not us doing the opening.

Trainee: So, it's not you managing or controlling it in some way. It happens.

Supervisor: It's a happen-ing, it's moving, and it is out of your hands to control it, or make it happen.

So, if we think back to you being with your clients, the space is an open region, an openness in which a happening collects you and the client and everything else into a oneness.

Trainee: We're collected …

Supervisor: Yes. All this is the very opposite of how we would usually come to talk about it. The collecting is the most basic and fundamental way that we can describe it. If we try to describe it in terms of being active agents, we lose this basic sense of it and then fall into something else.

Trainee: I'm not sure what that 'something else' would be, or what it would look like.

Supervisor: It would be a different kind of thinking, that is, the current way in which we are prone to engage in thinking. That is, a representational thinking, which makes everything into a self-standing object that is 'opposite' us, which we call the 'subject'. So, there is a splitting, and moreover, the splitting has characterised us as grasping, controlling, mastering, having power over the object, because we acquire knowledge through science, which provides us with technology, and technology is our means to achieve ends. We then think in this way.

Trainee: So this way is distancing, not bringing closer?

Supervisor: It's an attitude of domination over things in the world. And ultimately, over ourselves.

Trainee: So can't we just say that we're going to put up a resistance to that way of thinking? We can oppose it and remove it from the possible ways that we can think?

Supervisor: If you try to do that, you just engage in that same kind of thinking as when you try to control it. That is, you objectify it, and in doing so, it's something to resist, overwhelm, master and so on.

Trainee: So, if we can't dominate it, we just let it happen?

Supervisor: Exactly. Letting be. But we can look at that in more detail a little later on. First, though, this collecting. You and the client are collected. I think it is even better rendered as 'gathered'. It's a gathering, and there is no objectifying that is happening in this. The client might be objectifying themselves, and that then falls into representational thinking, which is, for them, correcting, fixing, overcoming, solving, perfecting, through their own representation of themselves.

Trainee: So, instead of that, we as therapists, in being with the client, hold the space open for something else?

Supervisor: Yes, that's right. As therapists, we become more sensitive to what thinking is, and in the openness, the client experiences it as a space to open up their thinking in terms of *being* possibility, and not in terms of being an object. That means that the client relates to themselves differently.

Trainee: But isn't there an irony here, because clients are coming to therapy because they *want* to be gathered, even though they wouldn't say it in that way?

Supervisor: The difference is that they want to be gathered *in themselves*, as the object that they take themselves to be, since they relate to themselves as a self-encased, stand-alone being. They take themselves to be gathered, 'together', they might say, when their world is running smoothly, and then something unexpectedly happens that disrupts that, which then feels like a loss of the gathered unity that the person takes themselves to be.

Trainee: So, when that happens, we explore the way in which the world just keeps going, irrespective of the client, but that their involvement in it and understandings of it can be challenged by such disruptions. And then they are invited to be open to the ways in which meanings change as they come to further understandings.

Supervisor: But there has to be openness, an open space for that exploration to happen in the conversations. And in so doing, they give time to this, rather than relating to time as something that they control. In the openness, there is a happening in the conversation, the way in which we relate, and we are gathered in that happening.

Trainee: I'm interested in the idea of 'letting be', which you said you'd address. Maybe it would help to do that now?

Supervisor: 'Letting' is the key term here. If you try to read some of Martin Heidegger's later essays and lectures, he brings this out very well, although you'll need some patience with it as you read it. Heidegger has a playful approach to words and their meanings. And I think he said something about the significance of the prefix, Ge-, in the German, which I initially didn't understand at all. Ge- means gathering, collecting, unifying. Then he combines that with a word, and it then means something which is being collected. Let me give you an example. You don't need to know German to appreciate this. 'Ge-birge' means a gathering of mountains, or mountain range; if you wanted to present a simple list of individual mountains, you would use the word that is the plural of 'mountain', which is Berge, so there would be no gathering Ge- prefix there. Or take the German word 'lassen', which means 'letting'. He then introduces the word, Ge-lassen-heit, which is all the various ways of lassen that are brought together: freilassen, einlassen, zulassen, seinlassen. Gelassenheit is usually translated as 'releasement', but it is better rendered as 'letting be' in general. However, when translated as 'releasement', it captures the '-heit' bit in Gelassen<u>heit</u>. In English, we put -ness, or -ment, at the end of a word, which makes it into a substantive, or substantivized noun, if you prefer.

Trainee: That relates to therapy in terms of what you said about the open and opening up thinking.

Supervisor: Yes, it does. What I wanted to show is that the German language is so much better than English in showing the various links that certain words have to others. So, it's letting be, and what I said earlier about representational thinking also becomes relevant here. Letting be is a stance of not getting caught up in trying to control, exert mastery and domination over something, because that is just a way of getting enmeshed in a metaphysical understanding of ourselves. So letting be is the opposite in the sense of just being with it, but not getting entrapped in it.

Trainee: Right. I'm still a bit fuzzy on it. Can you give me an example?

Supervisor: Yes, certainly. I think a good example would be the way in which technology works. I don't mean smartphones and laptops, how the internet and quantum machines do what they do – that's the concrete detail of technology – I mean our technological understanding of what it is to be anything at all, how it unfolds in its essence.

Trainee: I'm looking to see how this also has some bearing on therapy. Actually, it will, because therapy itself is being drawn into that technological understanding, as you mention. So, therapists might need to become aware of how they can either be caught up in it and see it in only positive ways, or they can take a more 'letting be' stance. But I'm not yet sure how that plays out. Maybe you can open that up more.

Supervisor: Back to the German again! Ge-stell is a gathering of all the different ways of 'stellen', which is 'placing', 'positing', 'positioning', that is, a standing in place, and then we have the various ways of 'stellen', such as hierstellen, vorstellen, nachstellen, darstellen, bereichstellen.

Trainee: So, I now see how language is important here.

Supervisor: Yes, and when we look at Ge-stell in terms of the essence of technology, how it moves and sways in the way it does, it translates as 'en-framing'. Others translate it as 'positioning', whilst another translation has it as 'synthetic compositionality'. But to put it simply, it's like putting things into a frame, an ordered placing so that everything is in its place, or standing in place, ready to order, ready for use.

Trainee: So, this is a way of understanding everything?

Supervisor: Yes. There is a danger in that we are also in this enframing picture. We understand ourselves in terms of ordering ourselves, being 're-sourceful', being as efficient as possible, minimising error or deviation from the optimal and so on.

Trainee: Maybe that way of ordering is a disciplining that helps people to cultivate skills in a much better way.

Supervisor: Maybe, but look at the way we then relate to other people. They become objectified because they are a means to an end, because their skills and acquired knowledge are marketable, are sellable to the highest bidder. They might well succeed in their achieving high levels of competency, and that is rewarding in itself, but it's all enveloped in a machine-like existence, an age of machination, we might say.

Trainee: That is what therapy can explore, then. That is, not fixing in place, not this 'Ge-stell' way of being. You mentioned the subject mastering and controlling, and that relates to what you say here about positing and positioning of this 'Ge-stell'.

Supervisor: It's an *imposing* of positionality.

Trainee: But if that's a reflection of the client's world, and it's the age in which we live, there's nothing that we can do about it, right?

Supervisor: It's about our openness to the letting be of the imposition of positioning, the Ge-stell way of ordering and placing.

Trainee: OK, but that sounds very passive to my ears: just let be, let go.

Supervisor: No, it's not. The alternative to letting be is not about opposing a certain way of thinking that controls and dominates. Instead, it 'lets be', lets technology 'be' to do its thing and order, optimise, control, whilst we avoid getting caught in blindly surrendering to it and getting sucked into it as if it's the *only* game in town, existentially speaking. For example, I order a new passport online. I have to go through numerous checks, I have to take a selfie, then take a photo of my photo in my expiring passport, and submit it all online. Then I go through various other checks and am sent codes to enter to verify that all this is being done on my personal smartphone, and so on and on. All the data and information is being cross-checked as I'm doing all this, and it's online because it's more efficient, quicker, much more economical. But I recognise it for what it is, let it be the way it happens, and then maybe go on to spend the rest of my afternoon enjoying some time with others.

Trainee: So, you're *in* the Ge-stell way of ordering, but not caught up in it. You can just take it for what it is.

Supervisor: Yes. The two examples that I gave, the first of being online and having to go through all the steps to order a new passport, and then, say, of being with friends, or walking in a park, bring out something of what I think is an important distinction that relates to the way that I understand therapy.

Trainee: The online ordering is a kind of dispersing, and being in the park or with friends is a gathering.

Supervisor: Technology is a separating so that it can control and order according to how it wants to compose things. It de-composes what comes together of its own accord, and *artificially* places them in some kind of ordering. In a way, things aren't 'near' to each other, but completely detached, and are seen only in term of their functionality.

Trainee:	So, having a technological approach to therapy, in its widest sense, doesn't bring near, but distances.
Supervisor:	The client doesn't come into her own, or to what is 'proper' to her. Think of 'proper' here as 'being oneself', being a whole. Another term that we can use is to be finding oneself owning, or owning up to, much like confessing to the truth about something, which is one's existence as uniquely one's own: being 'authentic', in that sense.
Trainee:	So, therapy is a gathering that is not a positioning, placing, putting something in place. It's a letting something be in its unfolding.

Event-ing

Event-ing, as the term is being introduced here, conveys something active and temporal. It can refer to something that is happening in the moment, or over a considerable span of time, even centuries. The event 'events', is event-ing in its unfolding. When we experience an event that is event-ing, it is not something that we can see, but, rather, we *hear* it in its occasioning of the moment in its significance, of being moment-ous. Just as a world 'worlds', that is, moves and sways, as in the case of the world of theatre, for example, so an event 'events', that it is an unfolding of a particular kind. Examples of this can be found in attending sports events, where we are swept up by a feeling of being at one with the many other spectators who chant, sing and applaud in support of their team. Or we find ourselves invited as guests to an awards ceremony that is meaningful to us in acknowledging the achievements that certain people have attained. In the event-ing, there is a gathering, or gatheredness, that gathers of its own accord.

Gathering as 'Letting', 'Allowing'

In gathering, there is a letting what unconceals itself *be* in its lingering presence. That is, it is a leaving be. For our part, this is not something that we relate to as a resource for our use, as if a mere object that stands neutrally and indifferently, opposite or oppositionally placed, and standing before us. Instead, it is an open stance or attitude towards whatever it is that reveals itself in its being manifest. The ways in which we can embrace a letting be is in relation to things, but also in our openness towards others. In the openness, we also embrace the listening that hearkens to the other's speaking. Listening is a stillness and a silence that is a letting be of the other's way of being manifest in their speaking. We are gathered into the other's speaking, and it is only on the basis of our listening that we can then engage in speaking. However, in our openness towards the other, we at the same time let them come towards us in how they appear to us and in the way that we encounter them.

Gathering as Con-versation and Language

As mentioned, we think of an event, or event-ing as a gathering gatheredness. What it gathers is the moment in which there is an appropriation, which we can otherwise describe as a bringing into a unifying unity. We can also understand it in the sense that one thing appropriates itself to something else. For example, soft clay is an inappropriate soil upon which to build a house or building, which means that neither the soft clay nor the building appropriate themselves to each other.[1] In order for there to be an appropriating, there has to be a mutual appropriation of one to the other: the building can only stand if the appropriate earth supports it, and the earth can only be a building bearer if it appropriately 'serves' what stands upon it. Building an igloo in the middle of the desert, to use an obvious example, is an absence of appropriation. In mutual appropriation, therefore, there is a relation in which each appropriates the other, such that each is not wholly independent of, or ex-propriating, the other. In appropriating each other, we can say, perhaps more casually, that they *are* appropriate *to* one another.

When considered in a more therapeutic context, such gathering, unifying, the sense of 'one-ing', is where and when a true conversation happens. It is disclosive, which is exactly what it is that *makes* it an event. As well as being disclosive, it clears the situation, opens it up *as* an openness. We are not in a position to make such a situation happen, just as it is not possible to make a conversation happen. Just as was mentioned earlier in the case of gathering, a conversation unfolds of its own accord. It is in the very happening of the conversation that the therapist and client experience it *as* therapy, or as therapeutic.

To recapitulate so far, then, in considering gathering, an easy misunderstanding that we can fall into is that we take ourselves as the agents who *actively* collect and bring things together through the enactment of our will. Instead, it is the gathering gatheredness (Heidegger, 1953/2014:135), as Heidegger puts it, that gathers of its own accord. Nothing, or no-one is 'doing' the gathering, in other words, but, rather, it is a gathering that gathers us into it, in relation to things and other beings.

Having arrived at this point, then, we ask, how is gathering possible? It is brought about, or enacted, through language. But what does it gather? It gathers ourselves, things and beings generally, into a relation that is the event. What holds all of them together into one, or one-ing, is language. When we speak, and do so in a way that is 'true' to what we are attending to, or in other words, is 'authentic', or 'proper', such language can be said to hold things and ourselves in a relation to each other, such that it binds or holds them together. When we do not speak in a way that is 'proper' to what we are addressing, language 'disaggregates' or disperses this relation.

Heidegger provides a clear though intricate account of gathering in the following way:

> "[t]o collect", to gather, means: to bring various dispersed things together into a unity, and at the same time to bring this unity *forth* and hand it *over*. Into what? Into the unhidden of presencing. Λέγειν [legein] means to bring together into a unity and to bring forth this unity as gathered, i.e., above all as present [...] to let it be manifest in its presencing.
>
> (1976/1998:213)

'Presencing' is a showing up of something, emerging out of the 'hidden', that which has not revealed itself and therefore is not presently presencing. Heidegger shows a strong predilection for drawing on ancient Greek terms that capture something significant in relation to his enquiries and where meaning has been covered over and forgotten over the course of the many centuries of our historical past.

Although gathering might be understood as bringing things and people together and therefore cultivating and maintaining a certain safety in the relation, this is not its predetermined goal, aim or intended purpose. Rather, where there is gathering, there is *already* 'safekeeping'. In fact, in the absence of such safekeeping, only dissemination and dispersal follows. In other words, in dispersal, nothing follows its own essence, much like a tree's essence that is a temporal unfolding, first as an acorn, then germinating with the emergence of a shoot that is a seedling, then to a sapling over time, and eventually as a mature oak tree. In this example, where there is no gathering of the conditions of climate, nurturance and light in supporting the acorn's eventual becoming a tree, it destroys this unfolding.

Gathering the Phenomenon in a Phenomenological Exploration

Our general tendency is to approach an understanding of words in terms of something fixed, but they are only pointing provisionally towards the basis or essence of a phenomenon. Take the phenomenon of frustration for example. It has a certain everyday sense to it that we already claim to understand when we encounter it. It carries something of the sense of the situation not meeting our desires or expectations in some way. For the therapist, however, the challenge is to stay with what the client is naming as frustration, and then inviting a deeper descriptively-based exploration of its essence. The essence, to remind ourselves, is the way in which the phenomenon is structured and unfolds or moves, temporally speaking, and which is the very way in which it shows up as the thing that it is. The phenomenon that has been initially named by the client has not yet gathered itself into its structural unity through the explication of its elements. The therapist engages the client to open the conversation in the attempt to bring out the phenomenon of frustration in its gathered unifying unity.

Ways of Gathering

Karen Blixen's short story, 'Babette's Feast' is an example of gathering, or eventing. It is an unfolding experience in which a number of guests attend a dinner; they 'come together' in gathering themselves and enfolding in and with one another. Virgina Woolf's novel, 'Mrs Dalloway' similarly shows something of the way in which people coming together and gathering becomes something 'sacred', a unique and inimitable experience that is not repeatable. We might recall a particularly wonderful and pleasant holiday, say, on a Greek island, which prompts us to make plans to return and re-experience what we had savoured in our remembering how exhilarating it was. But once there again and in the very same place, we fail to re-live the exact same sense of joy.

Gathering can show itself in various ways and in different contexts. As well as having a celebratory aspect to it, as in the case of being in good company with others and enjoying the experience in its sense of occasion, a gathering, namely, the event, might also be attributable to the birth of a child, or a moment of falling in love with another person. But an event can also gather itself into a moment of sorrow, such as a funeral, in which people attend the burial of a close relative or friend, or a commemoration of a past historical event that bears a considerable significance on our current existence and way of life. With this in mind, the therapy session might, at times, gather itself into the client's experience of freedom, and, at other times, have a gathered sense of more vulnerable and sorrowful moments, as they reveal something truthful in relation to their existence. Certain therapeutic approaches only seem to consider and emphasise the 'positive' aspect, presumably to bring the client (as well as the therapist) away from any mood of passivity and resignation to one of agency and expression of their will, so that they can enact change. This, however, overlooks the ways in which the exploration and expression of our thoughts and feelings already gather themselves into revealing meaningful insights about ourselves.

To take another possible scenario, a client might recall a celebratory family meal as it happened some time ago in the past, and with the passing of years, certain family members are now dead. Such an event has become more a remembrance rather than a celebration. One remembers with fondness and love how the event gathered itself into something meaningful, but also, in the remembrance, one is gathered into the experience with a certain gentle sorrow and lamentation of it not being in any way reproducible. It carries an event-ful-ness in its being possible only once (in a lifetime), we might say.

A Personal Example of Gathering and Being Gathered

In my much younger past as a philosophy undergraduate, I attended a particularly demanding evening lecture, grappling with some tortuously subtle lines of argument presented by our lecturer. Mercifully, he eventually brought our time to an end. As we started to leave the lecture room, a couple of my fellow students suggested that the three of us take ourselves out of the academic setting and visit a local traditional Greek restaurant for a meal, to which I readily agreed. On our arrival, a table was designated for us, which fortunately was quite near a group of musicians playing and singing traditional Greek songs with a real passion, energy and gusto. We set about ordering food and drinks, along with, according to Greek custom, a stack of smashing plates.

With our meal quickly dispensed with, the evening began to open up. An energy drew us more and more into a welcoming atmosphere as the music hypnotically enticed the room full of diners to their feet. By this point, they were singing along and dancing in a *choreia*, or circle. Several people even got up and danced on their tables. Others demonstrated their artful skills in plate-smashing, which was now taking on an almost ritualistic frequency. Looking all around the room, we took a certain pleasure in being present to others enjoying themselves. Having discussed his work earlier in the philosophy lecture, it was now clear what the Scottish philosopher, David Hume, meant when he talked about the 'pleasing sentiment of approbation' that we feel when we witness something of which we approve. This event was a 'coming together' of its own accord, a feeling of being gathered and collected into it.

Gathering is the way in which we are pulled or drawn into a certain attunement to, or in, a situation. In a sense, this reflects something of the way that we can relate to others, and to things or objects. On the one hand, we can see things as mere objects that stand separate to and independent of us, and that can easily be replaced by, substituted for, or disposed of in favour of similar objects that would fulfil the same function. On the other hand, we can relate to certain things that we don't treat 'object-ively', but very much as things that mean something to us in their having a place in the experience that is being visited upon us at the time. For example, the old terracotta jug of wine on the table in the restaurant allows me to pour the wine into my friends' glasses, whilst exchanging comments and approving glances at each other. The wine jug is set upon the table, but it takes on a significance in the overall setting in which we find ourselves. We are, in effect, gathered around meaningful things that we see before us, such that the jug, in this case, has an orienting force that plays its part in the gathering that reflects what is happening in the overall experience. The jug, to put it differently, makes a certain 'demand' on me, or is 'calling' me, to see it as a thing rather than as a resource that is a source of indifference to me. If I related to it as a resource, I would simply see it in terms of its function as a receptacle for holding liquid refreshments. In that case, we would simply be adapting rather 'functionally' towards the situation, and not taking in the sense of occasion in which we find ourselves.

Gathering and Therapy

In coming to a close, several points can be made in the light of the preceding sections.

In some cases, the therapist and client don't gather themselves into therapeutic conversations; that is, the encounter does not seem to unfold, and thereby becomes stilted or stuck in certain ways. There is a kind of withdrawing, and perhaps even closedness, or concealedness. Much of what happens in conversation, therefore, has to do with openness, and the extent to which the therapist and client are attuned to one another, such that a genuine happening emerges. The client, for their part, is, therefore, being invited to involve themselves in the conversation, such that they can focus on and disclose the phenomenon itself and not some semblance of it, nor talk in a 'false' way. Talking falsely is not a moral judgement or criticism, but simply a recognition that at such times we speak in a way that *seems* like the truth, but in fact covers over what needs to be uncovered, unconcealed and revealed.

A therapist can attend to making the therapy meeting room as comfortable as possible, by introducing soft lighting, arranging comfortable and relaxing sofa chairs on which to sit, and ensuring that no particularly distracting noises, objects and disruptive clutter are present. But this only attends to the setting. Where gathering is concerned, it can only emerge out of itself, rather than it somehow having to do with our willing it to happen. Planning and controlling in order to anticipate the course of a meeting or session gathering itself misunderstands the way in which such a gathering emerges of its own accord. Both the therapist and the client release themselves into the encounter in order for the gathering to gather itself. In more concrete and familiar terms, it is a bonding and connecting that enters the experience for the two participants, or partners, in conversation.

In letting something be, and not attempting to will it into being, we submit to the way in which something unfolds and emerges, rather than directing it through some form of pre-prepared idea of how things should go, managing it through some kind of already available knowledge or conviction that places everything in a way that is considered the best and most successful outcome of all. Of course, in many spheres of our lives, we organise events and situations to certain degrees, according to the importance of the occasions where such levels of attention are deemed necessary. But in a therapeutic setting, this stifles and prevents the unfolding emergence of the encounter and the space to embrace openness.

Note

1 I develop and adapt this from Daniel Dahlstrom's account of appropriation, p.26.

Bibliography

Dahlstrom, D.O. (2023). *The Heidegger Dictionary*. 2nd Edition. London: Bloomsbury Academic.

Heidegger, M. (1953/2014). *Introduction to Metaphysics*. 2nd Edition. Trans. G. Fried & R. Polt. London: Yale University Press.

Heidegger, M. (1976/1998). *Pathmarks*. Ed. W. McNeill. Cambridge: Cambridge University Press.

Chapter 4

Converse-ing

Introduction

Understood in its simplest way, therapy is a space for engaging in conversations between the therapist and the client. This much seems to be uncontestable. But what is it that makes a conversation essentially therapeutic? What is the particular way in which the conversation unfolds temporally within a therapeutic context? In the course of this chapter, attempts will be made to bring us closer to unveiling the way in which a conversation between therapist and client moves and sways, and in a way that is very different in character to everyday conversations and dialogues.

Converse-ing

Two experienced therapists, Tad and Marek, meet in Hyde Park, London. Having previously first met at a conference a year ago, they promised to meet again to discuss aspects of therapy, since there were points of interest and differences in their thinking.

Tad: I originally trained in the psychodynamic approach, but now see myself as just practising without real alignment with any particular school or orientation. I wouldn't call myself 'integrative' either, because I'm not trying to absorb various approaches into some kind of coherent whole. It's more to do with being in dialogues with clients and supporting them to arrive at their own insights, questions and answers.

Marek: I see. I think of myself as working from an existential perspective, taking a specifically phenomenological approach in my work with clients.

Tad: You add the 'phenomenological' part as being important to you in some way. Don't all existential therapists work phenomenologically, though?

DOI: 10.4324/9781003638698-5

Marek: That's a topic all of its own, as there are different ways that therapists might also think about phenomenology.

Tad: So how do you understand phenomenology?

Marek: In brief, the phenomenological approach draws on two main thinkers: Edmund Husserl and Martin Heidegger. Husserl introduces 'bracketing' as a way of just staying with the client's experience as it manifests in their consciousness. That means describing it as extensively as possible, without thinking about the world and context of meanings and significance in which we find ourselves. Heidegger, the second, thinks of phenomenology as always already finding ourselves in a world, which is where we start from in our exploration. So the contrast between the two is how they think about the world. That is what Husserl brackets, or shuts off, because he only wants to see what's there in consciousness, and not veer away from it. Heidegger says, no, you can't do that, because you lose the very basis of being a human being. He also avoids any talk of a consciousness. But there's a longer story about that which I won't go into here. Husserl's is a transcendental phenomenology, whilst Heidegger's is a hermeneutic phenomenology.

Tad: OK, that's already quite a lot to take in, and very concise too. I take it that the existential approach is very philosophically-oriented, and that puts me off it because I'm not philosophically-inclined.

Marek: Yes, it does draw on philosophy, and on particular thinkers, including Sartre, Merleau-Ponty and others, but they aren't necessarily all integrated into one way of thinking, because some are simply very much at odds, philosophically speaking, with others. But, as far as existential therapy goes, I think the important aim is to really get the basics in place, and not get too caught up in trying to *be* a philosopher. I don't think of myself as a philosopher, and it takes a little time to acquaint oneself properly with some of the ideas. But certain therapists and authors have tried to make it more accessible, which itself is a challenge.

Tad: Yes, I have come across one or two, and they make it a little easier to follow. But isn't philosophy too speculative in using and applying it to a therapeutic approach? We need something more solid than that, surely?

Marek: That's a really good question. I have a view on why I think we look for something more solid and grounding for us. Whenever we try to think about the human, we come up with some theory or other so that we can provide a permanent or enduring foundation of some kind. There is something really powerful about theory, if we think about it for a moment.

Tad: I have to say that theory, for me, is the basis of any therapy, so I think that's how we should proceed.

Marek: Say more, because I have a different view to yours on this.

Tad: Theory gets us to the truth of things, because it says something that applies universally, and in all relevant cases where certain features or behavioural aspects of a person are present. So, we have theories of personality disorder, various theoretical approaches to therapy and so forth. It is grounded in amassing 'data' or information, based on researchers' extensive investigations, gathering it all into themes or clusters that are then brought together and taken as the foundation for that theory.

Marek: So, you now have theory. OK. What does that then afford you?

Tad: Well, I can understand the client on the basis of certain ways of behaving. I would take time to explore what is going on for the client in terms of the issues that they find challenging or problematic, and then eventually identify the overarching reason for these issues by drawing on theory.

Marek: But then, what must you be assuming about being human that inclines you to follow that way of thinking about your approach to therapy in the *first* place?

Tad: Well, the person's behavioural patterns, their cognitive style or frame through which they behave in certain ways, certain inner tensions that manifest as symptoms, their inability to engage in more socially acceptable ways, the degree to which they can't regulate themselves in certain situations and so on.

Marek: But that wasn't what I was asking you. What you provided here is already drawing on a lot of theory, but my question is geared more around the following: what is it that you presuppose in order to talk in the way that you just have?

Tad: This is moving towards the philosophical more than I'm inclined to pursue. Let me think. (Long pause). I draw on a theory about the human. I need something that can explain what is happening in the person's experience in terms of something that goes *beyond* that experience.

Marek: OK. So that's the job of theory. What I hear you doing when you draw on theory is that you go from what is being presented, and then you link all that by subsuming it under something general and universal. When you do that, theory fixes in place the explanation for the experience. It's immovable, in other words. You can't have theory moving around and constantly transforming itself. It has to stay still. That provides it with a sense of stability, a ground, as I like to say. We no longer have to think, in a way. It simplifies things for us, because something is already laid out in advance for us to then use and draw on.

Tad: OK, I see that. And at the same time, it does feel unsettling if I had no theory to draw on. But what's the alternative? That we abandon theory?

Marek: I think it's more about first trying to understand how powerful theory is. It is very compelling. The question for me is, why live in theory at all? The alternative, as you put it, is something that we can come on to shortly. So, what is it that attracts us to theory?

Tad: We can make knowledge claims, which itself places us in a more empowered position, I suppose. Knowledge allows us to feel entitled to make certain truth claims.

Marek: Yes, I think so. The move that we make is that we look to something beyond ourselves, which is more reliable than *our* thinking. Thinking involves staying with what shows up in and around us. But thinking is hard, and we might also come to the point where we are reluctant to do this. So we move towards the conviction that staying with the experience is not enough.

Tad: That makes me think about the way in which you asked me the question about the human being. In a way, I'm presupposing that the human being can't provide its own insights, it can't pull itself up by its own bootstraps! It can't stand on its own feet! There is an underlying sense of being insufficient to the task of understanding ourselves, I suppose. I assume that the human being can only really understand itself by drawing on something that is abstract and general, that is, that captures what is true for *all* cases and that is then applied to something that shows up in a person's experience. To take an example: if a person disregards others, tends to be very aggressive and even violent towards them, has no sense of guilt or regret about their behaviour, is deceitful, impulsive, reckless, callous and shows very little understanding of personal responsibility and trust towards others, then I would be inclined to say that this person is anti-social in personality, and that therapy needs to take an approach based on this.

Marek: But in making that move we already commit to the idea that we're getting in touch with what is universal and absolute, unquestionably true, that has a lucidly transparent and complete access to what is going on for the individual. At the same time, we begin to build a technical language around all this. In order to feel that we are in control, we have a tendency to position things by naming them, but we do it in a way that removes the element of the temporal and dynamic, and instead says, in positioning something, it is in place, placed before us so that it doesn't sway, and that then enables us to control it, first by labelling it, that is, diagnosing it, and then placing it under an established explanatory framework that we call theory.

Tad: I have the feeling that we've been circling around the fundamental question of what we take the human being to be, which then determines how we approach our work.

Marek: Yes, that's been my line of thinking here. My approach is to stay with the person's experience, and not jump away from that. I think that we can get into all kinds of problems if we try to make that jump, however tempting it might be.

Tad: So, staying with the experience. Let me see if I can 'stay' with that as a possibility. If I remain at the level of the experience, then I face the client in their way of expressing themselves, the way that they see others, the situations that become challenging, the possible feelings that might underlie how they live at times.

Marek: Yes, I think it's extremely complex, and it's not suggesting that there is a standard way to think about all this, or that something magical happens. It's more to do with the experience of being with the person and letting the space unfold in a way that isn't already prefiguring how things need to go. It also offers the person another way to experience being in a relationship, and is very likely one that hasn't ever been experienced by them before.

Tad: But in bringing out the client's experience through the exploration, where does that leave the client?

Marek: Well, there is a lot going on that we can call the 'background', if I can call it that.

Tad: Which is?

Marek: As the client is revealing or discovering something or other in the course of the conversation, because nothing is scripted, and words just come to them as they speak, they are also disclosing themselves.

Tad: Disclosing themselves? You mean that they are saying something about themselves as they speak?

Marek: That's right, but I'm not sure we're hearing the words that you just used in the same way. I hear what you said as true, but it's all in the meaning of 'saying'. The client is saying a lot about themselves as they speak and talk about the weather, for example. It is the weather that they're talking about, sure, but they are conveying something about themselves in the speaking, if you see what I mean. They are disclosing the kind of person that they are, whether it be their disposition, the way that they are open to their existence, or somehow closed off to it, and so many other things.

Tad: Yes, I can see that. When I think about our work as therapists, much of what goes on is in the 'background', as you said just a moment ago. For one, it's the way in which we and the client are relating, how we are being with each other.

Marek: I agree, though I wouldn't quite put it like that. The way that we think of language and how we use it is that it's a 'me and you' of the therapist and the client that is the relationship. It's a focus on two separate entities, if you like.

Tad: But it is, surely? There's myself as the therapist, and then there's the client! There's one person, and there is another person.

Marek: Yes, but that gets caught up in not seeing the true phenomenon at is most fundamental level. We both used the word, 'background'. So, what is backgrounded?

Tad: In the background?

Marek: The language here is now getting really tricky! I don't go along with the word 'in', in asking, what's 'in the background'. That's similar to the way that you just talked about two separate entities.

Tad: OK. How do you see it, then?

Marek: The relationship is not something that you can point to or objectify. Language as we use it, certainly at this stage of our history, renders everything in terms of this dualism, an opposition, or what is positionally opposite to me, namely, an object. So, I am the subject set over against the object. We then talk about the relation of two separate subjects, rather than the way in which the relating is pervasive, hidden, so to speak.

Tad: So that accounts for the incorrect way of thinking about 'me and you'. But what about it being in the background? You commented on that as well.

Marek: OK, but before I do, it's not incorrect to speak in that way of there being two people; it's actually correct!

Tad: Now you're playing with me! But I don't think you're trying to undermine me. Maybe this is another example of how language might be covering over something else.

Marek: What you just said is true in terms of language! But to your point about the relationship question, it is *correct* to speak in the two-person way that you mentioned, but it's not true! There is a distinction. When I say it's not true, I mean that when we address the way in which the relation is backgrounded, it's what I think of as being-with, which is true, rather than being correct. It's a fundamental aspect of being human, or our kind of being. I'll throw in a term that we can maybe get onto some other time, but I don't think we'll get to talk about it today, which is the 'ontological'. The ontological reflects the way we enquire into the truth of our way of being.

Tad: OK. I'll have to reflect on that more. But what about the 'in' that is in the background?

Marek: If it's in the background, it's as if you put something inside something else. It's back to the dualist way of thinking again. We take 'relationship', and then we put it inside the 'background', as if it were a box. It's just that that thinking approach mischaracterises the very way in which our relating happens.

Tad: That's taken us a way away from where we started, but it's opening up another way of thinking for me. I'm mindful of time, maybe we can put this on hold until later.

Marek: That sounds good.

Dialogue and Conversation

The English language has two words for the discourse that takes place between two people: 'dialogue' and 'conversation'. How, then, are we to understand these terms, since they both seem to refer to the same thing? What is it that distinguishes them, if at all?

The word, 'conversation', can be traced back to its Latin origins, with the more archaic prefix, 'cum-' later rendered as 'com-' (Lewis & Short, 1879:395), which means 'together with', 'with', 'in connection with', as with, 'combination'. This was subsequently modified in order to help with the pronunciation of words, and so was changed to 'con-'. It was then brought together with 'versare', which means 'to turn', or 'versatio', 'turning', and this led to various forms, such as 'converso', and 'conversatio', which means 'to turn about with', or 'to turn together' (Lewis & Short, 1879:395).

Attending to words with a similar meaning in the German language, however, at least two terms for 'conversation' are available to its speakers: 'Gespräch' and 'Konversation'. Heidegger's preferred term is 'Gespräch'. This is because it is composed of the prefix 'Ge-' which is then combined with 'spräch', which comes from the verb, 'sprechen', to speak. 'Ge-' is a term that collects and gathers, and in this case, gathers speaking, or speakers. This was chosen in preference to the

German 'Dialog', that is, 'dialogue', because 'conversation' is the way in which language itself gathers. It is the gatheredness that speaking necessitates. 'Conversation' isn't a mode of description, or a means of conveying facts or information, which is an instrumentalised understanding, but rather, it conveys how conversation actually *is*: language in its own conversation. Language, in Heidegger's sense of the word, is not meant as a system or tool of communication, the totality of words and its grammar, but, he claims, more fundamentally, that language speaks *us* insofar as we are always already 'languaging' beings, living or being 'housed' in language.

Even if we agree with what has been said so far, why not use these terms interchangeably? What is the fundamental basis for not using 'dialogue' in favour of 'conversation'? After all, we might express a preference for 'dialogue' in describing the way in which the therapist and client are two people with distinct characters who are speaking and listening to one another. This, however, is precisely what Heidegger takes issue with, which is the *metaphysical* character of language that is reflected in the inherent dualism in this word. 'Dialogue' suggests a conversation between two, because it is composed of a *dia-*, that is between, or across two people rather than con-verse-ing, versing together as one. Dialogue also intimates more of a pushing of the two towards one another. Underlying this is a very Parmenidean point that Heidegger is making about conversation, as opposed to a Levinasian stance that thinks of it more as a dialogue. He reads the Greek thinker, Parmenides, very closely as his source for this, going back to the ancient Greek language and its understanding of the difference between the active, passive and middle voices. If I use the active voice, I might say to someone, 'the postman is delivering letters later today', in which case, I am telling you something. If I use the passive voice, I am being told something, say, that, 'the letters are being delivered by the postman later today'. But when I use the medial or middle voice, we speak together, or we speak '*between*' ourselves. We therefore might possibly try to render this as, 'the delivering of the post is in its later receiving', although this is obviously unwieldy, and reflects the limits of making good sense when drawing on our modern Cartesian way of speaking. In a conversation, the middle voice conveys more of mutuality or oneness, a gathered relevance to it as it proceeds. By contrast, our modern Latinised western language has been dominated by its active and passive elements. The middle voice, though still identifiable, is less used in our speaking to one another in our daily everyday encounters. Where we might see this more at play, however, is in poetry, where words come into a more intimate relation with each other.

As for the metaphysical character of dialogue, Katherine Davies elaborates on this more comprehensively in the following passage (2024:5):

> a dialogue presupposes the availability of the object about which subjects speak. Dialogue relies on what Heidegger calls metaphysical or representational thinking, which reduces things to objects and human beings to subjects. A conversation, on the other hand, endeavours to wait for non-metaphysical thinking – that releases any reliance on the subject/object metaphysical distinction – to

> unfold. It does not presume that the topic of which the conversationalists would speak is available in advance. Conversation instead calls for its speakers to remain open to the possibility that the event of conversation will fundamentally change them. Where dialogue depicts subjects carrying out a detached examination of a given object, conversation unfolds an unforeseeable and uncontrollable transformational event.

This captures well what is essential to a therapeutic conversation, which is that it allows a way in which its 'happening' opens and unfolds of its own accord.

A possible way in which conversations in therapy sessions can deviate from their open movement is when there is a certain reliance on knowledge and theory, which reflects a metaphysical approach. It introduces a knower who imparts knowledge towards the other, but this results in the closing off of true conversation. Plato thought that we must have knowledge of something in order to be or enact that quality, characteristic, tendency or attitude. For example, I require a prior knowledge of courage in order to be courageous. This approach reflects a tendency in our time to draw on various kinds of literature, or other sources that are taken to be authoritative, that will tell or explain to us how to cope with feelings, situations and other people. This, however, means that we deny ourselves the opportunity to engage ourselves on a path of thinking that stays with the experience in order to explore its nuances and tensions, so that we might alight upon insights and deeper understandings. Instead, we are presented with an immediate and painless route that saves us the time and effort, because knowledge is presented as if it is factual and infallible. This may be advantageous in certain respects, for example, in practical, everyday life, but when it comes to the larger and more important questions that are concerned with the way that we live and make sense of how we find ourselves in the world, we open ourselves in addressing this through conversations.

Clients who are in search of therapy might assume that a Platonic approach is the underlying basis of the therapeutic conversation. Therapy, however, offers something more Aristotelian, in taking the position that clients become more courageous, to continue with this example, *through* the conversations that expose the assumptions, feelings and challenges that they hold in the face of situations and in being with others. In fact, clients already undergo a process of becoming increasingly courageous within the very sessions themselves, by embracing openness, and disclosing what feels vulnerable or uncertain for them. In doing so, they are more receptive to transcending previously more rigid and seemingly immovable stances by now recognising other possibilities that they had not considered, or that now made more sense for them as viable options in their lives. In this Aristotelian sense, then, moments in which being courageous emerges is through the embodied sense of be-coming, or a continual 'always on the way' to being courageous. By contrast, no Platonic abstract knowledge of courage automatically seeps into the client's way of being as courageous. To think in this way reflects a more mechanistic approach towards oneself that might even take hold for a time if adopted, but that does not constitute change in an enduring sense, because it relies on a representational way of thinking. In other words, it is reflected more in a case of rule-following.

We Are a Conversation

Discourse, for Heidegger, is the general way in which we make manifest, through articulation, the intelligibility of things, how they are understandable in the first place. Language is the means by which we do this, but discourse provides the framework within which we express ourselves in using language, through words, gestures and the various ways in which we make ourselves intelligible to ourselves and others. Katherine Withy identifies four 'moments' in discourse (2021:133): what is spoken about, what is said, the communication, and what is made known. We speak through assertions that we make, such as, 'the world of technology reduces things to mere resources'. Another person hears what is being spoken about, that is, follows the content and understands it at face value. But this might be different to what is being *said.* The person speaking might actually be saying that they are feeling caught in the loss of closeness with others and experiencing difficulty in trusting them. In that case, what they are saying is something *of* the world, but not explicitly speaking out *about* it through words. Here we should not overlook the fact that both speaking and saying are part of discourse. Next, in the communication, the speaker is *sharing* their world with the other person. It is a form of discourse that reflects their being-with-others. Lastly, what is made known when the assertion is communicated is the speaker's way of *finding themself in the world.* This might show itself in any one or more number of possible ways, from anger, isolation, worry, to frustration or resignation.

Taking these four moments or elements and considering them in the context of a conversation, the conversants are uncovering what matters to them, sharing this with the other(s) and allowing the conversation itself to unfold as more is unveiled over the course of time. The conversation provides a space for being-with another in a way that being with oneself does not. It invites the hearer to be attuned to the other's world, and to be moved by it. In fact, when genuine conversation takes place, our world is re-shaped, altered or even transformed, given that it addresses us in our way of *being.* In other words, since to exist is to be-in-the-world, the way in which our world can be challenged and even reconfigured is reflected in our being. We are, to put it concisely, worldly beings.

Reflections on Conversation

Hans-Georg Gadamer

Hans-Georg Gadamer says that a conversation is hermeneutic (1960/1989:385, 388). Hermeneutics is, in brief, the process of coming to an understanding through interpretation (1960/1989:385). We make sense of something that we hear by interpreting it, and disclose our having understood what we have heard through our reflections and responses. There is also a logical structure of openness, Gadamer says (1960/1989:361, 362). When we are open, we are then able to hear a question that lies within our experience. In fact, he adds, we encounter questions in all experiences (1960/1989:361, 362).

Interpretation itself, as it unfolds in the conversation, is reached according to the interpreter's world horizon, or perspective on the world. The horizon is not a clear and distinct line, as such, but a backdrop, or background that configures the world in a certain way. Gadamer describes it as,

> the range of vision that includes everything that can be seen from a particular vantage point. Applying this to the thinking mind, we speak of narrowness of horizon, of the possible expansion of horizon, of the opening up of new horizons, and so forth.
>
> (1960/1989:302)

In more concrete terms, then, I have some measure of understanding of the client's cultural world, for example, even though it is very different to mine. In engaging in conversation, our world horizons 'fuse', as Gadamer puts it – 'understanding is always the fusion of these horizons' (1960/1989:306) – and 'the horizon of the present is continually in the process of being formed because we are continually having to test all our prejudices' (1960/1989:306). These 'prejudices' are the cultural and historical pre-formed judgements and norms-based 'facts' that we have made meaningful to ourselves in our own way and are the basis of our understanding of the world, including what it means to be human. Once we engage in conversation, we open ourselves to the other person's horizonal world, and are brought to experience significant moments in which our own horizon of understanding is challenged.

Jan Hendrik van den Berg

Van den Berg takes a very pronounced phenomenological approach in exploring the conversation in his essay, 'The Conversation', written in 1953. Highlighting just a very selective few points that he develops in his enquiry, in conversation, we 'see' the other, that is, we relate to them as another person who has their own understanding of the world. We also 'move' the other, appealing to them (perhaps through a question, or a challenge) whilst also staying true to what we are seeing in the topic under discussion. In other words, we are not 're-moving' ourselves from the conversation. We see the other and also remain true to how we are orienting ourselves towards the issue that is before us in that moment. It is also a seeing of the other's differing perspective that might lead to a disruption in the conversation, or some form of 'illusory sharing' (1953/2021:37), where we realise that we are not on the 'same page'. However, this also opens the possibility of re-entering a conversation. That is, we can dip momentarily out of conversation, perhaps because of a comment that feels like a deviation or disengagement from the topic, or a distraction that might occur, such as the intrusive sound of a car horn nearby. But disruption can also give way to resumption of a coming together. Lastly, for van den Berg, as for other writers on this subject, some conversations are already focused from the outset on reaching a certain aim or goal. In such cases, any sense of a shared world based on togetherness is compromised or even lost, because having a goal-oriented focus is 'hardly contained in the togetherness' (1953/2021:37).

Maurice Blanchot

Maurice Blanchot opens us to the possible impact that the therapist can offer by reflecting back and summarising what the client has just expressed in the course of the session. He offers a vignette that conveys this very powerfully (1969/1993:341):

> I recall being present at a conversation between two men who were very different from one another. One would say in simple and profound sentences some truth he had taken to heart; the other would listen in silence, then when reflection had done its work he would in turn express some proposition, sometimes in almost the same words, albeit slightly differently (more rigorously, more loosely, or more strangely). This redoubling of the same affirmation constituted the strongest of dialogues. Nothing was developed, opposed, or modified; and it was manifest that the first interlocutor learned a great deal, and even infinitely, from his own words repeated – not because they were adhered to and agreed with, but, on the contrary, through the infinite difference. For it is as though what he said in the first person as an 'I' had been expressed anew by him as 'other'[*autrui*] and as though he had thus been carried into the very unknown of his thought: where his thought, without being altered, became absolutely other.

Blanchot captures a significant aspect of a conversation between two people. It reflects the depth of understanding that the one listening discloses to the speaker through what he calls, 'the infinite difference' between the two people. That is, hearing one's own thoughts put back to oneself opens one to hearing the 'very unknown of [one's] thought' (1969/1993:341). As Blanchot also says, there is something infinite about the conversation. In its infinitude, there is openness and freedom.

Taking our cue from Blanchot, then, in conversation, there is both a way in which we are separate, but also a unity, through intimacy. The conversation is a holding together by a holding apart. If we happen to think of it *only* as a holding together, there is no space to open up any difference-ing. That is, there is really only distancing and oppositional binary thinking. That difference-ing is only possible if there is a holding together, an intimacy. In other words, we intimate something to one another in the conversation by 'versing together'.

Conversation in Therapy

A conversation in a therapy session is special in kind, since it differs from the kind of conversation that takes place with a priest, lawyer, our employer, a relative or a friend. Given this difference, then, we return again to the question, what kind of conversation is it? Perhaps a first point to make is with regard to the therapeutic space. Therapy sessions most commonly take place in a convivial setting, a certain ambience, which involves privacy, comfort, appropriate furniture, lighting and so on. Conversations with a therapist disclose those aspects of a client's way of being that are not introduced in conversations with one's neighbour, or even partner, since the therapist holds no place in the client's personal, historical or social 'life-spaces'. The client steps out of their familiar world, and into a new one in which they become increasingly able to express whatever comes to them, without the constraining feeling that they would experience were they to do so in their everyday public and social worlds.

The conversation between the therapist and client is both temporally finite and infinite in character, since only a set time is provided for the duration of the session; there is a point at which it stops, by prior agreement. During the session, the conversation can, in principle, be infinite in the depth and extent to which something is explored and discussed. At the same time, given the time limitation, there is an inherent inability to talk about and cover everything within the session, since something tends to remain outstanding for the client in addressing an issue. However, this does not mean that the conversation has exhausted the possibilities of continued exploration, since further elaborations and perspectives of the same topic can unfold over time. This also raises an interesting aspect of being in a session, namely, that the client experiences time differently, whether this be in relation to a temporary pause from living according to 'clock' time, or a way of relating to the time in the session as their *own*, rather than reckoning with the compromises that arise when it is shared with others. However, whilst it is true that, in the therapeutic space, time is *shared* with the therapist, it is not 'owned' by the latter.

The conversation between therapist and client delivers itself over to a playful engagement in exploring topics and issues, in a way that is imbued with a seriousness and meaningfulness. It moves in a way that is more 'poetic' in character than having a more scientific and technical intent. Where the conversation might take on a more technical orientation, however, it presents a danger of moving towards a more manualised and calculative way of thinking.

In a conversation with a client, there is a need to find the language that brings both therapist and client in a 'speaking together'. But speaking is possible only on the basis of listening. That is, the essence of language is to listen; it is a hearing, and speaking takes a complementary role. How so? It is the stillness of listening and hearing that beckons. As the therapist listens to the client talking about their feelings of love, for example, it is simply an initial pointing towards something more rather than being taken as a definitive term that conveys instant transparency as to its meaning. Certainly, the therapist hears the word, 'love', and understands it as it relates to their own world, but it is the client's understanding that is of crucial importance here. It is in the conversation with the client that a search for further clarification follows. In the course of the conversation, the attempt to grasp the word by now seeing it as a concept closes off further exploration. The search for clarification ends prematurely, because a concept is encased in a way that resists phenomenological enquiry. When we take a word as a concept, we objectify it and pull it out of its context, such that we fix it in place, so that it can be observed independently of its contextual circumstances. Doing so in this way leaves it with out a world in which it manifests as love, we might say. Instead, the therapist's intended approach reflects a way of exploring the world in terms of an experience that moves and sways, i.e., has a dynamic sense to the way it happens temporally.

Bibliography

Blanchot, M. (1969/1993). *The Infinite Conversation.* Trans. S. Hanson. Minneapolis: University of Minneapolis Press.

Davies, K. (2024). *Heidegger's Conversations: Toward a Poetic Pedagogy*. Albany, NY: Suny Press.

Gadamer, H-G. (1960/1989). *Truth and Method.* 2nd Edition. Trans. and Revd. J. Weinsheimer & D. G. Marshall. London: Sheed & Ward.

Gadamer, H.-G. (1976). *Philosophical Hermeneutics*. Trans. and Ed. D.E. Linge. Berkeley: University of California Press.

Lewis, C.T. & Short, C. (1879). *A Latin Dictionary*. Oxford: Clarendon Press.

Petropoulos, G. (2021). Heidegger's Reading of Plato: On Truth and Ideas. *The Journal for the British Society for Phenomenology*. 52:2: 118–136.

Van den Berg, J.H. (1953/2021). The Conversation [Het Gesprek]. Trans. M. van Manen & M. van Manen. In M. van Manen & M. van Manen (eds.) *Classic Writings for a Phenomenology of Practice*. London: Routledge. pp.31–46.

Vilhauer, M. (2010). *Gadamer's Ethics of Play: Hermeneutics and the Other*. Plymouth: Lexington Books.

Wiercinski, A. (ed.) (2011). *Gadamer's Hermeneutics and the Art of Conversation*. London: Transaction Publishers.

Withy, K. (2021). We Are a Conversation. In C. Engelland (ed.). *Language and Phenomenology*. London: Routledge. pp.132–148.

Wrathall, M.A. (2011). *Heidegger and Unconcealment*. Cambridge: Cambridge University Press. pp.11–39.

Chapter 5

Listen-ing

Introduction

The capacity to listen sits at the very heart of our understanding of therapy. The therapist listens intently to what the client is expressing about something that concerns or preoccupies them. Listening to what the client has to say orients the therapist towards the issue that then invites further exploration and clarification. But is the therapist's listening the same as every other possible kind of listening? The listening that the therapist embodies seems to be intuitively different in kind to what we encounter in our everyday situations and encounter with others. The attempt in the following sections of this chapter is to bring the therapist's listening into a clearer view of what we might call 'therapeutic listening', as opposed to everyday listening.

Conversation on Listen-ing

Student: So much mention is made of listening in therapy training courses, and in the various introductory books that cover it on our reading lists.

Tutor: Yes, I remember it all during my own training too.

Student: Yet it seems obvious to me that it could do with further exploration. It would be good to do that here, perhaps.

Tutor: Many courses don't really spend as much time discussing it as they perhaps might want to.

Student: Do you mean that we could define it more, go into it more deeply?

Tutor: I'm not so sure about defining it, but going into it more deeply, absolutely.

Student: So, how would you go about that? What would you say about listening?

Tutor: I don't claim to have the answers, and I don't think just giving answers to questions is all that helpful. I think that the more we open it for

DOI: 10.4324/9781003638698-6

further discussion, the more we get to see what therapeutic listening is in the way it happens, 'live' in the session, so to say.

Student: Practising listening in triad sessions during our training was a bit of a revelation to me. I missed things, I guess I was nervous and I wanted to feel that I was getting good feedback when I was in the role of therapist. I was then thinking about it in the discussions after the role-plays in the triads, and it just suddenly came to me that it wasn't how I experienced it as a client in personal therapy. My therapist listens differently.

Tutor: Differently?

Student: Yes. I don't think I can just say what she does, or how she does it, but it feels very different with her. When I was being the therapist in the triad skills exercises, I just felt the urge to say something and not just sit there like a lifeless thing.

Tutor: Is that what you were concerned about? How you were in danger of being? It's obviously a contrived exercise, but it helps to start somewhere, because the feedback could open up some really interesting points.

Student: Yes, I can see that. (Extended pause). What came to me just now is my experience at work meetings; there's the power structure, the protocol for how a meeting should go, someone chairing the meeting, what to say and what not to say, being close with some people in the room but not so much with others. We also have to get through the agenda, and there's someone taking the minutes. It's very business-like, as you'd expect.

Tutor: But they're public meetings and they have a particular purpose.

Student: Yes, I know, but I listen very differently. And I listen to the way that others listen to me and the way that they don't. It's like there's particular agendas that certain individuals have in the room, and it's actually energy-draining. I don't generally like being there. You mentioned 'contrived' earlier: there's something contrived there as well!

Tutor: OK. So, when you're in the therapy room as a client, what's making it feel like it's therapy?

Student: Lots of things. But if we're just talking about listening, then it's like I'm really seen by my therapist, because I can see her whole body listening, it's not just her ears doing the listening!

Tutor: How can you tell?

Student: She's absorbed in what I'm talking about. Her face has this expression of intensity, that she is drawn in to what I'm talking about. Now that

I think about it, it's as if she's leaving herself – that sounds strange – as if she has let go of being her and is in this open space ... it's the opposite of having answers, just like you said a minute ago, a kind of being very present, and in an active way.

Tutor: How do experience that?

Student: Oh, I really have this sense of her being all-out to try to 'get' me, understand me, get a feel for what I'm trying to express, whilst staying in that space that's between us, rather than saying, 'I get you now'. She doesn't *do* anything, it's a space that she doesn't close down by offering anything other than trying to get clearer on something.

Tutor: It reminds me of a phrase that Heidegger uses at the very end of an essay he wrote, *The Origin of the Work of Art*, which has been translated as 'dim confusion'.

Student: Yes, I think that sounds quite harsh and judgemental, but it is somewhat like that when I experience my therapist listening to what I'm talking about.

Tutor: I suppose the question that I have is, when your therapist is listening, why is she listening? What's the purpose?

Student: Well, she needs to hear what I'm feeling, or thinking, what's going on for me. As I'm talking, I'm expressing my feelings, some thoughts and questions for myself. It feels good when a person is just listening to me. But when it's a therapist listening, it's therapeutic for me.

Tutor: How does that make it therapeutic?

Student: So, I talk for quite some time, the therapist is listening, and I feel different as I'm talking to her. When she does say something, she doesn't break the flow. I'm not distracted when she says or asks something.

Tutor: Something about her way of coming in?

Student: Yes, it's very brief. Her comment or question can be a word, or a very short question, just to clarify or add or even challenge. But mainly I get the feeling that she has a way of staying in the silences. We sometimes come to long silences, and she can be in them, and with me. I feel self-conscious that I'm not saying anything, and I then get a little anxious, and start reflecting on what else I can talk about.

Tutor: Has it happened that you stayed with the silences rather than trying to stop them?

Student: Yes, I tend to do that more now.

Tutor: And that might be a special moment to actually reflect on what is going on for you.

Student: What, talk about how I'm feeling in the silence, or not knowing what to talk about?

Tutor: That, and the way in which it might be throwing a light on how you feel when you are *standing* in the space, or standing out in the silence.

Student: You mean, how it says something about my relationship to silence?

Tutor: OK, it wasn't quite what I was asking, but let's stay with what you just said: your relationship to silence.

Student: I suppose one assumption is that if I'm silent, it might suggest that I'm just not being a good client, that I'm not doing it right.

Tutor: Is there a 'right' way, then?

Student: Talking, working on myself, trying to work things out, being open and expressing myself. So, when I don't have anything to say, when I'm silent, I'm not doing that. I'm not expressing myself and working on things.

Tutor: But what if you really listen to the silence? And listen to yourself listening to the silence? What then?

Student: It ... comes back to what you said a moment ago about standing in the space, I think. In a way, it's similar to when I'm with other people. If there's a silence, even for a second, one of us fills it, with laughter or a smile or an off-hand comment, and then off we go, chatting again. But gossip does a great job, as well. It fills and fills ...

Tutor: And that's when we *really* have nothing to say. It's chatter that is speaking but actually saying nothing at all.

Student: And if it's not saying anything, we're listening to nothing at all, we're just listening to the words spoken, but not hearing something in any of the speaking. Is that right?

Tutor: Yes, I think so. So, bringing it back to the therapy, is there any bearing that this has on talking about something?

Student: Well, maybe the first thing is that I'm not resorting to chatter when I'm there. When there's a long pause of silence, I don't do what I'm inclined to do, which is to come up with something that fills it. I could say that I admire the bust on the mantelpiece, but that would be an obvious distraction.

Tutor: But the therapist listens to it *all*, the way that you are being with them in the room. We all fall into chatter at times, but in the context of therapy, it tends not to happen so much. I think we can allow for an initial exchange of greetings before the conversation starts. When it *does* move towards a conversation, we have before us a clear distinction between the everyday exchanges and the conversation.

Student: So the silence might be throwing light on how much we can listen to ourselves.

Tutor: That we can fall away from ourselves into distractions, yes.

Student: It also makes me think about the therapist's listening to *my* listening to myself.

Tutor: Yes, and that's a radically different kind of listening than our listening in a conversation with a colleague.

Student: It just dawned on me, that when I was talking about the way I experience my therapist listening, it's those moments that I actually really listen to her listening to me, if that makes sense. I feel listened to, and I listen to that when I notice it. It's like a certain glow that I feel inside, and being at home with where I am, in a way. It probably carries on in the background, though, because the mood in the room changes for me.

Tutor: You see a meaning to the listening?

Student: Yes.

Tutor: I use the word tentatively, because people think of it as a morally-loaded term, but it's more 'authentic'?

Student: Genuine, you mean?

Tutor: It's more to do with what I mentioned about standing out, but in the listening in this case.

Student: The listening isn't a speaking, but it's saying a lot.

Tutor: I completely agree. The therapist might have a lot to say, but is most herself, that is, authentic, *as* the therapist, in listening, and being silent. In the silence, she listens, and only in being silent can she *then* speak. In the silence, she listens to herself listening to you and the silence between you.

Student: Could it be that the silence is saying something about our being with one another?

Tutor: Yes, I think so. I think we listen to our being, our existing.

Student: So, using Heidegger's term here, I listen to my way of being-with, the inescapable fact that I am always in a with-existence. But I listen to how I have shaped and manifested a style of being with others that is meaningful to me.

Tutor: And the therapist is the other to you who is also being with you in a certain way that also manifests a certain style, or way of being. The question then becomes, how open can the conversations be that listen to, and are able to reflect on, the layers of listening that you spoke so well about?

Student: (Long pause). I have to say, I think we have moved quite a long way along from where we started, and I see a big distinction now between everyday listening and therapeutic listening. One of the most significant things that has emerged is the significance of silence to listening.

Tutor: Yes. As therapists, we hold ourselves in a kind of 'restraint' so that the open can be preserved, and that we listen in that openness.

Student: What I heard in what you just said illuminated something for me. If we step into that openness, say, with some kind of theory or explanation, or model that can try to ground what we hear the client is saying, we drag it into metaphysics. That way, we subtly take away the tension, the uncertainty and possible *cul de sac* that we might arrive at in the exploratory process, and give it all a ground, a metaphysical ground, a theory that itself plays at being God as the ultimate ground.

Tutor: That's very Heideggerian. And you mentioning all this is helping me see more here too. This seems to be what Heidegger meant by 'the clearing'. Are you saying that we stay with the clearing, the openness, rather than turning the clearing into some-thing?

Student: Yes, I think so. It was when you mentioned the open, and holding and preserving it that sparked something for me. You illuminated the clearing! Not that you can *do* that, though. We have been turning the clearing into something for 2500 years, and counting! So, the therapist listens to the clearing, and she shows restraint and thereby preserves, maybe 'cares for' it *in* the restraint. Theory does the opposite: it doesn't listen to it, and in that way abandons the clearing by totalising it into some-thing.

Tutor: So, now we're in the clearing, as it were. What interests me as the therapist is the listening in that clearing with the client, the other.

Student: It actually feels scary. I'm not anchored in me as the 'subject', or taking a strong stance as the therapist. Of course, I'm in the role of being a therapist; I agree. I think of this more like being, I don't know, a teacher, I suppose. If you're always trying to project yourself as a teacher, and *only* a teacher, you lose the human touch, let's say. It's a bit like Sartre's idea of the waiter who is so mechanical about being a waiter that he is nothing else *but* a waiter as he serves food and drinks. Sartre says he's in 'bad faith', which is a bit of a harsh caricature, I think. He's only trying to do his job, after all!

Tutor: So, back to the clearing, and listening.

Student: So, it's both clearing the clearing, which means staying in the clearing, and also that I *am* the clearing! If you *don't* clear the clearing, in comes metaphysics, and it takes over.

Tutor: OK, say more.

Student: I am the kind of being who cares. I am care. So, we can understand care through an old Greek fable that Hyginus rewrote into Latin, which always brings me back to a way of understanding it in a more poetic form. It sings to me! The goddess Care was crossing a river and as she did so, picked up some wet clay that she started to press into shape. At that moment, Jupiter, the sky god, came along and she asked him to give this shaped clay 'spirit'. He agreed to do so, but then the two got into a fight over who was to choose the name for it. While they were arguing, Terra, the earth goddess arrives on the scene and says that *she* should decide on the name, because the material originally comes from her earth. Because the three of them can't come to an agreed resolution, they ask the god of time, Saturn, to arbitrate between them. He says that Jupiter, who has given it spirit, will get the spirit back upon its death; Earth, having bestowed it its body, will get its body. Care, however, owns it as long as it lives because it moulded it in the first place. Finally, Saturn adds his own touch and names it 'homo', because it's made from the earth, which is 'humus'.

Tutor: So, we're care. It's 'moulded' into us that we *are* care. And how is this related to the clearing? I'm listening to you, but I think it would also be good to eventually get back to the topic itself, listening. And to therapeutic listening.

Student: Yes, I know, but I like wandering about on a path like this. Care gives light to the clearing. The clearing is the constant opening that is always there. We are always in a 'there', in the open, in the clearing. Care makes it bright. Saturn is the god of time, temporality. So, to give it a little of my own spin, he sprinkles humus, or homo, with temporality, even though it does have spirit too. But homo is always temporalising the 'there'. When it really ***listens*** to itself as being in the clearing and being temporal in the clearing, owning it as its own, it exists *truly*, or authentically. It listens to itself as a homo who is care, and care fundamentally understood in its temporality.

Tutor: That's putting it extremely concisely.

Student: I think it's important to say something about the listening to oneself *being* in the clearing. Now I've just remembered the idea of 'filling', as in, filling the silence. 'Filling' is relevant, I think. We listen to ourselves falling into *filling* the clearing with metaphysics when we speak in certain ways. Speaking is structured in such a certain way that we can't just prise ourselves out of metaphysical language and switch into something non-metaphysical. But we can listen to the way in which we grab for things to fill the clearing. We fill it with theory, abstraction, concepts, mathematical language, measurement, technological thinking and so on. We listen to the vulnerability of collapsing the clearing itself or ignoring it. If we *don't* listen to this, we then lose our understanding of *being* homo, humus, care.

Tutor: This sounds like a good place to stop, though I feel reluctant to do so.

Listening and Speaking

Firstly, we should note that there can be no speaking without listening, and we can be listening to a person speaking without really hearing them. Heraclitus said as much in the following aphorisms: 'Not knowing how to listen, neither can they speak', and, 'we should not listen like children to their parents' (Kahn, 1987:35).

Hearing is fundamental to being human because we are discoursing or discursive beings. This is also reflected in Heidegger's claim that, 'we are a conversation' (Heidegger, 1980/2014:62), which is a line that he draws on from Hölderlin's poem, *Hölderlin and the Essence of Poetry*: 'since we are a conversation *[Gespräch]*, and can hear from one another' (Heidegger, 1980/2014:62). Discourse, in this sense, is the way in which we are always disclosing ourselves both to others and to ourselves. It is the most general way in which speaking, hearing, being silent, having something to say (as opposed to speaking, uttering) and expressing ourselves in different ways, reflects our way of being human.

Since we commonly take listening to be simple and straightforward, a little further clarification is warranted here. Importantly, hearing, particularly when understood in a therapeutic context, is a term that distinguishes itself from listening insofar as it means more than simply listening to the other person's words. Everyday listening, we might say, has more of an 'acoustic' meaning to it. Hearing, however, is more primordial. If the therapist only listens, her listening might move towards a diagnosis of the client, for example. In other words, her listening can 'reduce', i.e., be reductive. Therapeutic listening, however, also includes the hearing of what emerges, comes out, moves outwardly. In hearing, the therapist hears the client in the disclosing of their existence. The therapist's hearing seeks to understand the client in what they are saying in their speaking. In their having something to say, the 'saying' is the meaning, or the whole of what they want to convey by putting this into the many words that they speak out. The therapist hears the way in which the client is enveloped in their mood, the degree to which they embrace and live in possibility, their way of being temporal, how they embrace their placedness in the world, the extent to which they are living on their own terms, and much more. In hearing the client, however, the therapist might also 'hear over' them. This can take the form of not hearing them at all, or missing what is to be heard. In what follows, I will use the terms, 'listening' and 'therapeutic listening' to mean a listening and hearing as they have been described above.

The Act of Listening

Perhaps it helps to initially reflect on the kind of listening that is at the extreme opposite end of therapeutic listening. It shows itself in a context in which listening is instrumentalised in a certain way, and could be described as a 'calculative listening'. This is a kind of listening that already has certain aims in mind, and is more interested in using listening as a form of control or domination of the situation and the other person. In this scenario, the other has a certain value only insofar as they are seen as a means that can be used to reach particular ends. At certain times, listening is a means to win an argument against another person rather than to engage in a listening that attends to the concerns that are embedded in the other person's stance on some matter or other. In such cases, listening becomes so narrowed because it confines itself to a zero-sum, win-lose form of argumentation. Fiumara reflects this well in quoting a passage from Lakoff and Johnson:

> We don't just *talk* about arguments in terms of war. We can actually win or lose arguments. We see the person we are arguing with as an opponent. We attack his positions and we defend our own. We gain and lose ground. We plan and use strategies. If we find a position indefensible, we can abandon it and take a new line of attack…It is in this sense that the 'argument is war' metaphor is one that we live by in this culture; it structures the actions we perform in arguing.
>
> (1990:108)

At such times, words are tools, and powerful ones at that. They can, in extreme cases, be used to demean and subdue the other person, by attempting to, for example, exhaust, threaten, enforce, degrade or monopolise them. Listening then becomes, to use visually-oriented language, distinctly 'foveal' rather than 'peripheral': we safeguard ourselves from the specificity of the threat in the situation, rather than taking in the wider contours of our experience. In such cases, even possible moments of silence take on a 'deathly' tone, rather than the 'peaceful' silence that receives and welcomes the other.

Listening to Being

In the experience of listening to the other, we listen to their being as we encounter it in the relation that holds us together. How do we listen to someone's being? Being, after all, is not a thing, or entity that can be objectivized, even though different metaphysical positions throughout the different ages have reduced being to a being. Listening to a client's being, therefore, can easily fall into a metaphysical listening that enframes what is heard and interpreted in the hearing. For example, the therapist hears the client saying that her relationship with her partner is becoming increasingly strained because they no longer talk to each other. Rather than being open and receptive to the unfolding narrative and the fact that the client has yet to disclose what has not yet been put into words, the therapist already listens to his own patterned way of putting what he hears into a certain interpretative framework. He draws on his acquaintance with a certain theory, or his own assumed conviction that routine and difference, or the changes in the client and partner's worldviews, have now distanced and estranged them to the point where they no longer truly encounter each other.

In listening to the client's being, they disclose themselves, but this is not related to speaking. Rather, such self-disclosing is the unconcealing of the client's being. The conversations during sessions unveil and discover a number of aspects of the client's concerns that are articulated and spoken in the words that they use. They discover and reveal something in their understanding of themselves that was previously veiled and concealed.

When we listen for particular things, or beings, rather than the *being* of things and beings that are constituted in a *wholeness*, we are somewhat distracted from what is at issue. For example, a client might say that he can't seem to do the things that he needs to do in order to have a more comfortable life. He focuses on finding a better-paid job, a promotion, or a relocation to another part of the country, and focuses, understandably, on the practicalities and the significance of each of these aspects of his life. The 'what' that he feels needs to change, however, also requires a listening and attending to his 'how' he is living, and his being a whole that is really at the centre of his existence. His existence, granted, can only be addressed by attending to the various aspects or features of being human, but these are all constituted as a whole, and not as separate, stand-alone elements. To put this another way, we are constituted by certain necessary and ineliminable features of our being that have, in turn, been shaped by us in the very way or style of our existing. In listening to the client, we open ourselves to hearing for the ways in which such features are being expressed by them. In doing so, we can attune ourselves to what appears to show itself as an issue for them in terms of one or other aspect of their being. I devote a little attention to a number of these in the next section, by way of example, in the attempt to illustrate our way of hearing the client in how they are expressing themselves.

An Example of Listening to a Client's Way of Being

As I listen to my client, Diotima, talking about her relationship with her siblings and parents, and then going on to reflect on her friendships and challenges with work colleagues, she expresses her way of being with others that has been moulded and fashioned over the course of living her life with others. This has manifested itself as an accustomed pattern that has become actualised in her way of being. As she opens up and elaborates on her experiences, she discloses something about the continual challenge of being in a harmonious and settled orientation towards such others. She explores this further as our conversation develops, and as she does so, she also uncovers her way of being 'in sync' with others, trying to find a commonality with them so that there is a minimal sense of discomfort or distance between herself and other people. Diotima expands on this as being her way of trying to be aligned with others in some way and not being 'anti-social', as she puts it. She says that there are times where she feels anxious around others. We explore this anxiety as a way of clarifying how it discloses something deeper about herself.

So far, then, I have been listening and hearing Diotima express her way of being-in-the-world. Three aspects of her being-in-the-world have been brought out in the conversation as the therapist attends to her through listening: her way of being with others; the particular way in which she wants to belong and experience safe relations with others, that is, to 'get along' with them; and the way that she is already captured by a certain disposition or mood when in such encounters with others. She experiences a certain level of anxiety, though she says that this can vary from being more subtle as an underlying feeling to being more prominent and even overwhelming at times, depending on the person, the situation and the circumstances. From the therapist's perspective, much has already been expressed in Diotima's way of disclosing herself.

As we proceed further, Diotima reflects on her world, particularly her world of work, since this is a topic that she returns to frequently. Her work world is one that identifies her in the role of a manager in a medium-sized company, where she experiences various pressures to meet deadlines and outcomes. Her challenges as a manager come both from her staff members who report to her, and from the directors who make demands that she finds difficult to resist. She wants to maintain good working relationships both with her reports and with the directors, or as she puts it in more hierarchical terms, those both 'below' and those 'above' her. Being in the 'middle' of this arrangement exhausts her, and at the same time, draws something out of her that manages to bring tasks and outcomes to fruition. In this regard, she feels that she holds a strangely intense attitude towards her work, and realises that she also, somewhat paradoxically, experiences some form of satisfaction in all this. As she further explores this, she says that it maintains and sustains her identity, a way of knowing herself in relation to her role. In some moments, she ventures to add that she feels special, but as she hears herself saying this, also feels embarrassed. She thinks her specialness sounds arrogant and haughty, as if she is not like others. She doesn't want to stand at a distance from others, but rather, continue to be accepted and embraced by them. She also fears the prospect of others' judgement, as they might criticise her for behaving as if she *is* special. In all this, Diotima's world is very familiar to her, she feels embedded in it, grounded in having acquired certain skills in her role as manager. Throughout the session, then, I listen intently, hearing what it is like to be in Diotima's *world*.

Another aspect of Diotima's way of being is reflected in her not having much space for anything else in her life. Her job and her responsibilities in maintaining certain obligations towards her parents, keeping up her contact with friends and fulfilling various chores and errands that take up her spare time at weekends, means that she has little time for herself, or to just do nothing and 'chill', as she puts it. In my listening, I hear Diotima's experience of not having sufficient room to be, to be 'is-ing' in her own space. Space becomes filled, which is reflected in having no time for herself. Managed time is ordered and set in a way that excludes time for being, a time and space that does not schedule for any doing. Only when she has time for herself does she find space to be. However, I hear the way that Diotima experiences a certain *tension* in this, since space and time become something akin to a burden or weight to carry rather than somewhere that she can dwell.

Diotima reflects on the way that she lives her life according to facts, data, evidence and reports. She considers these as objective, she says, and surrenders to this as a source of reliability and stability. Whilst taking time to explore this in greater depth, I listen to, among other things, Diotima's way of dampening or immunising herself from any opening to choice and *possibility* in her way of living and of expressing herself. She sees her circumstances as given and inviolable. They don't require questioning. The idea of questioning itself feels threatening to her world, and so it is kept at arm's length. To think of possibility, for her, also feels like opening a gaping abyss. These are possible experiences to resume at later points in the sessions that follow, and so, in this regard, I listen for what can unfold as a future possibility.

Finally, I also listen for the way in which Diotima relates to *endings*. I hear that nothing must end for her, or change, for that matter. Change invites the unsecured and unmoored experience of cultivating uncharted new worlds, which feel too unpredictable for her.

Therapeutic Listening

Flickinger on Therapeutic Listening

Listening, to reiterate, is a feature of being human, and is commonly described in terms of one of the five senses that we all possess. But to listen as a *therapist* is what Aprile Flickinger calls, 'therapeutic listening'. It suggests a particular kind of listening that is different in some ways to our accustomed everyday practices. As Flickinger says, we might all listen to the same reflections and narratives that someone relates to us, but 'what is heard depends on who is listening. And the way we listen depends on the way we stand in the world' (1992:186).

Flickinger, rightly, points to the kind of relationship we have towards the other person insofar as it determines how we listen. As a parent, or relative, or partner, it is very likely that my listening is shaped significantly by the role or relation that I have to the speaker. Friends might offer advice and even some form of directive if I open up to them about some difficulties I am experiencing in my life. Similarly, a medical doctor might well offer me quite firm and decisive advice about my indulgences in sweet foods. But they both listen in order to assess my level of awareness about my circumstances, and the need to inform or challenge me to take other courses of thinking and action.

In each of these instances, the ways in which we take on certain roles and identities reflect the way that we take a stand in the world, as Flickinger says. In the case of the therapist, however, listening is particularly central to the *identity* of being a therapist. To extend this, the therapist listens in different ways, whether this be intuitively, practically, realistically, narratively, phenomenologically, analytically or ethically. In the last respect, listening therapeutically is a *just* listening, as Steven Gans and Leon Redler insist, emphasising the centrality of an ethical listening in the therapeutic space.

In a therapeutic setting, the client talks about the difficulties, challenges and tensions that they experience in their current circumstances. I listen. As I continue to do so, my listening reflects a respect for what they disclose. I sense something of their sense of uncertainty and perhaps at times even hesitation, because their speaking is so personal and also possibly somewhat new and even surprising to them, as they put into words, for the first time, what they are feeling. As I continue to listen, I honour the space in which we encounter each other, experiencing it as a 'sacred place' (Flickinger, 1992:188). In a certain unforeseen moment, the client touches on something that seems to be coming from the very depths of their own being, and I feel a sense of awe. It seems to resonate with the sacred in this case, but it is completely unrelated to any kind of religious experience, as we might think of it. Rather, it is something akin to what the German philosopher, Immanuel Kant, called the 'sublime'. These terms can sometimes be used hyperbolically, or are overdone, as in the phrase, 'that was awesome!', or 'the moment that he asked me to marry him was sublime'. But staying with something that overwhelms us or seems unfathomable nevertheless makes a very strong impression on us. We become somewhat humbled by what we experience.

When we touch on the sublime and the sacred, we feel a sense of awe, because we experience something that our perceptions cannot take in and make coherent, in some way. We can think here of standing in the presence of the Egyptian pyramids, for example, or visiting Cathédrale Notre-Dame in Reims, France, and looking upwards and marvelling at its vaulted ceiling. In such moments, we tremble and experience a kind of transcendence insofar as what we experience is humbling. It overwhelms us, and does so in two ways: we are *perceptually* overwhelmed, in that we perceive something before us that we experience as being *beyond* perception, and which we can't grasp through reason and logic; secondly, we are overwhelmed in an *embodied* sense, insofar as we experience ourselves in our limitations and 'smallness' in relation to what is before us.

Being overwhelmed by the client in our listening is to hear our smallness in the face of the overpowering 'height' of the client's being that towers over us. It exposes, as Flickinger says, the therapist's own inadequacy, fragility and limitation. It might have to do with the client disclosing something that they have lived through that is unimaginably horrific, or with the way in which they unexpectedly disclose something distressing and disorienting. This leaves the therapist in the realm of the unfathomable, since the deep mystery of that which cannot be grasped by logic and reason leaves a void, or a 'nothing' that we peer into as human beings.

In the course of listening to a client, and their possible expression of sadness, despair, uncertainty, anxiety, confusion, and fear, the therapist experiences a certain resonance, because they listen care-fully, as a listening that is imbued with care. It is not worry, or a caring *about*, as we might say when we are fond of someone, or a caring *that*, which points towards what matters in one's relations to others. Rather, such care arises when the *whole* of the client is seen, and *as* a whole, rather than as any one aspect of their existence that expresses a particular issue that concerns them. It is *through* the issue, and listening care-fully, that the client as a whole being, or being in their wholeness, is encountered. This wholeness is reflected in their temporal nature: this poignant moment has a particular significance, as it brings something of the client's 'how they have already been being themselves in their life' as well as their presently pressing into a future. Their future is always shaped and configured by how they have been in their lives. That is, they come from the future into the now, the present, through the way that they have already been being who and how they are up to the now. It is only through listening deeply that we really hearken to the client's temporal way of being.

In therapeutic listening, there is also a form of gathering. Gemma Corradi Fiumara takes up Heidegger's exploration of the old Greek terms that point to listening as a 'gathering of itself' (1990:3), which comes from laying-down, laying-before and bringing together in such listening. To elaborate, Heidegger thinks of laying down as a laying one thing beside another, or laying them together, such that to lay is to gather. We, for instance, see sentences written as a form of gathering, namely, the gathering of words. In our listening, then, we attend to speaking, and in doing so, we lay-down and lay-before the speaker. This is reflected in an openness and a sense of being in communion with them. We gather ourselves with and towards them. But the listening is a gathering that also 'houses' difference.

Wilberg on Listening

Drawing very directly on Peter Wilberg's work on the therapist as listener, I make several points here that reflect what I consider to be essential to the act and process of listening. I attempt to flesh out the way in which listening 'happens' in the therapeutic encounter by taking up Wilberg's own terms, though I endeavour to interpret them somewhat differently.

1 Listening as Withholding – the therapeutic space is a holding. The holding is not a handling, as we might encounter in the phrase, 'I can handle this', or 'I am handling the project that I am running'. Rather, it is a sense of the be-holding of what unfolds, or what holds forth, with the client. It is therefore a holding-with, also expressed as a with-holding. The with-holding is not a trivial play with or on words and their order, but rather, places 'with' as more fundamental, and therefore existentially prior, to any holding, as such. Listening is a

with-holding that is not something spoken, but a holding with in its silent yet present listening.

2 Listening as Hearkening – when we hearken, it is a hearkening *of* something *as* something or other. The client's speaking hearkens us to hear something in a certain way. In a more general sense, I hear the sound that breaks the silence as the church bells ring. In being with the client, I am called to what hearkens, that is to say, calls on the therapist to be an attentive listener, and who attends to the 'as' of what is spoken by the client. For example, the client is talking about the encounter *as* threatening, or *as* ominous, or *as* uncertain, and I hearken to the nature of this 'as' in the client's speaking.
3 Listening as Heeding – the therapist pays heed to the client's way of being in the former's way of listening. In other words, the therapist does not take for granted what they hear, but rather attends closely to the words that have *come* to the client as they are speaking. Perhaps the way that they speak is very formal and guarded, or they speak in a very measured and tentative way. In their way of talking and expressing themselves, the therapist heeds the client in what and how they are unveiling, in the sense of dis-covering, and at the same time dis-closing, that is, what is not put into words but is nevertheless said. A way of heeding the client's unveiling in their speaking might, for example, be hearing what is being dis-closed *in* their being mortal, and in their way of speaking *as* a mortal, but not speaking *about* their mortality, *per se*.
4 Listening as Homing in – the therapist's listening is a process, and not a computational absorption of information and details. That is, a deepening unfolding of the listening happens as the therapist is nearing a sense of being at home with the issue that the client is attempting to bring forth in their speaking. Coming to be more at home, then, is a listening that is described here as one of 'homing in'.
5 Listening as Holding – holding is a supportive listening in the therapist's way of being. In their being present in the therapy session, the therapist extends a holding listening to the client in their openness, vulnerability, uncertainty and possible anxiety. A client might say, 'I feel held', which reflects a certain 'holding together' what might otherwise be deemed unsteady and even chaotic. In the therapist's listening, we might also understand this in Levinasian terms, namely, that the client holds the therapist 'hostage', insofar as they are being held responsible to the client in their listening. Being 'hostage', however, intimates a 'positive' meaning here, namely, that of therapist's guest-like stance of being 'hosted' to enter and dwell in the client's world. In the main, the listening here is asymmetrical, as it is the therapist who holds themself responsible for listening to the client, whilst the client is not obligated to reciprocate, or at least not in the same (therapeutic) way.
6 Listening as Beholding – when with-holding, there is at the same time a beholding, which is an appreciation and receptivity to what appears or manifests. The therapist is, in this sense, beheld in their listening to the client.
7 Listening as Taking to Heart – the therapist is present as a whole and not as a part that performs a certain role in relation to the client. Taking the other person

> to heart is a 'letting in' and leaving oneself open in the listening. This leaves the therapist receptive to the possible resonances that might emerge in touching similar concerns in their own life, but not becoming self-preoccupied by them while listening to the client.

Wilberg touches on other aspects of listening that have not been addressed here, though those presented above reflect something of the richness of the process of therapeutic listening by further elucidating various aspects of its essential character.

Bibliography

Fiumara, G.C. (1990). *The Other Side of Language: A Philosophy of Listening*. London: Routledge.

Flickinger, A.T. (1992). Therapeutic Listening. *Phenomenology + Pedagogy*. 10. https://phenomenologyonline.com/sources/textorium/flickinger-aprile-therapeutic-listening/

Gans, S. & Redler, L. (2001). *Just Listening: Ethics and Therapy*. Bloomington, Indiana: Xlibris.

Heidegger, M. (1980/2014). *Hölderlin's Hymns "Germania" and "The Rhine"*. Trans. W. McNeill & J. Ireland. Indianapolis: Indiana University Press. p.62.

Kahn, C.H. (1987). *The Art and Thought of Heraclitus*. Cambridge: Cambridge University Press.

Wilberg, P. (2004). *The Therapist as Listener*. Eastbourne: New Gnosis Publications.

Chapter 6

Question-ing

Introduction

Questioning is pivotal to the therapeutic process, since it is a way of exploring and clarifying a phenomenon or issue that the client brings to the session. In other words, it moves the conversation towards a mutual search for deeper understanding through open exploration. Questioning here means something specific in a therapeutic context. How might it differ from a questioning that takes place between friends, or even a questioning directed towards oneself in one's quieter moments? The same term is being used, but its meaning has a more nuanced sense when we consider it in different contexts and within certain relations in which we find such experiences of questioning.

Conversation on Question-ing

Therapist 1: Over the years, as I continue to work with clients, I almost always arrive at the most basic of all questions, which is, what sense can we make of being human? It seems to me to be a question that is greatly overlooked and ignored, because we already have ready-made answers.

Therapist 2: OK, to play devil's advocate for a moment, why is that so important to you? We already have an understanding of what it is to be a person, and that's the client that we meet in the therapy sessions.

Therapist 1: But I think we do two things when we do this: we close down the question, as if we have arrived at a final body of knowledge, and we then also build whole systems of thinking that just stack and load more and more layers of 'knowledge' on top of it. As a result, we lose all sense of the original question.

Therapist 2: So it's not to approach it with, 'I have a question, what's the answer?' type of thing, it's more to do with an activity that respects the question rather than trying to step over it.

DOI: 10.4324/9781003638698-7

Therapist 1: Yes, that's right. But it goes further. The activity is a question-ing. It's a path of questioning. It follows a path, which is very Heideggerian. He does this in his later essays, in his lectures, everything he writes. Wilberg puts it nicely, I think, with the phrase, 'quest-ing'.

Therapist 2: Yes, I see. It's a journeying. But it's not just *any* old question, is it? It has to be something meaningful, something that is 'questionworthy', I think Heidegger says somewhere or other.

Therapist 1: Yes, worthy of questioning. For him, it comes back to the question, or question-ing, of being. So, he undertakes a questioning of the essence of such matters as technology, language, freedom, history, of truth and so on, and it's a lifelong project. What that means is that he comes back to the question of the essence time and again, but in different ways, from different directions.

Therapist 2: On different paths, yes. There's a questioning that isn't just questioning *per se*, it's the questioning of the *essence* of something. That's very different. I guess the anthropologist or the psychologist would ask about the human being itself and not the essence of being human. So they would say something about the features of being human that distinguish us from animals. They would also possibly talk about memory, learning, social organisation in communities, symbols and so on. They take the human being as an object of study, focus on it in an anthropocentric way, and in doing so, might introduce any number of methods to undertake the study, such as the phenomenological, empirical, ethnographic, or participant observation, and so on. And they study humanity.

Therapist 1: It's humanity as *humanism*, though, isn't it? That is a very significant difference. On the whole I agree with you in the way you have clarified the idea of questioning. I started our conversation with my question, what does it mean to be human, but you've made it so much clearer, that it's the *essence* of human being that I'm interested in. That puts us into a ground-level, fundamental questioning that doesn't overlay it with our framework of knowledge which we've inherited down to our own time.

Therapist 2: And what is that 'framework of knowledge'?

Therapist 1: It's the way in which we have even lost touch with questioning the assumption that our knowledge is already taking a position on what it is to be human. We live in knowledge, make claims to knowing as our bedrock to everything, but underneath knowing, more basic to it, is being: what it is to be as anything at all. But for our kind of being, it's the question of what being human essentially means.

Therapist 2: So, we've gone from one era to another trying to gain knowledge and understanding of what's ultimately true about us?

Therapist 1: Yes, granted that it *is* a questioning, but it stays within the framework of, what can I know? And how can I *know* that I know?

Therapist 2: And knowing is the basis of our current framework, so we just take it that what we are, at bottom, is knowers, and that when we really know what there is to know, we just keep going in that trajectory, that direction, because there is always more to know.

Therapist 1: That's how it has been. The fundamental thing that we've always been searching for is the ultimate explanation: it stops the search. We come to a point where we can say, it's God who is the ultimate explanation for us and for everything; or, it's substance that is the ultimate explanation for everything, that everything is made up of atoms, and so everything's material 'stuff'. Or, as we already claim to know in our time, on the most fundamental level, we human beings are consciousnesses encased in bodies. No-one questions that: no questioning, and, hey presto, it's beyond question that it's true knowledge.

Therapist 2: It's so ingrained, isn't it? I find it hard to think in another way, to be honest.

Therapist 1: Absolutely. It's a real challenge for me too.

Therapist 2: Well, what if we try to engage in a questioning. How might we think of questioning?

Therapist 1: That's the most important thing to ask from the outset: what does it *mean* to be a question? What sense does it even make or have to talk about a question at all?

Therapist 2: We can try and approach it slowly, that might allow it to unfold in terms of its essence.

Therapist 1: I think we need to ask first what the question is *about*. It's about something, surely?

Therapist 2: Yes, absolutely. And what is it asking *of* the questioner, as the questioning being?

Therapist 1: And third, what is the question ascertaining? That is, in what respect is this question being asked?

Therapist 2: OK, questions, questions! I think that the being who is questioning is asking about the question of being human.

Therapist 1: Well, I think that would be to ask about the human being as an entity, a being. And to ask in that way goes back to the idea of not asking about the *essence* of our being.

Therapist 2: So, what we are asking about is crucially important. We are asking of ourselves what it is to *be*, the essential way that our kind of being happens temporally, and not asking about us as beings. There's a difference.

Therapist 1: So, we are certainly addressing ourselves as beings, but not staying with that. And if we think of ourselves only as a being, we would be on a pathless path if we took ourselves to claim that we are a conscious mind and a material body. That excludes any recognition of the *being* of that being that we call a human being … if you follow me!

Therapist 2: That would then mean giving up on the idea of what's internal and what's external to our way of being, and the conviction that there is something at work inside our heads that then needs uncovering. That would be to place the world as being 'out there' and that it needs to somehow be brought into a relation with the internal. That's the question that thinkers have grappled with over the centuries.

Therapist 1: It's starting from the wrong place. We're already worldly beings. It's a 'there-ing' that characterises how we are. I don't see that in a piece of driftwood, for example.

Therapist 2: And the key thing to add is that we care. So, it's 'there and care', if you like!

Therapist 1: 'There-ing' is existence. The '-ing' part is the verb-like sense that reflects the temporal. Again, driftwood doesn't care, it hasn't got care woven into the very fabric of its being. And if it *did* have, its sense of being would be grounded in its temporality. But only our kind of being is temporal, and, to take it further, a temporalising of the temporal.

Therapist 2: And because we care, that is, we *are* care, we open ourselves to questioning.

Therapist 1: But, to repeat, we can take up a questioning of some aspect of the way that we're living, for example, or we can undertake a questioning of our essential being, our 'is-ing'.

Therapist 2: It means questioning what it means to *be* as our kind of being.

Therapist 1: And to just say it out loud straight away so that we get to the bottom line, the essence of our way of being is *existence*, as Heidegger says.

Therapist 2: As opposed to saying that our way of being is to be rational, an animal that employs reason as a thinking thing.

Therapist 1: That takes us back again to the beginning of our conversation, which is the idea that we take ourselves to be, at bottom, knowing beings, beings who are, to use the more technical term, epistemological.

Therapist 2: As we already agree, we stop there. We don't take up the most primordial issue of the ontological. Ontology is the address of being.

Therapist 1: So, questioning is to address our being, what gives sense to our way of being, that is, existence.

Therapist 2: And questioning is thinking.

Therapist 1: Yes. It dawns on me that if we undertake a questioning, we introduce a way of relating to the task of thinking itself. Thinking in terms of questioning means that we gradually bring out some aspect of what we are addressing, what we are question-ing. If we are question-ing, we need to listen closely to language.

Therapist 2: Yes, we always need to be sensitively attuned to the language.

Therapist 1: Right.

Therapist 2: The language that we are 'housed' in, so to speak, and that speaks *us* rather than the other way round.

Therapist 1: The 'other way round'?

Therapist 2: We assume that language is only a grammatical tool that we use to communicate. That we place ourselves at the helm, the centre, whenever we speak.

Therapist 1: Yes, we do use language to communicate. But if that's the *only* way of relating to language we miss the *essence* of language. As a tool, we assume that we lord it over things that are not us, either by just observing them and then finding out certain things about them, or we go further and we exploit them in some way, exert control over them.

Therapist 2: And just think about the way in which we can get sucked into believing that the algorithms that AI uses to generate large language models are accurately capturing language in its essence.

Therapist 1: We are already embedded in language so that the world shows up through the 'sieve' of language that is already there. We also get so caught up in thinking that we *will* the questioning, and use it to get answers, and as quickly and efficiently as possible.

Therapist 2: Instead, we can let things be, and let them come to us. That way, a questioning path opens itself through such questioning. There's no willing involved, because to think in that way is to undertake a questioning that engages in a means-ends form of questioning. But when we are on the path of questioning, we are being questioned, called into question. And the questioning takes *us* somewhere.

Therapist 1: I agree. The questioning 'gives' itself to us rather than it being something that we project onto what is being asked. We receive something as we undergo the questioning. The very path of questioning is a thinking, as I said, and the thinking is a gift that moves us to receive something that comes to us from beyond. This isn't anything supernatural, though, in case that's how it comes across.

Therapist 2: No, I completely agree with you. And I think that what we are doing here in discussing questioning is undertaking a questioning about our questioning.

Therapist 1: Yes, we are. And, to add, I assume that neither of us is trying to lead on this, or adopting an attitude that we have to get to an answer, or questioning whether this is going to be worth our time. But I think that there are certain kinds of questioning that look as if they are doing something like an open questioning, but actually aren't.

Therapist 2: What did you have in mind, exactly?

Therapist 1: Well, I was thinking about the way in which dialectical thinking, as presented by certain German philosophers – I have Kant, and particularly Hegel in mind here, but also the French thinker, Merleau-Ponty, to an extent – is systemic thinking. It totalises rather than keeps open the question-ing.

Therapist 2: OK, just to rehearse our understanding on this, what is dialectical questioning?

Therapist 1: Simply and briefly put, we start with a claim or assertion, which we call the 'thesis', what I put forward as a position. I build a convincing case for it that supports it. I then make a turn, where I offer as powerful a critique of it as I can, showing its flaws and failings, because it's an inadequate account of what we're addressing. That leaves us with the opportunity to take an opposing stance, and build a set of arguments in support of it. We make as convincing a case for that too. We call that the 'antithesis', because it opposes the thesis. At that point, we look at the antithesis, and see that it *too* has flaws and lacunae in it, it hasn't raised itself to the level of an adequate and complete description of what we're after. But both the thesis and the antithesis have something that they have each illuminated. Moreover, the antithesis couldn't have been presented if the thesis hadn't been made in the first place. So, given where we have got to, the next, and final move is to carry out a synthesis of the thesis and antithesis. There has been a process of thinking and questioning, and it involves a surpassing, transcending of what was posited. The synthesis takes the thesis and antithesis and brings out a resolved position. It is now complete. Thinking and questioning can still continue, though, by taking the synthesis as a new thesis.

Therapist 2: I think that's very tidy and powerful.

Therapist 1: Yes, I'll accept that. But it suggests something pre-set in its whole approach to questioning. It also reduces phenomena to concepts, which don't really let us stay with the phenomenon and uncover it through questioning. And it doesn't really open us to the concrete, in my opinion. Because it is so wedded to the dialectical process or movement, it already takes us out of the everyday and into something abstract.

Therapist 2: So we could call it 'metaphysical' questioning.

Therapist 1: It's steeped in the last vestige of metaphysics as a whole, yes.

Therapist 2: So, we have questioned a form of questioning that can easily fall into metaphysical questioning.

Therapist 1: Yes, I think so.

Therapist 2: I think we have addressed the three elements of a question that we mentioned.

Therapist 1: We could keep our questioning going, but it may be best to leave it here for now.

Kinds of Questioning

An example might help us here as a way of getting clearer on understanding this term and also on what it means. A police inspector comes to my house and requests my presence at the local station for questioning. However innocent I am, this still leaves me quite unsettled about the imminently unfolding process of being questioned. 'Where were you on the night of the 15th at 21:00?', I am asked, as the enquiry probes for further details on my movements on that particular evening. Was I with someone, or alone, what were my intentions in being in a certain location? These are questions that are directed towards me with a persistence that is somewhat uncomfortable for me. I feel increasingly disoriented as I now recognise how much I have taken my freedom for granted, and normally able to go about my business without having to answer to anyone. Eerily, as I suddenly recall Joseph

K's experience in Kafka's novel, *The Trial*, I ask myself, where is this going? And where will it end? Such an example is just one form of questioning that has a particular end goal towards which it is directed, namely, trying to establish the truth of my whereabouts, but also a possible confession and admission of guilt in the case of having committed a crime. What is most relevant to note here, however, is the particular mood that such an experience of questioning evokes.

To now take a very different scenario, think of the child who is hiding something, a secret that they are holding *within* themselves, and withholding *from* others. The child's parent becomes aware that something is wrong, and is becoming concerned that someone or something is compromising the child's safety, for example. Any attempt to subject the child to questioning in a similar fashion to the police inspector's interrogative approach is unlikely to bring about the desired or intended outcome. Heavy-handedness and manipulative questioning simply deepen the child's refusal to engage with the parent, whether out of fear or stubbornness. Instead, a gentler, milder, softer form of questioning conveys a genuine care and concern towards the child, such that they come to understand something more about the meaning of the parent's questioning. A background mood of trust between both parent and child opens the space for possible revelations.

In yet another context, questioning the government's foreign policies during a lively group debate is seen as the lifeblood of a participatory democracy, and the chair encourages such questioning by ensuring that as many voices are given room for expression, and from a range of perspectives. In such cases, questioning serves as a means of both expressing and promoting further learning for all in the public arena. Its purpose is not to exclude or accuse, but to probe each others' opinions and beliefs on matters that concern them as citizens. In this setting, the mood tends to change and at times even become volatile, but this is leavened and balanced with the sense of freedom that all participants cherish and defend as being most fundamental to their existence.

In the course of our lives, we tend not to engage ourselves too much in a questioning attitude, whether this be in relation to ourselves or the world, because it suggests or intimates uncertainty and perhaps even a sense of weakness. On a more general and practical level, however, questioning through the posing of questions is something that we all encounter in the day-to-day situations that we face: do I buy these trainers or the more expensive ones that I find very appealing? Which job offer should I accept, and on what basis? How will I spend my summer months? Who will I invite to dinner, given that I only want to invite a small circle of people? In each of these scenarios, it seems that the extent to which we are open to questioning is related to what is at stake for us in doing so.

Questioning as a Way of Being

The overriding concern in our way of living in the world is to arrive at answers. The answer provides the solution and resolution to an unwanted set of circumstances in which we might find ourselves. In other words, answers are ways in which we can avoid and pre-empt uncertainty and ambiguity. In the end, we ride roughshod over the process of questioning, because we have come to place little value on dwelling in the questions themselves. We react to, by turning away from, the anxiety and the sense of powerlessness that we might experience were we to stay with the questioning. This inclines us towards reaching for answers. But the question that we then also face is, from whom or what do these answers ultimately come? Ourselves? Or from the various sources that we gravitate towards in our daily routines, such as social media, insightful newspaper articles, gurus or teachers?

It is a truism that life itself is constantly changing. This is no less true when we are caught in the moment in which we arrive at a definite answer to something that is based on both the feelings that we experience as well as the degree of access to relevant information available to us in finally reaching a decision. But since life moves on and never stays still, so to speak, we might question the decision that we made at an earlier time. In that sense, we focus more on the decision rather than the difficulty of the process of *questioning* that, in fact, brought us to actually experience ourselves as our *authentic* selves. Such authenticity is reflected in the fact that we are, in the final analysis, the *sole basis* for the decisions that we make, even if we happen to draw on others' advice or support. The responsibility ultimately falls entirely and inescapably on ourselves and on no one else. The other aspect to this is that, when we experience what we come to assess as a 'failure', because we made an entirely wrong or bad decision, we undergo a form of 'existential death'. At such times, we typically say, 'I wish the ground would swallow me up', expressing a deep disappointment in ourselves. Authentic questioning recognises that our decisions may not necessarily turn out to be ideal or perfect for us, and so might leave us feeling somewhat 'dis-located', but at the same time aware that a decision reflects our own limitations in not having an omnipotent God's-eye perspective on matters. In acknowledging this, we take the responsibility for the decision that we have taken based on our very own questioning.

An Excursus on Historical Questioning as a Deepening of Understanding

When we are open to questioning, we are also putting out of action our usual way of knowing something. This attitude or disposition of questioning can enter into the therapy conversation when we recognise that there are various ways in which the phenomenon of guilt, for example, already carries along with it various different historical facets that lie as hidden remnants within our experience of guilt in our own time. In questioning, we also deepen our understanding of the phenomenon through its more historical origins.

When we consider past societies, for example, the phenomenon of guilt was understood in terms of honour, and of being of good character, which was central to being a valued, accepted and respected citizen or member of a community. Any lapse in being able to perform courageous acts, for instance, reflected a lack of commitment and loyalty, such that one's reputation and standing in the community was put into question. The consequence of this was a public sense of shame, but also private feelings of guilt that weighed upon oneself when alone in one's more private moments. Guilt, as we understand it today, directs us towards a socially and communally-oriented meaning and context in which the way that we appear to others is of some concern to us.

In ancient Greek times, the need to take a stand was central to being human. It was the heroic figure who stood out, by speaking truthfully, with all the attendant risks that this might have brought them. In the Christian era, however, the meaning of guilt changed in its meaning by becoming associated with sin. That is, guilt acquired a more internal, or individualistic, rather than communal dimension. But it also introduced the idea that there is a moral standard that we must conform to, a 'height', something that stands over and above us. The Judeo-Christian epoch placed God as the 'beingest being', that is, the all-seeing, all-knowing supreme being who had the power to punish us for our misdeeds and malign thoughts, unless we sought repentance and genuine forgiveness. He is the Absolute, or the Form of the Good, to draw on Platonic language. On this picture, therefore, we are beings who are dependent on that which is 'external' to us, namely, God, for Him to grant us absolution from guilt, or sin. Our relation to God is the only means by which we can be freed from our guilt, given that we are *not* God, and that salvation is possible only through Him. The key point here is that we come to relate to ourselves more as individuals, such that something 'internal' to us is being addressed, rather than being already understood in terms of us all falling within a unity, that is, a group, tribe or community. This is reflected in the fact that the Greeks had no sense of the 'person', or 'individual', which might sound altogether strange to us in our time. But this shows something crucially important: that there are different understandings of being, and that being itself is historical in character.

Rather than experiencing guilt as an individual, our being a member of a community means that we uphold the identity of the whole. When we fail in this, we dishonour and disgrace the unity or unified whole, and are therefore guilty, in this sense. A more Mediaeval understanding of guilt might be prevalent in our current ways of living through certain constraints and prohibitions on our behaviour, such that the State empowers itself through laws and acts to ensure that certain punishments or, alternatively, expressions of leniency, or, to use a more familiar term from past times, grace and redemption, are brought to bear on the individual. However, we should not miss the fact that the 'internal' element here identifies us as the kind of being that has a conscience, and that it has a 'voice' that speaks to us, albeit silently. Again, the Greeks had no sense of a conscience, as such, and it only came into our understanding from the Christian era onwards.

In our Modern times, guilt takes on an even *more* individualistic meaning, and becomes more centred on the degree to which one attempts to maximise one's possibilities within the time schedules that one has available in any one week, month or year, for example. The professional lawyer, for instance, works for over 70 hours a week, bringing additional paperwork home to complete in the evenings, and then starts his daily schedule by attending the gym early each morning before work.

Time becomes a resource, such that it is considered a waste if squandered. Any slip from the daily and weekly schedule would incur self-criticism for inefficiency and loss of control. Time, according to this way of living, becomes the basis for the lawyer's existence in a way that previous ways of living in past times did not. That is to say, time becomes much more prevalent as the measure by which efficiency and making the most use of it become important. One values and relates to oneself as 'good' or 'bad' according to this measure, that is, leading a flourishing life, or falling into guilt because of lapses in doing so.

Therapeutic Questioning

Insofar as we move through time, and our circumstances change, this leaves us with a realisation that our life is one of a continual questioning. But, as mentioned previously, this is something that we rarely embrace in the course of living our lives, except at times when we are called to do so because something significant is at stake for us. As we undergo ruptures and encounter 'dead-ends' at certain moments, whether it be the end of a long relationship, or a transition to retiring from our careers, it is at these times that questions and self-questioning become more pressing for us. Since many find this difficult, for various possible reasons, the space that therapy offers is a clearing or opening that invites the possibility of exploring as-yet unarticulated issues. In the background to this is the opportunity to cultivate an increasing ability and skill to undertake a process of self-questioning as a way of life.

The openness to questioning is a stance that both the therapist and the client take towards themselves, rather than it being exclusively focused on the latter. This does not mean that the therapist is immersed in a certain self-preoccupation when in conversation with the client, but that questioning necessarily addresses the essence of the human condition, and so frequently raises strong resonances in the therapist as the client pursues their own path of questioning. For example, a client talks about her experience of loss as she approaches her older age. She reflects on the mysterious and unfathomable nature of what constitutes a well-lived and meaningful life. She goes on to reflect on the way in which she experienced several losses, in relationships, work redundancies and even in certain physical respects, such as a past complete loss of hearing for a period of several months. In all this, she concludes, it is the losses that opened a path to appreciating simply being. It all brings her to an awareness of the gift and privilege of having lived through them: being intimate and close to another human being, the vulnerabilities and fragilities that this exposes, the caring for one another, the loss of a particular world (the work world, for example, or the theatre world) in which her identity withers and eventually dissolves, the realisation that the centrality of being human is to be a world-discloser, of hearing a poetry recital that brings her to tears, the sound of birdsong, the rustle of leaves, the relentless tapping and drumming of raindrops against the kitchen window, and even the sound of the silence that announces itself on waking up on a Sunday morning. In such moments, the therapist hears and opens himself to the questions that weigh on all of us: the questioning of what it means to be human.

In every field of enquiry, whether it be therapy, teaching or research, a questioning attitude is central to all those who are engaged in a process of further understanding. For example, Heidegger reflected that, 'the teacher must be more teachable'. In this, I hear a certain humility and vulnerability that I think is also centrally important in the therapist's way of being. This speaks all the more strongly when we read an extract from a lecture that Heidegger gave on thinking:

> The teacher is ahead of his apprentices in this alone, that he has still far more to learn than they – he has to learn to let them learn. The teacher must be capable of being more teachable than the apprentices. The teacher is far less assured of his ground than those who learn are of theirs. If the relation between the teacher and the taught is genuine, therefore, there is never a place in it for the authority of the know-it-all or the authoritative sway of the official.
>
> (1954/1968:15)

From this passage, 'learning to let learn' is a letting-be-to-learn, and in order to learn, questioning is central. Although teaching is a very different enterprise to being a therapist, we can take from the above that therapists comport themselves in a mode of questioning, which itself is a process of thinking, and true or authentic thinking is a letting *be*. The therapist's questioning comes from a stance in which they are not in a position to have privileged access to a complete understanding of the client's way of being, i.e., that they 'must be capable of being more teachable', which translates as the therapist's questioning of and with the client insofar as they also find themselves questioning *themselves* through the therapeutic dialogue.

Question-ing, as Wilberg puts it, is a *questing*, opening and pursuing a path of thinking that ventures openly and uncertainly, without attempting to draw in already established ideas that determine in more certain terms the topic under exploration. Questioning comes from a certain disposition of wanting to learn something, but, most importantly, it is actually *learning* to see and to hear something. The moment we try to determine it by settling upon a final answer or explanation, we lose the sense of the questioning that is a kind of 'hovering over' and playing with what we are putting into question. In other words, questioning takes a completely different path to conceptualising. Concepts wrap things up and clothe them into a tidy whole such that, when packaged in such a way, show distinct limits that mark them off from other concepts. Concepts are therefore a way of ending questioning, as if everything has finally been said about the matter at hand. The space, or opening has been filled, and the process of moving and meandering along a path has been replaced by a positioning, putting in place what is now taken as true about the phenomenon put to question. When we are questioning, we are exploring ways of moving around the phenomenon, and not trying to leap into deductive conclusions about it. A phenomenon does not immediately show itself, because it has gone through so many layers of historical, i.e., accumulated meanings and interpretations, that it requires a careful unpicking and unveiling or revealing in order for it to show itself. This requires a certain attitude of patience and reverence for the phenomenon in order for it to unconceal or show itself over time.

Questioning, Openness and Hermeneutics

Hermeneutics is a study of our fundamental way of always already interpreting ourselves, others and the world as a whole. As a client brings an issue to a therapy session, for example, he opens himself to various questions as he proceeds. As he alights upon certain thoughts, he takes some time to consider their relevance to the topic at hand. He then expresses himself in the course of his further reflections that move and change the direction of his questioning, discerning an important distinction between what seems important and what appears trivial or unimportant to him along his path of thinking. Such a process is a certain unfolding of thinking as he ponders and takes in what comes to him, rather than having it already pre-prepared in his head, so to speak. After some time, he is challenged to question his current understanding of the issue, based on the process of thinking that he has undertaken thus far. He opens himself to this challenge, and now sees something else that he hadn't previously brought to the fore. He undertakes a questioning of whether this new insight is now addressing an aspect of the issue that previously had been overlooked.

The next session begins with the client commenting on his further reflections since the last session, and has now found himself taking a different stance to one that he had previously expressed. In all this, his thinking has taken a more interpretative turn or movement. In other words, the activity of thinking and questioning has been a process of continual and continuing openness towards the question that he has brought to therapy and that has been transformed from being a question to being a *question-ing*. Expressed in another way, the substantive form of the question has now become verbal in form. Moreover, in this transformation of the client's world, his own change in stance and attitude towards the question is *itself* a transformation.

Gadamer and Openness

Gadamer attends more closely to the 'logical structure of openness', that is, how openness is gathered into a structure that characterises it in that particular way. He states, rightly, that the structure of the question is implicit in all experience. When a client talks about a troubling or uncomfortable experience in their relationship with their partner, for example, questions arise, since we always find ourselves in hermeneutical situations, that is, ones that are always already interpreted and understood in a particular way. The client has made a hermeneutic interpretation of the situation, and they come to understand it in the way that they do in the light of this. However, since this understanding has effectively closed off other possible interpretations, further questions remain open for continued exploration. In other words, it invites a process of hermeneutic questioning. As Gadamer clarifies, 'we cannot have experiences without asking questions' (1960/1989:362). Having, or asking, questions is the sense of openness that is key here. Moreover, this openness has the structure of a question.

Gadamer's remarks on the idea that experience leads us to the realisation that our finitude and fallibility – that we are only able to grasp things from a limited perspective, and not able to enjoy a privileged God's-eye view of everything – culminates, for him, in a 'knowledge of not knowing'. This was Socrates' stance when engaging in dialogues with others on a questioning of what they claimed to know, whether it be concerned with piety, for example, or courage, or being virtuous. He knew that he did not in fact know, and so sought the assistance of others through a maieutic questioning. This surely turns on how we understand 'knowing', and what constitutes knowledge as such. For example, it seems strange to assume that Socrates knew absolutely nothing about any of the themes that he explored with his interlocutors. Rather, the standard of knowledge that he set was one of arriving at 'justified true belief', unless he was in pursuit of absolute knowledge, which is somewhat doubtful. In other words, Socrates was simply underlining the need for questioning rather than holding on to prejudices, or pre-judgements, as Gadamer refers to them. In this sense, therapists participate in questioning, but in the crucially important respect that it has a therapeutic dimension rather than a purely philosophical one.

In order for there to be a possible process of questioning, the question, says Gadamer, has to have sense, otherwise it offers no direction from which any response can come. It strikes me as an example that a child can ask the simplest questions, such as 'why is there the sea?', and yet we have no grasp of the sense of direction from which to address it. But if we were to be asked, 'why is the sea so blue?', 'what is it to *be* a sea?', we might at least have some chance of offering a response that speaks to the sense of the question.

Bibliography

Fiumara, G.C. (1990). *The Other Side of Language: A Philosophy of Listening*. Trans. C. Lambert. London: Routledge.

Gadamer, H.-G. (1960/1989). *Truth and Method*. 2nd Edition. Trans. and Revd. J. Weinsheimer & D.G. Marshall. London: Sheed & Ward.

Heidegger, M. (1954/1968). *What Is Called Thinking?* Trans. J.G. Gray. New York: Harper & Row.

Wilberg, P. (2004). *The Therapist as Listener*. Eastbourne: New Gnosis Publications.

Chapter 7

Think-ing

Introduction

This chapter is dedicated to thinking, and its relevance to therapy. We usually describe thinking as a cognitive process. But this does not get us very far if we are interested in the act of thinking. We think about something by attending to it and reflecting on the issue before us. In doing so, the question that surfaces is, how does thinking manifest *as* thinking? Rather than addressing it from a biological or scientific perspective, thinking is a movement of thoughts unfolding. How and what we think bears significantly on therapy, since it is, amongst other things, a space for deeper reflection. Such reflective thinking already suggests something wholly different to a process of logical analysis of various arguments presented, or a purely rational approach towards ourselves, although this also falls within the process and experience of thinking.

The therapeutic space does not confine thinking to an arrangement of thoughts that necessarily need to follow a sequential order, and a certain consistency, in the attempt to formulate valid and sound conclusions from certain premises. Therapy, moreover, invites a 'thinking about' and 'thinking on' ourselves, others, our everyday situations, as well as significant moments that linger in the background of our daily lives. Therapy extends the possible kinds of conversations that do also include common-sense thinking, but also opens clients and therapists to the larger question of thinking itself.

Conversation on Think-ing

The following dialogue is an illustration of a possible way in which thinking manifests in a therapeutic context. I provide imaginary excerpts from two consecutive sessions, five and six, in which the therapist and client meet, with the conversation in this case being centred around the client's experience of death. The focus is on certain experiential

DOI: 10.4324/9781003638698-8

aspects of the phenomenon of death, rather than exclusively attending to its more conceptual or biological perspectives.

Session Five

Client: I've been thinking about Dad's death. It happened after a decline in his mobility. But he was 88, and becoming more and more fragile. I'm just thinking about it now, it's been a year already.

Therapist: Time itself has moved on, but he's still with you, in a sense?

Client: Yes. He *died* (with emphasis). He's not in the space that I've been used to seeing him in. The world's the same, but he's not in it.

Therapist: He's there, but the world doesn't 'reveal' him as being there?

Client: How do you mean?

Therapist: Your experience of him when you walk into, I don't know, a room, or somewhere that he would have sat, is that you feel his presence?

Client: Yes, exactly, his presence …

Therapist: But that presence is also an absence: him 'not being in it', not in the space, as you say?

Client: Yes. I know that he's dead. That's what happened. He died. It's the end of life. Intellectually, I know that. But, as well as that, there's a kind of weirdness to it. And it's not reachable by the intellectual part. There's something else to it.

Therapist: You say, 'weirdness'?

Client: Yes.

Therapist: Maybe we can explore that more.

Client: OK. When I'm in the house, I might go into the front room, and as I walk through the door, I get into moments where I look over at the comfy armchair where he always sat, and in that moment, I see him just smiling back at me. It's so vivid, and yet, it's an empty chair. It's as if I'm having a hallucination.

Therapist: When you're in that moment, what's it like?

Client: I'm here, part of everything, but also not part of it at all. Like a moment of madness.

Therapist: The being part of everything <u>and</u> not being part of it can't be put into one whole? Like they're completely separate?

Client: Yes, and it's like something goes into a momentary disarray …

Therapist: What, like a picture puzzle that doesn't have the pieces all put together properly?

Client: More like a completely broken and shattered vase, I think.

Therapist: OK.
Client: It's like I've lost a footing to stand on for that brief moment of time.
Therapist: The floor has dropped through?
Client: Yes, something like that.
Therapist: As you are in that moment, if you could capture it, what's it like for you?
Client: I'm … scared. I feel alone. *Really* alone. I get the memory of him in that moment, and at almost the same time, he's dead, biologically dead (a distinct change in the client's embodied way of holding himself).
Therapist: You say alone …
Client: Yes, I can't hold things together, something I usually have, that isn't there. The glue is missing, has gone.
Therapist: That familiar world that's the same, as you put it earlier on, isn't holding together.
Client: It's like a gaping hole, that world comes apart at the seams and I just see something of what keeps it together.
Therapist: What's that 'something'?
Client: It's … reality. The reality that keeps things whole.
Therapist: And *you* also experience it as not being held together.
Client: So, it's something in me that's having a problem in not keeping it together. It must be me. Because the reality is that everything is still as it is, it's whole, *that's* reality, and in that reality, Dad's not here. He's dead.
Therapist: And that there's something that *you're* not doing, which is keeping it whole?
Client: Yes, Dad is dead. That's clear. But I'm having these moments where I fall into a kind of wobble: I can't keep it together. That's what I have been trying to say.
Therapist: Reality is always keeping it together. And you can't keep it together. So, that's the difference that brings the wobble?
Client: Yes.
Therapist: And that the wobble is because your experience isn't matching up with the reality?
Client: Yes, that's right.
Therapist: But what if it might be the other way around?
Client: How do you mean?
Therapist: Well, you've put this reality first, and then your experience comes second.
Client: (Incredulously) Well, how *else* could it be?

Therapist: What if your experience is the glue, as you just put it, and it's gluing together what it experiences of that reality? There's something out there, I agree, but you can only make sense of it through your putting it together for yourself.

Client: But what if I've put it together in a distorted way?

Therapist: Distorted? How?

Client: Well, that I should be putting it in a way that keeps it glued, solid, stable ...

Therapist: You say 'should' ... how do you mean?

Client: I'm sure others would have moved on from this, but I'm still having these experiences.

Therapist: But you're moving into a way of thinking that's looking at others and then comparing yourself with them.

Client: I suppose I am.

Therapist: You're *you*, not others, and you're expressing something about your unique experience, even though everyone goes through an experience of some kind when someone close to them dies. But it's *their* own unique experience.

Client: I guess I'm mourning in *my* way.

Therapist: Yes, it's tied to all kinds of things that relate to who you are.

Client: (Long pause). Yes, I can see it hinges on my relationship with my Dad.

Therapist: Yes, the sense or meaning that you hold about him as your father, you as his son, the world you shared together.

Client: Yes, it's a world that was ours, and incomparable. The fishing trips we went on together, the conversations, the way we could talk to each other as father and son, the way in which family life held itself together ... the ways in which we lived through difficult times together and came through them.

Session Six

Client: I've thought about our last conversation. I couldn't help but reflect more on how Dad's dying has made me think about the fact that I'm *also* going to die one day.

Therapist: (Lengthy pause) What comes up as you say that?

Client: It's scary. I mean, I've hopefully got some way to go yet before that happens. I'm not ready for that.

Therapist: Is there a way of being able to see what 'ready' would look like?

Client: No, I guess not. But I think it's shaken me up a bit.

Therapist: Mmm.

Client: That I thought I was going to live forever! And Dad now gone has changed the picture completely. It's just that I now see that it really will happen someday.

Therapist: And that feels shaky?

Client: Yes. It's like an awakening.

Therapist: That there's an end-point …?

Client: Yes, like an end-point. Anything happening sooner is a tragedy, a kind of betrayal of being granted a life and then having it taken away before your time …

Therapist: That sounds like a kind of linear timeline that extends out from now into some far-off future, at the other end of life.

Client: Yes, that's how I see it.

Therapist: What's that like when you hear it? A linear timeline at the other end of life?

Client: A little relief, actually. It's not 'close' to me. Like it's something separate and almost 'not me'.

Therapist: Like it's something that shows up when you get to a certain age and then it hovers over you?

Client: Something like that. I love living. I've got my hobbies, my friends, my work colleagues, I travel. So I've got plenty to fill my life. Death doesn't have a place for me while I'm enjoying life.

Therapist: Yes. But there's something about the way that your stance has changed as you reflect on it more?

Client: Yes, I think so.

Therapist: In what way?

Client: It throws me into more questions about how I'm living, whether I'm doing what I want, or whether I'm just in a familiar groove.

Therapist: Yes. And *are* you?

Client: Well, there's always this feeling of looking for the easy path, comfort …

Therapist: And what comes up if you *are* living in that way?

Client: I suppose … I avoid certain things. Challenges … new experiences … taking some risks.

Therapist: Yes. And what would it be like to take up those challenges, then?

Client: (Long and extended pause). I think I'd feel out on a limb. On my own with whatever it is I'm doing.

Therapist: And being on your own with something … what would that bring up?

Client: I … could fail. It would feel scary, I'd get anxious.

Therapist: And the anxiety … what might it be 'saying', if anything?

Client: (Long pause as client reflects). Well, I suppose it's something like a mini-moment of dying. Like falling into chaos.

Therapist: Chaos?

Client: Yes. Nothing to guide me into something, give me a steer on how I need to deal with whatever it is I'm up to.

Therapist: So, *you'd* usually be steering it?

Client: Yes. But then I think, if I hold back, I just go back into keeping things safe, and that feels like I'm living comfortably.

Therapist: Rather than risking the 'mini-moments' of dying, as you put it?

Client: Yes, I think so.

Therapist: But do you *really* die when you are going through something challenging?

Client: No, of course not!

Therapist: So, what would 'dying' be for you in those moments?

Client: I suppose it's more accurate to say that it's unsettling, that I'm not settled, sort of unbound to something that would make it more comfortable.

Therapist: OK. I'm wondering what it might also open you to as an experience.

Client: Open me? That's interesting. I guess I've been thinking along the lines of closing off, closing down, rather than opening up. The other thing that's come to me is the sense of time. The fact that Dad's no longer with me makes me think again about all the moments that pass, and that I take for granted. I kind of keep them contained, if that's the right way to put it.

Therapist: Contained? In what way?

Client: Well, that's what I meant when I mentioned the closing off. I distance myself slightly from moments that might be welcome challenges, and I contain them, as if I'm a spectator. I don't jump in, in other words.

Therapist: And those moments pass?

Client: Yes, I think that it's to do with time, and how I relate to it.

Therapist: And how *do* you relate to it?

Client: As something ineffable, but that makes it containable with clocks and watches and diaries and calendars ... I suppose time passing, moments passing, are not only those moments, but *me* passing *by* those moments, rather than coming *into* those moments.

Therapist: Coming into them ...

Client: Yes, I'm not 'owning' time, if I can put it like that.

Therapist: Owning it ... I hear it as 'your own', 'your only' ...

Client: Yes. Dying is *time* dying. Time passing. And I think it's about living in a way that keeps me in touch with it being *my* time.

***

The above conversation between client and therapist has tried to show that thinking is what happens in a gathered being-with-one-another, in this case, between the two people who meet in the same space. The therapist embraces his role as therapist here in not aiming to direct or lead the conversation in which thinking happens. He is aware that his speaking can take up the space of the client's thinking, and that the client's thinking happens in silence as much as it does in his own uttered reflections. The therapist lets thinking itself guide the conversation, that is, a certain 'letting go' in the case of both the therapist and client. This also invites the client to sense the mood in which the conversation is unfolding. His thinking is respected for what it uncovers, rather than a thinking that bases itself on certain familiar ways of speaking. We can also see here that the thinking that happens is not a simple, linear, logical thinking, but, rather, meanders, or moves in, we might say, a more circular fashion. This circularity opens, rather than 'viciously' closes or blocks enquiry. In the course of the conversation, both therapist and client surrender to the process, which means that they both abandon any standpoint or conviction towards which they might have previously become invested and attached. That means that either of the two might refute the other's thought at any time. What emerges is a thinking together, rather than 'across', from one to the other.

Session five attempts to, among other things, bring out a way of thinking that sees the world in a certain way, such that we either adjust and accommodate ourselves to the world, or we fail to do so. Underlying this is an assumption that the world has an ultimate 'rightness' about it, and that any difficulties that we experience are attributable to something being 'wrong' about us. The conversation comes to question this, insofar as we, in fact, *construe* and *interpret* our world rather than understand it as something that is wholly independent of our thinking about it. The conversation reaches a point where the client experiences something of a transformation, or moment of transcendence, but only in the context and actuality of the conversation itself.

The conversations also implicitly suggest the significance of time. This can only be experienced, but is not itself made explicit, or concretised, otherwise it becomes a more conceptualised and even possibly 'technically-oriented' mode of conversation.

The client mentions 'presence' in terms of his experience of his father being somehow present to him at times. This reflects the way in which a person is present to us in a way that is very different to the presence of an object, or something non-human. The death of a relative or a person close to us leaves us experiencing their presence *and* absence. We miss the permanent absence of discoursing with them, their standing out and expressing themselves in world-illuminating ways, the way that they press into possibilities, and the mood that had gathered itself on the occasions when they were present to us. This is what we now long for again. Objects, in a different way, are present to us, and absent when we are not noticing them or moving away from them. Their absence, so to speak, is not an issue for us, unless we have lost something valuable, such as our house keys, or the memento that is a reminder of a memorable experience from our past.

The conversations from the two sessions also attempt to convey something of the non-subjective element in the thinking that develops. Another element to this is that we don't come to thoughts, but, rather, thoughts come to us. That is, we might be immersed in a conversation with another person whereupon we experience an upsurge of thoughts, perhaps suddenly, or even surprisingly. Such thoughts can't be forced or willed by us.

Thinking About Thinking

Lee Braver (2024) identifies various ways of thinking that we might encounter in a therapeutic context at one time or another. In what follows in this section, a number, though not all, of these are addressed, whilst also considering the ways in which they bear on therapy itself.

Pragmatic Thinking – we think in order to find ways to cope and deal with situations and others. Thinking is embedded in our everyday activities, and in our know-how, or general understanding of how to do things, such as ordering a coffee, surfing on the internet, or driving a car. Our overall understanding of how to do these things does not require us to stop and think about what we are doing, though it *does* necessitate a *form* of thinking in order to complete a set of actions or tasks. At times, such reliable and trusted thinking does not tend to adapt itself to any sudden change or disruption in the particular circumstances in which we find ourselves. When this happens, we are brought out of the familiarity of the flow-like experience: it arrests us, pulls us out of that which had absorbed us and either forces us to think again, or leaves us dumbfounded, anxious, uncertain or despairing.

Our reliance on pragmatically-oriented thinking might be considered to be what is most fundamental and grounding for us when coping with everyday matters. Some clients might typically see therapy in a similar way, namely, of addressing issues in more pragmatically useful ways. Whilst this might be helpful at certain appropriate times, it also limits and constrains the scope of what therapy can offer in terms of a deeper exploration and understanding of the client's way of going about the world, that is, in their being. Therapy opens the space to challenge the assumption that this is the *only* way to think about the world, oneself and others. It therefore invites clients to think more broadly about themselves by thinking in other ways.

When clients approach therapy with certain pragmatic expectations, their initial engagement in sessions takes a somewhat solution-focused orientation to thinking. They present issues that then motivate them to view a therapist with the expectation that therapy will provide such solutions. The therapist is assumed to be a fount of knowledge, an expert, and able to modify or rectify the client's path through responses, suggestions or even advice that will optimise and satisfy the client's expectations. It is in that sense that the client is taking a pragmatic approach to therapy. This, however, might disclose something important about the client's way of dealing with the world, such that, over the course of time, it can be explored, questioned or challenged. In a wider sense, it also reflects something about the age in which we all live. We take a closer look at this in a later section. However, for the time being, we can say that there might be a variety of possible reasons for this. We see this in the case of the client who is perhaps anxious to 'correct' some aspect of their relationship with their partner, and to do so quickly, because they feel that it is very close to coming to an end. Or the client who has a certain understanding of therapy based on a friend's recommendation that attending sessions will provide a 'remedy' for them. In these and all other such cases, however, therapists can show a measure of understanding towards the client's initial assumptions whilst also keeping in view that the *unfolding* experience of therapy over time tends to reveal something quite different for the client.

Interested Thinking – our thinking directs itself towards what is of concern to us, matters to us, rather than our being wholly indifferent to what it is that we are thinking about. Thinking conveys a certain effort and intensity of reflection that the thinker is moved towards in their preoccupation with something that is of interest to them. What interests the client tends to be a greater understanding of their own way of being-in-the-world, or existence, given that the world 'comes to them' with certain challenges. In the course of thinking, the client becomes increasingly interested about themselves, as they engage in the exploratory questioning that addresses them. Aristotle thought of this as the highest form of activity, which he called the *vita contemplativa*, that is, the contemplative life.

Interpretive Thinking – thinking always already construes the world in a certain way, rather than accessing it without any mediating element to it. When we assume that we have unmediated access to things and the world, we look at objects and things around us and experience a direct and instantaneous perception of them. In this sense, everything is placed before us, such that we then draw on already familiar ways in which the world is carved up and categorised according to what common-sense tells us is real and independent of our thought, talk, knowledge and experience. This, however, ignores, or is ignorant of, the fact that we happen to first interpret our world and everything that we encounter *as* something or other, *prior to* being able to make a claim of any direct access to it. Our thinking is always interpreting what is before us. When on my way to meet a friend, or making a cup of coffee, for example, I deal with what presents itself in the moment *as* something, that is, through prior interpretation. The thing before me shows itself to me *as* a cup, just as the place in which I meet my friend shows itself *as* a restaurant, for instance. It doesn't show itself as, say, a department store, since that is not how it is always already being interpreted.

Therapy attends to clients' thinking insofar as they already interpret others, themselves and the world in certain ways, which, in turn, shapes their existence. Two people, for example, attend an awards ceremony and, given their experience of it, differ in their attitudes, beliefs and predispositions towards it. Or it might be the siblings who don't see 'eye to eye' when they discuss family matters. In both cases, each person relies on and trusts what they experience as being true, such that it anchors them in the world and provides them with a solidity and meaning as opposed to a sense of ambiguity and uncertainty. When something more disorienting and unnerving begins to enter into these experiences, such as an outbreak of intense disagreement, they either entrench themselves in their own stances and convictions, or they enter into a conversation that is sufficiently open to recognising themselves as interpretative beings.

Temporal Thinking – thinking takes its time to actually unfold; it 'whiles', such that not all possible thoughts can unfold within a single instant of time.

Reflexive Thinking – thinking can be pragmatic, insofar it is 'about' something. In that sense, it is representational. But thinking is at the same time *self*-disclosive as it unfolds, as well as disclosing the 'what' and 'how' of the topic that is being addressed.

Transcendental Thinking – thinking has the capacity for us to move beyond the customary world in which we actually live. For example, I might be reflecting on accepting a new position in my workplace. On further reflection, I might begin to think more about *how*, rather than *what*, I might be engaging with in my new role. On a third level, which we might call the transcendental, I might begin to consider *who* I am being in taking on this new role, whether this relates to my reassessment of my commitment to this kind of work that I do, or to the question of considering a different way of life that takes me away from a work setting, for example.

Changing Thinking – thinking itself opens new possibilities, and so is prone to meander, or move in an interpretative circular motion, by returning to what might have been previously articulated but now expressed in another and possibly enriched way.

Nihilistic Thinking – nihilism questions the point and purpose of existence, one's commitments and projects, and has the sense of nothing mattering. However, thinking opens us to reflect on this rather than falling into an abyss that hardens us towards the conviction that this is a permanent and inevitable 'nothing'. In other words, we are beings who can think the nothing, absence and emptiness, which might itself enter the therapeutic space on many occasions.

Wondrous Thinking – thinking mirrors our wonder that something is *at all*, that it is there in the first place. Thinking of, and thinking about thinking is the experience of think-*ing*, that is, following a path. It is not some kind of staccato-like hopping from one thought to a completely separate, random and unconnected thought. In wondering about ourselves and the world, as we find in a therapeutic setting, we are being taken somewhere new and freeing.

This is also captured well in Maurice Blanchot's writings (1969/1993) on the French philosopher, Alain. He writes that, 'Alain used to say that true thoughts are not developed. To learn not to develop would thus be one part, and not the least, of "the art of thinking"' (1969/1993:339). This seems to reflect a way in which we can think more aphoristically, as Alain himself did, which means that thoughts require no self-justification, proof or even logical argumentation, because they are not under any social or political constraints for their free expression. As Blanchot says:

> True thoughts are thoughts of refusal: refusal of natural thought, of the legal and economic order, which imposes itself like a second nature, and of the spontaneity, without research and without caution, which is merely a habitual movement that pretends to be a movement that is free. True thoughts question, and to question is to think by interrupting oneself.
>
> (1969/1993:340)

Historical Thinking – in reflecting historically, we come to see what we have been saddled with in our tradition. But this also invites us to see that past ways of thinking were different, and, in some cases, more insightful than in our own time, for example. From a therapeutic point of view, clients can come to appreciate that thinking historically about themselves allows them to discern the changing meanings that grounded them at different points in their lives. This opens them to see the historical contingency of such different understandings, rather than one necessary meaning that is fixed and immutable.

According to the renowned sociologist, Max Weber, we are all captured by a world that is an 'iron cage', and, as he puts it, a 'disenchanted' one at that. But Weber presents the world as something seemingly static, hardened into eternal stasis. This mischaracterises our experience of being in a world. Instead, we should see ourselves as the kinds of beings who *cultivate* worlds, we are world-formers. This is because we ourselves *are* imbued with possibility, rather than locked into actuality. Certainly, our world becomes stabilised in various ways, shaped by politics and the state's governance over us, the influence of the media and the impact of social and cultural norms, conventions and practices that embed us in ways of living that rein us in whenever we stray too far from the effective centre or accepted hub of what is considered 'normal'. If we want to see how our world is more open to possible change, we only need to consider the transformations that took place over the past 120 or so years, including the fall of the USSR and the Berlin wall, as well as the more recent resurgence of far-right politics and populism. Such changes were unthinkable prior to these historic moments taking place.

All this is to remind ourselves that thinking is never final and complete. The dominant tendency is to attempt to arrive at a conclusion, the truth of the situation, which means that no further enquiry is needed or warranted. The impact of this is that it closes off the original question that initiated the enquiry, thereby placing conclusions into a tidy box that is usually labelled, 'theory'. By that point, thinking has stopped, or become constrained and reduced in certain ways.

Groundlessly Grounded Thinking – this is a thinking that acknowledges that *we* are the basis for the stance that we take towards ourselves, rather than relying on what society thinks or says how we ought or need to be or think. In other words, we ground ourselves in the world rather than surrender completely to an 'external' ground that we take to be fundamental and 'real', in some sense.

Forms of Thinking

Representational Thinking

This is a form of thinking that mediates between what is 'inside', or 'internal to' the subject, i.e., ourselves, our minds or our consciousness, and what is 'outside', or 'external', namely the material world, nature or reality. Everything that is outside the subject is the object. In the mediation, the external object – let's say, the table, in this example – is represented internally, in consciousness, or the mind, by the subject, such that the presented object is re-presented internally, in thought, or as a proposition or idea. In other words, the table, as it is presented externally in the world, corresponds to the thought, idea or proposition of the table that is a representation of the external object that has been presented experientially as a table.

Representational thinking is the standard account of our current understanding of thinking and thought generally. It is language that provides the setting for representational thinking, since it sets into place the subject, object and predicate, i.e., what is said of the object. Tobias Keiling elaborates on this in the following passage:

> According to this view, specific subjective forms of the representation of an object mediate and in this way determine how the object appears as meaningful to a subject. The semantics of setting and positioning expresses how this medium is brought to bear on what it is to represent: it is a *set* form of representing objects in thought, prior to any particular object that is to be represented; it is *positioned* in such a way as to capture what it should represent; their representation is *imposed* upon objects.
>
> (2019:101)

This account, however, depends on a metaphysically-oriented dualist account of subject and object, internal and external and the mental and material. It takes the subject as 'imposing' itself on the object, which is a metaphysical position, rather than one that attends to the way in which we apprehend or encounter a thing.

Representational thinking, when considered from a more practical orientation, manifests in all manner of ways, including fixing, mending, rectifying, optimising, reengineering and correcting. It is also associated with competitive, transactional, binary, categorical and systemic approaches to thinking. Barbara Dalle Pezze (2006:98) articulates this kind of understanding that we commonly assume as the *only* possible way that thinking happens:

> When we use the word 'thinking', our thought immediately goes back to a well known set of definitions that we have learnt in our life or in our studies. To us thinking is a mental activity that helps us to solve problems, to deal with situations, to understand circumstances and, according to this understanding, to take action in order to move forward. Thinking for us also means to have an opinion, to have an impression that something is in a certain way. Thinking means reasoning, the process of reaching certain conclusions through a series of statements.

Thinking, she adds, quoting this all from Lovitt and Brundage (1995:586), is 'a means of mastery'.

Technological/Calculative Thinking

One form of representational thought is calculative thinking.

As Crowell explains (2019:81),

> Calculative thinking replaces things with functions, names with variables, in order to follow a path of its own construction. With such thinking entrenched, it is the function that counts, not the thing. Things are [...] indifferently valid; individually they count for nothing. Their ordinary names remain, of course, and with them we are still fully capable of correctly marking distinctions in practice and discerning their "value". But all this has the air of the human, all-too-human, and we *behave* toward them as though what really is [...] lacks all meaning.

We relate to the things that we encounter with a certain indifference, which is to say that they only mean anything to us insofar as they have a use, rather than as things that are meaningful in their way of being present. When we treat such things in terms of their functional benefit to us, reduced to simply standing there in being available for use, we are not truly thinking, as Heidegger characterises it.

Mark Wrathall has called the calculative form of thinking 'cybernetic rationalization', that is,

> the establishment of a system that guides itself without deliberative intervention. It requires a kind of thinking that succeeds in uncovering the precise, replicable, calculable unfolding of causal interactions, and in arranging a system so that those interactions can be predicted and governed.
>
> (2019:23)

Cybernetic thinking here has been most notably brought into the public domain through the 1948 publication of Norbert Wiener's *Cybernetics: Or Control and Communication in the Animal and the Machine.* Cybernetics very quickly established itself as a field of study of its own, attracting a number of academics and professionals from a wide variety of backgrounds. Wiener conceived of ourselves as animals that are cybernetic systems which regulate themselves through a process of feedback and control. In other words, we are thinking machines that possess 'cybernetic brains', as Andrew Pickering characterises us (2010). To use a very simple example of how this works, if I am trying to throw a ball into a basket at the end of my garden, my first attempt sees the ball landing a short distance beyond its target. My brain now recognises this as feedback for me to act upon and therefore uses as a means to calibrate my next throw. I try once again, but the ball now falls short of the basket by a small distance. Again, I draw on this feedback to then reassess my throw of the ball so that it will drop into the basket. The process of feedback and adjusted action repeats itself until I am successful in achieving my goal.

Whilst this whole way of thinking was applied extensively to various military and technological activities and projects, it has also turned its attention to addressing and claiming to solve issues and challenges that *we* as humans face in the course of living our lives. The result was 'Psycho-Cybernetics'. This was first introduced as a 'science' by the American cosmetic surgeon and author, Maxwell Maltz, in a book that was published under the same name. Over the years, this whole way of thinking expanded into the self-help movement, as well as in pseudoscientific approaches such as Neuro-Linguistic Programming, but has also influenced various motivational speakers and 'life strategists', such as Tony Robbins, who extended this to certain technical-sounding formulations, such as 'neuro-associative conditioning'. Some therapeutic approaches have similarly adopted this general approach to thinking, most notably in cognitive-behavioural therapy (CBT), which is to date the preferred therapeutic approach in the National Health Service and other Social Service settings in the UK and elsewhere.

Meditative Thinking and Gelassenheit

In thinking calculatively, or even computationally, we reduce the world to quantification, measurement and utility. The various entities in the world are treated as objects for our use, consumption and transformation. In order for this to be possible, we engage in a thinking that orders, optimises, controls and positions such entities, so that they are seen as resources that are conveniently on-hand for us whenever we deem them to be a relevant means for reaching certain desired ends. However, at the same time, we *ourselves* become objectified as resources, and moreover, relate to ourselves in this very same way. In so doing, we become entrapped or 'encaged', as Weber would have it, in a technological understanding of what it is to be anything at all. Thinking in this calculative way draws fundamentally on the will, and willing, as the means by which to exert mastery and control over things, entities and situations.

In all this, we fail to acknowledge that we are, most fundamentally, contemplative and meditative in our thinking, which Heidegger describes in terms of a 'letting be' (*seinlassen*). It is the very opposite of a will-oriented thinking, since we let an entity and the world be, rather than subdue and 'attack' it, as Heidegger puts it (Heidegger, 1982/1998:7). This is reflected in an attitude of openness and encounter with things, but one that is not passive and indifferent. Rather, it stems from care, which is the basis of our existence as human beings. The general way in which we relate to things, however, is one of 'releasement', which is a translation of Heidegger's term, 'Gelassenheit'. When released towards things, we let them manifest in their way of being. In other words, we don't 'get in their way'.

Thinking as Mortals

The open-endedness of living as mortals induces a certain anxiety, because it introduces uncertainty: my fate is something that is both certain – that I will die at some point – and also uncertain, in that I don't know when, or how. In the uncertainty, I also experience a sense of being thrown back on myself, with questions about the way I have lived my life, and also on how I am to live. As we age, our experience of ourselves as temporal beings changes, such that we acknowledge that our future has become shorter and our past longer, so to speak. In that sense, we might experience this as distressing, since it awakens us to the deeper questions about our existence. Questions as to what we have made of our time, the degree to which we have lived on our own terms, and the paths that moved us towards the further reaches of our existence in our wandering and adventuring, are likely to enter our reflections.

What is essential to thinking is to think being, which is only possible through language. Our overriding tendency is to relate to ourselves as *a* being with a name, identity, character, qualities, values, interests and so on. The 'a' singularises us, makes an 'item', person or entity of us that is contained in a world, but a world that we understand as a receptacle in which items, persons and things are held. What remains 'hidden', from view, however, is that everything 'is' or is 'is-ing'. We rarely think and reflect on our being, and being as a whole, or wholeness.

To embrace thinking in this way is to get away from a subjectivist metaphysics and into a relational world in which we, as mortals, are constituted in, through and by it. What are these constitutive elements?

The First Element

As mortals, we have been thinking for as long as thinking has been recorded or disclosed to us, that the world is constituted by an element or dimension that is 'the immortals', or that which is not mortal. This has been a considerable mystery to us in our thinking, coming to eventually express itself in various ways in language, as the gods, the divinities, God, the Godhead, Spirit, Allah, Yahweh and so on. Heidegger's talk of the 'flight of the gods', or Nietzsche's proclamation that 'God is dead', amount to a critique of living in an age of technological nihilism, where the gods are absent and have withdrawn, because we have 'forgotten' being. That is, we see only a being, or beings. This idea of the gods or the divinities is not intended here as an explanatory and fundamental metaphysical ground, namely, one in terms of there being a supreme being, first cause or ultimate origin, but as one that attunes us to being itself. This is wholly at odds with our way of thinking in our technological age, in which we live calculatively, without regard for our mortal being, because we are both increasingly and continually ordering ourselves as beings, as does the world in its using us as resources to optimise and order into an efficient overarching system.

The Second Element

As mortals, we recognise 'the above', that we are 'under' the sky, so to speak. We take this as a concrete phenomenon, such that we experience inclement weather, the (humid, or dry, or cold) atmosphere that envelopes us, the Sun's light that appears in the morning, and the various ways in which sun, rain, wind, the stars are the elements that speak to us in the form of what is 'beyond' us, reminding us that we are finite mortals limited in our understanding. In a more general way, it emphasises the fact that we are beings whose very way of being is to encounter ever-receding horizons that we can never contain or reach or transcend.

The Third Element

We are earthly beings, which means that the earth is our home. It is a non-negotiable fact that earth is our serving-bearer, and our building-bearer. This is an understanding of earth as that which withdraws and shelters humans, but also understood in a concretely explicit and physical way as land, property, fields, nations, and so on. In its being withdrawn and sheltering, earth serves us in allowing us to 'walk the earth', which is constitutive of being human. Space, directionality, bringing things close, existing communally, all relate to the earth and its sense of being in serve-ice to us. It nurtures, offers sustenance, as the land from which we can feed ourselves, and does so through its relation to the sky, which allows crops to grow, for example, and air to be released by the living processes that plants, trees and forests most fundamentally sustain us in our being.

Thinking and Therapy

The therapist invites the client to think. This means that the therapist is both present and absent, in a sense. Their presence is a being present to and relating to the client, being engaged in a conversation, but also not intentionally getting in the way of the client's space to reflect and think. But this isn't a mode of thinking that remains solely in a representational, conceptually-based, theoretical framework. Rather, it is a more holistic, engaged way of thinking that is at odds with any calculative approach. It is reflected in a letting be. To think in this way is the origin of freedom. That is perhaps why any restrictions on our thinking within institutions can feel un-free. The insistence on conforming to rules prompts us to think and undertake a process of questioning as we resist constraints being placed on our thinking.

Thinking, when we are open to it in the therapeutic session, is also reflected in the way in which we hold the space for this to unfold. We might describe this as an 'awaiting'. This is a more structured expectation of a particular outcome that will happen in the future. For example, I await the arrival of the guests and friends to my dinner party. We have agreed that they will arrive at a certain time, which has then enabled me to plan and coordinate my time accordingly in anticipation of the event. Or it might be the client who awaits the answer or solution to their presented issue, since they hold the therapist as the repository of expertise on the matter of problem-free living. By contrast, thinking that lets itself happen is a kind of *waiting* for thoughts to come, without having any advance awareness of when, or even how, they show up, let alone if at all. I simply remain open to the possibility of such thoughts arising and lingering, and where they do, they open us to a path that has been cleared for us to journey along. Thoughts, to put it more prosaically, take their time. When willed in some way, we lose the originary sense of thinking that lets itself be.

Bibliography

Blanchot, M. (1993). *The Infinite Conversation.* Trans. S. Hanson. Minnesota: University of Minnesota Press.

Braver, L. (2024). *Heidegger on Thinking.* Cambridge: Cambridge University Press.

Crowell, S. (2019). The Challenge of Heidegger's Approach to Technology: A Phenomenological Reading. In A.J. Wendland, C. Merwin & C. Hadjioannou (eds.). *Heidegger on Technology.* London: Routledge. pp.74–95.

Dalle Pezze, B. (2006). Heidegger on Gelassenheit. *Minerva.* 10: 94–122.

Heidegger, M. (1982/1998). *Parmenides.* Trans. A. Schuwer & R. Rojcewicz. New York: Harper & Row.

Keiling, T. (2019). Letting Things Be for Themselves: *Gelassenheit* as Enabled Thinking. In A.J. Wendland, C. Merwin & C. Hadjioannou (eds.). *Heidegger on Technology.* London: Routledge. pp.96–114.

Lovitt, W. & Brundage, H. (1995). *Modern Technology in the Heideggerian Perspective Volume II.* Lewiston: The Edwin Mellen Press.

Maltz, M. (1960). *Psycho-Cybernetics.* London: Souvenir Press.

Pickering, A. (2010). *The Cybernetic Brain.* Chicago: University of Chicago Press.

Wiener, N. (1948). *Cybernetics: Or Control and Communication in the Animal and the Machine.* Cambridge: MIT Press.

Wrathall, M.A. (2019). The Task of Thinking in a Technological Age. In Crowell, S. (2019). In A.J. Wendland, C. Merwin & C. Hadjioannou (eds.). *Heidegger on Technology.* London: Routledge. pp.13–38.

Chapter 8

Dwell-ing

Introduction

Our initial thoughts about dwelling might move us towards thinking about our architectural surroundings, and the buildings that are all around us. We might then think about the need for buildings as places in which we dwell. But there are buildings in which we do not dwell. When we dwell somewhere, we already say something about the dwelling *place*. The place in question is a building, and we call this 'home'. Such talk about home is associated with being 'at home'. I say to a friend, for example, 'yes, I'm at home now if you want to come over'. What I intend by this is that I am to be found at my home address. But another sense is found in the expression, 'I'm at home with that idea'. That is, I feel comfortable and agreeable to something expressed, offered or considered. It conveys a certain engagement and alignment with what is being proposed. However, when we talk about being at home, even this does not necessarily suggest that we dwell there. We might be living in an apartment on a busy and noisy main road and never consider it as a place of our dwelling, but rather one that we inhabit. In other words, it does not provide us with a dwelling space, but merely a space that we occupy and settle into, because it offers habitation. It offers shelter and a space for our belongings, as well as somewhere to eat, rest and sleep.

So far, then, we acknowledge that inhabiting is different to dwelling. We can think of other arrangements where a living space is not a dwelling space. For example, I spend a few days in a plush, comfortable hotel room. Even though this might be very welcoming and exciting, because it means that I can relax in my own space and allow myself special treats and indulgences while I am staying away, I am only inhabiting the room. I hold the key to the room, and it is a personal living space that I enjoy, but when the time eventually comes, I will need to leave the room and return the key. Inhabiting the room was temporary, only a period of stay, rather than something more enduring or permanent, in terms of my appropriating it as a place that is mine without pause or end.

As we consider these examples, they hopefully move us closer towards the idea of dwelling. They are ordinary arrangements that we can all relate to in some ways, but they also highlight the distinction that reflects the fact that we can dwell *at* these

DOI: 10.4324/9781003638698-9

places, but that we don't dwell *in* them. So, whilst there seems to be a way of understanding the term here, the sense of dwelling that I think is central to what we mean by it in its deepest, most existential sense, is still in need of further exploration.

There are places that we can inhabit and live in that are seen in terms of utility, based on the practicalities of living 'somewhere', and that is a mere means to meeting our goals and ends. When we relate to the idea of dwelling in this way, we see that the very language that we use, which is our very understanding of language itself – that language is communication, transmitting information, assertions and 'speech acts' – means that we relate to our world through language. If I see a house as an object of sorts, then it already shows up as a means to an end that satisfies certain needs towards which I am disposed. A house has a tangible value in terms of the property market's assessment of its sale price, and it can appreciate in value if I consider building various extensions to it, for example. Such an understanding of living and dwelling, however, constrains us from seeing that there is something more that is going on with dwelling, and what it really means.

To try to get to the essence of dwelling, then, we need to maintain a sensitivity to language, and hear the actual words that are being expressed. Hearing is different to simply seeing or perceiving when trying to discern and understand something. The challenge being presented is to hear language in non-utilitarian terms. Taking the word, 'inhabit', it comes from the Latin, *habitare*, from which we derive the English term, 'habit'. As we hear this, 'inhabiting' now begins to sound different. It speaks differently to us, that is, it is heard in a different way. We begin to hear language when it is taken away from its reduction to utility. That is, we move closer to hearing something that is essential.

When reducing language to communication and signs, we deploy it in a way that assumes a certain mastery, that we 'have' language and that it is under our control. In a certain sense, we *do* exercise some control over what we say or how we speak, but in its essence, we are always already given language and live in it: in this sense, it has *us*, rather than the other way around. As Heidegger says,

> there rages round the earth an unbridled yet clever talking, writing, and broadcasting of spoken words. [The human being] acts as though *he* were the shaper and master of language, while in fact *language* remains the master of [the human being].
>
> (Heidegger, 1971a:146)

We can get more of a sense of what this is saying if we think of the example of receiving a gift. A friend hands me a gift, and wishes me well. The gift is now in my hands. I am in grateful receipt of it. It is mine. In that moment, I am not in a position of controlling my friend's giving and of being given. The situation is one into which I am already thrown, and it has not involved any element of weighing up my possible options, much like my being thrown into a world and culture at this particular point in historical time. What I am given is what I have to reckon with. So, in this sense, we are already in language, rather than language being a tool that we use and over which we exert control and mastery.

It is when we *do* think that we dominate language and everything around us, including ourselves, that we can experience a sense of alienation (Heidegger, 1971a:146). In alienation, a certain homelessness, of feeling not-at-home in the world, overwhelms us. Both homelessness and alienation are important terms that we need to explore further here, as we attempt to unveil what is essential to dwelling.

Conversation on Dwell-ing

Thinker: I think that the idea of dwelling is a central topic when I think about the meaning of therapy.

Therapist: How so?

Thinker: Well, when you drill down into the depths of what therapy is addressing, it's the issue of human dwelling. What it means to be a human being is to dwell.

Therapist: OK, unpack that for me, because it's as if you've jumped from one end of the field to the other in one leap. I can't see all the steps and strides that you might have taken to get you there.

Thinker: OK, fair enough.

Therapist: I mean, I have my understanding of 'dwelling', but I have a feeling you're thinking something beyond that.

Thinker: Yes, you're right. We can try and tease out what that very word reveals, because if we just stay with its common, everyday meaning, we restrict ourselves to something that doesn't get to the heart of the matter.

Therapist: You even mentioned that it has a 'meaning', so I'm a little curious about that. I have a feeling that I won't find an answer to the question of meaning in a dictionary definition as you intend the term.

Thinker: Yes, when I think of 'meaning', I'm thinking about the *sense* of whatever we're talking about, that is, therapy. What sense does therapy even have for it to *be* therapy?

Therapist: OK. Again, I think we need to go slowly here, as I can see you're the one who thinks abstractly and is more comfortable with doing that than I am.

Thinker: That's fine, we can do that.

Therapist: Maybe we can start with how the word 'dwelling' speaks to me when I first encounter it. It's a belonging.

Thinker: Yes, a belonging. It then makes me think about belonging to what? If I belong, I belong to something, surely?

Therapist: Yes, but that's not meant in the sense of an object, like a pen that belongs to me. I own the pen and it belongs to me and no-one else.

Thinker: Yes, that sounds right to me. Human belonging doesn't have that sense of being an object that is then owned by someone. I can see how that is how certain people can relate to others though, and how this can also be seen in certain historical and cultural contexts.

Therapist: Yes. It's an objectifying attitude, and we can think of the ways in which it has been taken to extremes in the past. Some people attempt to humiliate, degrade, dehumanise others in various ways through claiming that someone belongs to me, the claim to own them, they're my property. But I think belonging, in the sense that we're thinking about it, is very different to that.

Thinker: Yes, agreed. I'm thinking of belonging in terms of 'this is where I belong', which is usually one's home or family, or country or culture. I can even say that I belong to the category of *homo sapiens*. But that is also moving away from what I think we're talking about, because it's just placing us in a taxonomy that looks for classification and ordering. But there is a certain belonging to, or in one's personal space when one is at home, the place where one eats, sleeps and lives. I belong because I can rightfully claim it as my home-space.

Therapist: Yes, when I enter my house through my front door, I can close myself off and away from the world at large. And I experience a very different feeling, as if a weight has been taken off me. I take off my coat and shoes and already begin to feel comfortable. I can be more myself, in a manner of speaking. I don't have obligations towards others, or roles to fulfil, as I do to a large extent when I am out there in the public world.

Thinker: That's interesting. I'm in two minds whether to stay with this, or to just strip things back again so that we go to the basics as much as we can.

Therapist: Yes, I'm all for that, if it helps us to understand what we're talking about here.

Thinker: Think of the way in which you think of going into your office where you see clients. As you get up, you're already there, so to speak.

Therapist: I'm not following you.

Thinker: Don't think of it in 'mental' terms, that you are thinking about going to the office, and that your thoughts are preoccupied with going there, that the thought is in your mind, and that your mind is picturing or representing you going to the office in your getting up to go there. Don't think of it as all being 'internal', in your head.

Therapist: But I'm the one going there, so there must be something going on inside me that's bringing this about, surely?

Thinker: That's the temptation, to start from there. I'm saying that you get a much more truthful sense of what's going on if you describe it in terms of its more 'outward' and worldly relation. You're in the world, involved in it and already going about it, actively up to something or other.

Therapist: So, it's the way in which we're not going about saying to ourselves, 'I'm thinking this' and then in the next moment saying, 'I'm now thinking that', as if we have a repository of thoughts that jangle around in our heads all the time.

Thinker: That's right. The thing to stay with is the idea that we are always already absorbed in our surroundings, our situation, our world and it's moving all the time. It's not like a dead weight, just statically put there as a thing and not up to anything.

Therapist: OK. So, now it's the idea that we're engaged, absorbed, immersed, enmeshed.

Thinker: Yes. And as you get up from your sofa chair to open the door of your office, your being on the way is *already* to be engaging with the door handle, opening the door, walking in and so on. It's not some kind of work of the imagination going on inside your head. It's that your being embodied and caring takes you right there in the way that you comport, carry yourself as a human being.

Therapist: Is this what some thinkers call 'phenomenology'?

Thinker: Yes, that's right. I think of it as everyday phenomenology, a careful description of what is happening, rather than the way that we tend to think about it.

Therapist: And what's the way we usually tend to think about it?

Thinker: Well, when we think about it, it's the idea that you're a physical object in space and time. We take it that space and time are both objectively independent of you, and that you are positioned in this container we call the world, which is external to us. So, you're enclosed in the position of your body in that container. From this perspective, you're not there in the room as I mentioned before, but an object that has to move through space and time to get to the room. You have a definite location in space, and that location is not in the room. So you're not there.

Therapist: Yes, I see. But how is this a gradual step towards what we're talking about: dwelling?

Thinker: So long as you see what I'm trying to show here, that the phenomenology of going to the office is different to our usual way of talking about it, then hopefully we're on the way to talking about dwelling.

As I get up to go to the office, I'm not alienated from the office, from the door, the door handle and so on. I am already somewhere, and it's a familiar 'somewhere'. Everything is available, within reach, to hand, handy. I'm already 'ahead' of myself, and concerned and preoccupied with being in my office.

Therapist: So, what happens if I get up from my chair, and as I walk across the room, I trip on the rug on my way to the office? Am I still carrying myself there in the way you described?

Thinker: That's a good question. In that moment, there is a breakdown and I now focus on my steps as I get up. I'm not ahead of myself any longer, as I was before I tripped over. The tripping has put me back *behind* where I was already, if you see what I mean. I'm going 'backwards', trying to attend to what happened, because I was already past this as I was moving across the room to go to the office. It's like the temporal moments have become momentarily jumbled and disrupted, and I'm now trying to go back to how I was moving out ahead of where I am now. I might conclude that I was too clumsy and didn't see the edge of the rug on which I slipped, or that I was in a rush, or that I was dragging my feet a bit, or that the slippers' soles have become very slippery, and so on. It brings me back to where I am now, and how I am embodied in this moment, now.

Therapist: It reminds me of one of my favourite thinkers, Maurice Merleau-Ponty. He talks about the 'solicitations' of the world, that we are drawn towards things that afford us their use. For example, the doorknob solicits me in entering the office, and it affords the door's opening for me. But this is not something explicit, or theoretical.

Thinker: The problem is that if we look at the world theoretically, we dim it down to a certain uniformity of what is simply observable and explicitly there, rather than how we are always already practically involved in the world, using things, getting somewhere, living our lives and so on (for more on this, see BT177). As well as that, we tend to be quite tranquil and settled when we look at the world through theory, because we have a sense of being empowered, and in control, when we use it. But we can become so attached and devoted to it, thinking it is the way to explain everything, or even that everything falls under explanation. It becomes a reliable tool, as many researchers like to remind us.

Therapist: Applying research to therapy is like mixing oil with water: it doesn't work. But look, let me summarise. So far, then, we've been talking about what it's like to be existing somewhere. The next step is to understand how we can be in a familiar environment, already there, and in a significant or meaningful 'there', not just 'anywhere' or 'nowhere'.

Thinker: If we think of the example we just spoke about, it is a 'somewhere', as you put it, but it's somewhere in which we feel comfortable, where we are 'at home' with things around us. The office has my desk, my laptop, my books on the bookshelves, my favourite writing pens and pencils and so on. It all 'hangs together'. So this 'somewhere' is where I dwell.

Therapist: It has a wholeness and coherence to it, yes. I suspect dwelling is something even more significant than that, though. I'm thinking of my clients, in particular. Many clients might be actually addressing the issue of dwelling in the world.

Thinker: Absolutely. It's an issue for all of us. We can live somewhere, reside in a particular street or town, but we might not dwell there.

Therapist: But if we just stop here for a moment, without getting to dwelling *per se*, clients come because they *feel* homeless, in a way. They have homes, a place to live, but they still have this sense of not feeling at home. When they are in their home it is more like a 'refuge' from the world and its cacophony of noises and demands, rather than the feeling of coming home to one's place of abode. Is there something about feeling homeless that we need to talk about first before getting on to dwelling?

Thinker: Yes, that would be a better way of talking about it. It has something of a dialectic quality to it, which I like to think of as a movement of thinking.

Therapist: I think of feeling homeless as a kind of alienation. I know that it has a currency in 19th century German philosophy, but I'm thinking of the uprootedness that people can experience, and it can happen in many ways. It can also be a tendency on the part of some people to feel that they *never* felt at home, that they were homeless throughout their lives. How do you think of alienation?

Thinker: That you don't feel you're connected to the world, whether because you feel rejected by it in some way, or the feeling that the world is indifferent to you and your existence. It can be an alienation from others, when someone just doesn't feel they speak the same language as others, that there isn't a sense of feeling part of a group, tribe, clique, collective or community.

Therapist: But there are clients that I worked with in the past who were very successful in their lives, in their education, their careers, lived in a way that society valued and endorsed, and yet they felt empty and estranged.

Thinker: Estranged from whom, though?

Therapist: Well, that's the other aspect of alienation, that we can feel alienated from ourselves. Some clients just feel that, where they happen to be at that point in their lives is not providing them with meaning. They feel they're just moving along from one week to the next, a bit like an automaton, living robotically. They were originally committed to some kind of meaning in their past, and then, as time went on, something was lost, for example. They got to where they wanted to be, and then something just stopped for them. Or they changed. Some go through a radical reassessment of where they were going in their lives, or how empty things are in the present, but have no idea of what they *now* want.

Thinker: That's quite a lonely place to be in. It's as if the world has stopped for *them*, but at the same time, the world itself just keeps moving on regardless. It doesn't wait for you to make up your mind and get back in the saddle, so to speak.

Therapist: It's not as if anyone can really step in to provide the solution, that is, propose a path that gets them to engage again. It's more about the way that they are opening their world and describing it in the sessions gradually brings them to glean insights and a greater understanding of how mattering shows up in their world. The 'what' of the mattering might not be so clear to them. Some realise that they just want to move away from being senior professionals in large institutions, whether it be the health service, or a global, powerful trading bank. As I said, it's the sense of the unknown of where they are and where they might be headed that feels alienating.

Thinker: So, this is the sense of homelessness as alienation – from others, or oneself, or the world – and the emptiness and distance it carries with it.

Therapist: Yes, and I think that the therapeutic space offers something of a possibility of experiencing a world, a way of being with, and a sense of the openness of being in the sessions together. It increasingly underlines the contingency of that world that they feel alienated from.

Thinker: Contingency in the sense of?

Therapist: That it isn't a permanent, static, immovable world. If that becomes an insight that the client comes to see, it can make a big impact on the client's predisposition. The space is an expanse rather than a confined, restricted place that demands something.

Thinker: And if the client had originally thought that there was something wrong with *them* in the *first* place, that this disorientation is something that only happens to them and not to others, that would presumably convince them that they need to see a medical specialist, a consultant or a psychiatrist.

Therapist: Obviously depending on the way that, say, the psychiatrist relates to their role and the extent to which they work in an orthodox way, that is, within a strictly medically-oriented model, that could elicit *further* alienation, or another layer of alienation. The client or patient might be treated for depression, or some diagnosed ailment, and that could distance them *further* from the world.

Thinker: The medical model is wedded to method and knowledge. But what about psychology? What if the client went to see a psychologist? Would that be a viable approach?

Therapist: I think that psychology, in almost all cases, assumes an empirical approach. But there may be more phenomenologically-oriented psychologists who work differently. That would still leave me very sceptical about psychology *per se*.

Thinker: What's the difference between therapy and psychology? I think that to clarify this would help a little, because it might point to how therapy might be able to address dwelling and alienation in a very different way.

Therapist: We can start to look at this from a slightly different direction. I think that much of psychotherapy has thrown itself into a 'psychologism'. So, it does offer a place, or space, but it also orients itself towards the client in terms of someone to fix, which is a way of seeing the client more as an object to correct, recalibrate, make functionally active again. It veers towards a scientific approach, because it is underpinned by causality and explanation. Science adopts a more detached and impersonal position.

Thinker: And therapy, as you see it, embraces an engaged, relational stance?

Therapist: That's how I think of it, yes. This highlights the difference between them when we think about this in terms of dwelling, feeling at home, as opposed to feeling alienated or not at home.

Thinker: So, therapy attends to the relationship, which itself is a welcoming someone home, in a way.

Therapist: Yes, but when I'm with my clients, I don't constantly have in mind that I'm working on the relationship between myself and them. It's rather a case of losing myself in being with them and on a path together.

Thinker: Right. As you just mentioned it, 'to-gether' just now also made me hear 'to gather'. It draws in, holds in one place.

Therapist: And it's not something I 'do'. It's the very opposite of being a tool or instrument that I have in my toolbox. That's to use technique.

Thinker: Yes, technical thinking. The 'it' that you mention is not a thing when you talk about the relationship.

Therapist: That's right, it's not. Some approaches might think of ways to understand what makes for a good relationship so that it can be brought out and made explicit. But a relationship is only possible if it is hidden, withdrawn, so to speak, and stays there. You can't teach 'relating'. Students who are undergoing therapy as part of their training only really understand it through the relationship that they come to experience when with their therapist.

Thinker: It's also something that moves and sways. Perhaps a better word for it is 'relation-ing'.

Therapist: Yes, or relate-ing.

Thinker: So, back to dwelling, because I think we've opened this all up a little now. I think that when we relate, we are being temporal in a certain way, which is dwelling.

Therapist: We let the temporal be, as it were. We also release ourselves into feeling at home when our world gathers, in being with others.

Thinker: And, I think, being open to the elements of the world, letting them be. But also caring for and about them. There is almost something sacred about the elements, which means not relating to them as manipulable.

Therapist: Yes, I agree. I think the letting be, letting go, rather than holding on, is central to dwelling. We lose the sense of really dwelling, being in place, when our world accelerates in its busyness and is always trying to get somewhere.

Thinker: Yes, that is a very utilitarian attitude and approach.

Homelessness

Our era of Modernity reflects a 'destitute' time, Heidegger says (1971d:91), because we are homeless. In our homelessness, we have failed to appropriate and engage with dwelling, make it our 'own', in a sense, which is not to say that dwelling has somehow been completely lost. Dwelling is *not* something that *can* be 'lost', since Heidegger claims that the essence of being human is to dwell. In other words, his message is that we need to recognise that we have 'forgotten' dwelling, and that we need to embrace this in order to then open ourselves to it. Our lack of dwelling, or homelessness, is particularly prevalent in our modern technological age, where all distances are brought near, but at the same time, that which is brought near has no meaning for us other than in the utility and advantage it affords us. In this way, we 'overlook' what is before us, because all we see is the exploitability and substitutability of one thing after another. Rather than being things, they become objects, which suggests a neutrality and distance. Paper coffee cups are discarded once their contents are consumed by us, for example, and we cease to think anything more of them. They served their use, and can now be 'forgotten'. They fit into our fast-paced world because ordering a takeaway drink and then enjoying it 'on the go' allows us to make the most of the time that we have. That is, time itself has become a resource that needs to be managed. This is a wholly different experience to drinking coffee from a fine bone china cup, enjoying the way we delicately clasp it and perhaps savour it in its lightness and elegant shape as we raise it to our lips. On such occasions, the china cup stands out in its 'nearness', thereby being preserved and let into our world, in contrast to the 'technological cup', which remains 'far' from us in being meaningful only in its functionality.

When we are in a position to see this meaningful difference between what is near and far, then, we can experience a certain 'homesickness'. We can perhaps notice this at certain times and moments, as we do when our weekend periods draw to a close and Sunday evening approaches, when we experience a gentle sadness at the thought of returning to our jobs the following morning.

Heidegger speaks about homesickness in his lecture course, *The Fundamental Concepts of Metaphysics*, where he draws on an excerpt from the work of the German poet, Novalis. Fundamentally, it is a mood or disposition, 'an urge to be everywhere at home' (1983/1995:5). In other words, it is 'not merely here or there, nor even simply in every place, in all places taken together one after the other. Rather, to be at home everywhere means to be at once and at all times within the whole' (1983/1995:5). This 'within the whole', he adds, is the world 'as a whole' (1983/1995:5). That is, our homesickness drives us to being as a whole, such that we are on the way to it, though at the same time we are drawn downward. This brings about a certain unrest in us, because we are not yet in the world, but, rather, simply striving towards it. In this striving towards, we experience a 'not yet' of our being underway that accompanies our restlessness. Here, Heidegger adds that this 'not', a nullity, discloses our finitude, that is, that we are mortal (1983/1995:6). Our finitude shows itself as a nullity – we can't step beyond it to grasp it, but instead face a 'nothing', like looking into a void – and this individualises us such that we now are more attuned to our being, namely, existence. Our homesickness as finite beings reflects the fact that we are at a distance from dwelling. The distance, however, draws to see this as a longing that we feel for *being* at home in the world. The longing opens us to coming home, or experiencing a homecoming.

Robin Cooper summarises homelessness in his own elegant way, when he says it is

> not the position of being without a roof over one's head but of having lost one's way; or not knowing one's way about [...] a sense of having lost one's way, where it is not simply a matter of following some directions back – for one may have lost one's desire, too. There are numerous different inflections to this 'having lost one's way', such as being out of touch, beside oneself, not knowing where to turn,

> going round in circles, up the wall, and so on. Many of these popular idioms are strikingly spatial; homelessness, we might say, is being 'spaced out' as distinct from 'homed in' [...] homelessness is, above all, disorientation. How does it feel, screams Bob Dylan in that anthem of the sixties, to be with no direction home?
>
> (1984:198–199)

Being Out of Place – Alienation

In considering the idea of alienation, we might say that it is constituted by three elements: (1) the background norm of how things ought to be; (2) what is lost and (3) how that is transformed into something else. There are a number of ways of understanding alienation, although we commonly take it as the feeling of being excluded from a group or community of others, and of things that belong together coming apart in some way.

For the German thinker, Karl Marx, for example, alienation is an important though complex idea, which he worked on for much of his life. His thinking was very much influenced by another German philosopher, Georg W.F. Hegel, who thought that our alienation was more a metaphysically-based issue. Marx, however, brought this back down to concrete reality and claimed that we are essentially labouring beings. In our industrialised and commercialised age, we sell our labour power to others, i.e., employers. Insofar as we create and produce things, usually seen as products, our labour can be exploited such that we become alienated in different ways: (1) alienation from what we produce – that things we produce appear hostile and alien to us because they take on a power of their own as commodities to be bought and sold; (2) alienation in production activity – this is a basic activity that we human beings show that distinguishes us from animals, namely, to *produce* goods and (3) alienation from our species-being (Marx's term for what it means to be our particular kind of being). Marx, however, was very much concerned with the economic, political and societal aspects of alienation, and the way this stifled, compromised and constrained human freedom; but perhaps his own contributions paved the way for thinking more about the technological age in which we live, and the way that alienation remains an important consideration as we continue to reflect on it. In this sense, it seems we need to understand the wider experience of *feeling* alienated.

Robin Cooper describes the feeling of alienation well in the following excerpts:

> "Alienation" here is used variously to allude to un-rootedness, set-apartness from the objective world, and from nature, technical outer-directedness, and loneliness; we are left less with a concept that has been clarified than with a feeling that alienation is a "bad thing", and the disease of our age.
>
> (1984:193)

> to "alienate" is to make alien, strange, or foreign; also to disown. Alienation, however, is usually used to refer to that state of being alienated or estranged – from something, someone, or oneself.
>
> (1984:194)

The renowned therapist, R.D. Laing, similarly brings this into the realm of our relation to others and the world. He introduces the distinction between, as he describes it, 'normal alienation', on the one hand, and the appropriation of the wholeness of experience, on the other. As a mark of the importance that he places on this, in his introduction to his *The Politics of Experience*, he writes that,

> [o]ur alienation goes to the roots. The realisation of this is the essential springboard for any serious reflection on any aspect of present inter-human life [...w]e are born into a world where alienation awaits us [and] is achieved only by outrageous violence perpetrated by human beings on human beings.
>
> (1967:12)

Heidegger on Dwelling

If we feel homeless and alienated, how might we undergo a 'homecoming'? It is through the realisation that we have oriented ourselves only to beings and not being, that is, that the beings that we encounter in the world are *being* in their 'is-ing'. This is important because treating everything as an object, including ourselves, leaves us homeless, uprooted and disjointed. In our accustomed way of living our lives, most if not all of us feel at home in metaphysics, though we don't see it for its underlying homelessness. It offers what *seems* to be a home of sorts, given its offer of familiarity, the promotion of convenience and an ordering of objects that are readily available to us. But this lacks a sense of *being* at home, in terms of truly dwelling in our being.

Heidegger attends to dwelling in a 1951 lecture that he gave and later presented as an essay under the title, *Building Dwelling Thinking*. The title's words lack punctuation, which already intimates the way in which these terms are deeply interwoven or, more correctly, a unifying unity. In the final sections of this essay, he addresses the 'real [i.e. proper] plight of dwelling' which he distinguishes from 'talk about the housing shortage' (1971a:161), in that 'we try to fill the need by providing houses'. Even though this is a continual challenge that has been with us for a long time, this is not the deepest issue that we face with dwelling. This 'plight of dwelling' has been with us for much longer.

As he elaborates (1971a:161),

> The real dwelling plight lies in this, that mortals ever search anew for the nature of dwelling, that they *must ever learn to dwell*. What if [the human being's] homelessness consisted in this, that [the human being] still does not even think of the *real* plight of dwelling as *the* plight? Yet as soon as [the human being] *gives thought* to [their] homelessness, it is a misery no longer. Rightly considered and kept well in mind, it is the sole summons that *calls* mortals into their dwelling.

The plight of dwelling is not, as Heidegger stresses, the same as the plight of homelessness, the lack of housing, the environments in which we happen to live.

Houses and buildings do the work of providing shelter, but that does not mean that we are assured of dwelling. Our thinking, it seems, has ignored, not explored, or sufficiently attended to, the question of what it means to dwell. We could even say that 'the plight of dwelling [...] is a form of forgetfulness. [The human being] dwells forgetfully' (Cooper, 1984:216). This, Heidegger says, is the plight of mortals (1971a:161).

Heidegger's reference to us as 'mortals' is distinguished from the term, 'the human being', or 'man', as Heidegger writes in this text. Why mortals? As mortals, we think of ourselves as finite, and thereby facing up to our finitude. In so doing, we exist authentically. In existing authentically, I 'own up' to and address my being, insofar as I am both 'stuck with' my being as a fact (that I am) and that I am called, summoned, addressed to take up my being in one way or another (in having to be) (Withy, 2019:158). I cannot shirk, or throw off my being, so that I bracket it in some way. However, human beings generally do find ways to deflect away from the issue of being mortals by absorbing themselves in distractions of one kind or another.

As human beings, we generally think of dwelling in more practical terms, namely, as having a home in which we live that offers comfort, privacy and freedom for us. As Heidegger puts this, our 'customary notion of dwelling'

> remains merely one form of human behaviour alongside many others. We work in the city, but dwell outside it. We travel, and dwell now here, now there. Dwelling so understood is always merely the occupying of a lodging.
>
> (1971b:214–215)

But as mortals, we are called into the question of dwelling. As human beings, whilst we might feel at home in our houses and dwellings, it is our *thinking* that is 'homeless', because our cleverness and the results that it produces has seduced us into a thinking that has actually left us ever more distant from dwelling. That is, thinking itself has given little consideration to what dwelling really means. Mortals are called to think about what it means to dwell, given that they face up to the question of being.

Dwelling as Fitting

Matthew King reads Heidegger in a way that introduces the idea of a 'fitting' that is reflected in dwelling. Drawing on his own examples, we usually talk in terms of 'fitting in' or 'fitting together'. We also think about our suitability for a particular role or way of living. To take some simple examples, given Jonas' very irresponsible attitude to money, he is not a good fit for working as a finance director; or, we might say, it is not a fitting life for Jenna to become a complete recluse if she is very sociable and enjoys being with other people. When we fit in, King says, 'we say that we are at home' (2009:11). In contrast to things and other beings that *are* in a place, humans *have* a place, and this relates to their being-in-the-world. Having a place relates to what it is to be human, which is care. The table *is* in a place, for example, but it does not care about the place that it occupies. For us, dwelling in a place matters insofar as we show and extend care towards it. We tend to it, as we might do in taking care of our garden, for example. This reflects the significance of the term, being-in-the-world, as the hyphenation emphasises the *placedness* of being human that is intrinsic to its existence. This contrasts with the isolated objects that are located and positioned in a space.

Dwelling and Therapy

The essence of dwelling is to be at home in the world, as opposed to merely residing in it. To be home, we build in order to shelter our placedness; in other words, we take care of our being-in-the-world. Such taking care is reflected in our sense of belonging. We be-long, which suggests a meaningful longing for our being in a place that is welcoming for us, a feeling of being grateful for the home in which we dwell. But, as Rogers adds, when we belong to a place, we dwell in it temporally:

> It is presently to have been in a place and to anticipate where one will be. The root of this temporal belonging is a kind of receptivity. One trusts that he will find a place of belonging, or that the place in which he finds himself will prove to be the occasion for enjoyment or fulfilment. It will be where one finds his home. If this is the case, then the place of belonging is already identical to the place wherein one finds his welcome [...] To bring into view the temporal structure of our experience of place, of dwelling, is simultaneously to discern a relational structure in it. To be human is to receive the gift of oneself wrapped in the gift of place and everything brought forth in place.
>
> (https://www.planksip.org/heidegger-on-human-dwelling/)

As existing beings, we either own up to our mortal way of being, which then shapes the manner of our existing, or we busy ourselves with continual activity in ways that deflect us away from our finitude. In the busyness, we are unable or unwilling to be still, that is, to reflect and meditate on our true longing to dwell, and what this means for us. Instead, we absorb ourselves in perpetual searches for what will only momentarily ground us through gain, consumption, mastery and control. When we embrace our mortal way of being, we acknowledge all that we have been given, granted and received in the limits, or finitude, of what has been bestowed to us. What has been given or bestowed to us has been 'thrown', whether it be our being mortal, our being embodied beings, our being the null basis of a nullity, along with the various limits of my existence that I cannot surpass and 'get behind', so to speak, such as my ability to predict the future, the possibilities that can emerge for me in the course of time, my ability to defy gravity, and so on.

For clients, there is a feeling of being gathered in therapy sessions, which is a way of being and dwelling. A deep sense of belonging in the therapeutic relationship manifests over time, even if the location and setting of sessions were to change. This is also reflected in the way in which care 'expresses' itself in the therapeutic setting, one that is markedly different to the everyday, public world at large.

Clients feel settled, 'well-placed' and open to the world in its totality as their home, rather than simply seeing the world in terms of particular entities and situations that are to be reckoned with in some way.

Bibliography

Cooper, R.A. (1984). *Dwelling and Hospitality: A Phenomenological Inquiry into Therapeutic Community*. Unpublished PhD Dissertation; Open University.

Hadjioannou, C. (ed.). (2019). *Heidegger on Affect*. London: Palgrave Macmillan.

Harries, L. (1998). In Search of Home. In E. Führ (ed.). *Bauen Und Wohnen/Building and Dwelling. Martin Heidegger's Foundation of a Phenomenology of Architecture*. Münster: Waxmann. pp.101–120.

Heidegger, M. (1927/1962). *Being and Time*. Trans. J. Macquarrie & E. Robinson. Oxford: Blackwell.

Heidegger, M. (1971a). Building, Dwelling, Thinking. In A. Hofstadter (ed.). *Poetry, Language, Thought*. New York: Harper & Row. pp.145–161.

Heidegger, M. (1971b). Poetically Man Dwells. In A. Hofstadter (ed.). *Poetry, Language, Thought*. New York: Harper & Row. pp.213–229.

Heidegger, M. (1971c). Language. In A. Hofstadter (trans.). *Poetry, Language, Thought*. New York: Harper & Row. pp.189–210.

Heidegger, M. (1971d). What Are Poets For? In A. Hofstadter (ed.). *Poetry, Language, Thought*. New York: Harper & Row. pp. 91–142.

Heidegger, M. (1983/1995). *The Fundamental Concepts of Metaphysics: World, Finitude, Solitude*. Trans. W. McNeill & N. Walker. Indianapolis: Indiana University Press.

King, M. (2009). *Heidegger and Happiness: Dwelling on Fitting and Being*. London: Continuum.

Laing, R.D. (1967). *The Politics of Experience and the Bird of Paradise*. Harmondsworth: Penguin Books.

Rogers, B.W. (2025). Heidegger on What It Means to Dwell. https://www.planksip.org/heidegger-on-human-dwelling/

Van Lennep, D.J. (1969/1987). The Hotel Room [Die Hotelkamer]. In J.J. Kockelmans (ed.). *Phenomenological Psychology. The Dutch School*. Dordrecht: Kluwer. pp.209–215.

Withy, K. (2019). Finding Oneself, Called. In C. Hadjioannou (ed.). *Heidegger on Affect*. London: Palgrave Macmillan. pp.153–176.

Xuereb, A. (2025). From Bayt to Baita: The Poetics of Dwelling. *The Wednesday*. Issue 203. Oxford: The Wednesday Group. https://www.thewednesdayoxford.com/2025/06/04/the-wednesday-issue-no-203/

Chapter 9

Care-ing

Introduction

Our accustomed everyday understanding of care and caring is expressed in terms of worry, concern, overseeing, attending, looking after, supporting, mattering and so forth. It shines forth, like a jewel in its own right,[1] in situations where we are witness to, or experience for ourselves, another person's assistance and help. When we are open to another person's support towards ourselves on certain occasions, we feel grateful and well-disposed towards them, based on an appreciation of their respect for our dignity as human beings. It is, in other words, a feeling that another is acknowledging both our being the kind of being that we are, but also, more generally, our basic sense of humanity towards each other. It reflects something deeper about us than our everyday understanding of ourselves. That is, it reaches into the very heart of the meaning of existence.

Various authors have approached the phenomenon of care in different ways and from different directions and orientations, including Joan Tronto, Annette M. Holba, Stan van Hooft, Jeffrey Blustein, Milton Mayeroff, Nel Noddings and Maurice Hamington, and, from a more therapeutic perspective, David Smail. However, suffice to say that, at its most basic level, our everyday expressions, such as caring about, caring for, taking care of, showing care towards and taking care with what we are attending to, all point significantly towards the way in which care shows itself. The intention in this chapter is to move towards an unveiling of the *essence* of care, which attends to the question, how *is* it with care?

The concrete expression of care manifests in many ways and in various worlds. The world of music and the arts, for example, expresses care more directly and resonantly with its questions and preoccupations. It addresses human existence in different ways and pursues projects that treat this question as one that matters. But it also shows itself in concrete moments, as in the case of musicians playing together as a unit, band or group. This is illustrated by an anecdote related by the noted Jazz keyboard musician, Herbie Hancock, about an on-stage appearance with the legendary Miles Davis and his band. Hancock was improvising on a jazz piece at a certain point, but as he did so, he reached a moment where he realised that he had played the 'wrong' note. It just didn't fit at all with the piece that was being played. He

DOI: 10.4324/9781003638698-10

began to panic. Davis, however, didn't hear it as a mistake, because he was acutely attuned to what he was hearing, and came in at exactly the appropriate moment and resolved it, in effect, making it 'right', as Hancock experienced it. Davis, in other words, 'took care' of what was before him. It was what we might call a 'playful care' on his part, though one that was, nevertheless, serious in attitude. Such play involved a certain openness to the moment, a certain attunement and receptivity that could be described as a light, caring touch.

Care, we might say, is an essential happening, temporally speaking, rather than a static definition that misses its temporal character. It is the very basis of what it is, or means, to be human. An understanding of care does not become immediately apparent to us, and so a starting point to our enquiry is to engage in a questioning that asks, what do we usually say when speaking about care, and what is the general grasp that we have in our everyday understanding of it? In the course of exploring this hermeneutically through deeper explorations, we see that what is essentially human about us is care. It is most primordially *structural* in character rather than simply an action or attitude that we perform at certain times or occasions, which is how it manifests at a more explicit and concrete level. This can easily be overlooked as our age of technology sucks us into a picture of seeing people as a resource, a form of inventory or supply that can be used as a means to achieve certain valued ends. In such cases, care is ignored, since it produces no economic value, or else is appreciated in certain ways only insofar as it conforms to an enhancement of economic performance and 'added value'. Treating people only as a means towards ends has led to the introduction of relatively modern terms, such as 'Human Resources', and 'head count', amongst others, in order to reflect our technological attitude towards desired outcomes. This has even seeped into the sports world, with the advent and application of statistical analysis to assess the value and best positioning, for example, of today's professional footballer. Detailed diagrams and extensive trackings of a player's movements throughout a game are produced in order to then speak in terms of percentages, numbers of tackles, distances covered, 'heat maps' and meaningful passes made, all with the intention of ranking the player in their overall performance, consistency and strengths. Given the high stakes of investment, care becomes relevant only insofar as a player is highly valued, both for their playing ability and also for their marketable worth. For the moment, however, the question of technology and its relation to care will be left to one side and addressed later in this chapter.

Conversation on Care-ing

Thinker: Various people have written about care, some offering definitions whilst others presenting theories. I think there are such a wide range of approaches to understanding it, even though we might think it's a straightforward, simple word that we all understand: care.

Therapist: Yes, I think it's so central to understanding who we are that we easily overlook or ignore it. It's a word that we use in a habitual way, but it's when we really sit down and spend time with each other that we experience care, perhaps really see it. It merits further exploration, I think.

Carer: I agree wholeheartedly.

Thinker: I like the very word that you have used there: 'whole-heart-edly'. I think it says something meaningful and appropriate about care. But *you're* actually <u>there</u> with others, caring, being caring, so you have a closer feel for what happens when you're with other people in your role as carer.

Carer: You say 'role'. That's right, you're correct. But I see it only as a convenient name that places or identifies and positions me in relation to my daily work and activities. It goes beyond that. I *feel* it when I'm there, I lose myself in it and just see myself as a human being who is engaged in what comes naturally to me when being around others who are being helped in some way.

Therapist: Yes, it's interesting to think of being in a role, and also seeing oneself standing out as someone who cares, has the other's being at heart, so to speak.

Thinker: Taking someone wholly to heart. You both express the heart when it comes to care. Maybe you can open your hearts to speak how this care manifests?

Therapist: Well, so can you, if I may say so. You seem to think we're especially privileged in having some understanding of what care means. I think we all know something about care when we let it in, open ourselves to it. Some people see it as too namby-pamby and weak to even think about care, that we're prone to self-pity or softness, that all everything amounts to is the need to be more bullish, resilient, autonomous, going out into the world and making it a generally richer place.

Thinker: Well, if you mean material wealth, that's also expressing care, but more focused on objects, things, money, ownership, accumulation, growth, development. It's when their world breaks down or becomes disrupted that care of the kind that you both attend to and speak about comes to the fore.

Carer: Yes, it's returning someone to well-being. But just getting on with things in daily living gives the impression that people don't even need to think about care, or about themselves in terms of care.

Therapist: I agree with that. Some people I have worked with have just lived in a certain way that just lacks self-care. When they talk about their lifestyles, they're preoccupied with getting the most out of everything. In many cases, they think it's something that they *should* be doing.

Thinker: How do you mean?

Therapist: In some cases, it might have to do with work, that people might bear heavy responsibilities, overwhelming workloads, staff to manage, incentives and opportunities that pull them into doing more.

Carer: I don't think that any of us escape that sense of feeling stretched and having a very busy and intense schedule.

Therapist: I agree.

Carer: It seems to me that an assumption that tends to float around in my role as carer is, 'the more the better': if I work longer hours, look after more people than I'm used to looking after, that I will be providing more care, and therefore *better* care. I think that the way we see care now is different to when I first started caring for others.

Thinker: Just on the last part of what you just said, you mean that the way that care has become professionalised so much over the years has impacted upon you?

Carer: Yes, but all of it is based on one thought, for me: that, as a society, there is too much focus on 'managed care', that care needs to be procured in some way. I agree that it has to be organised within a certain framework, within the health service and care services, for example, but it's just that something starts to change the way that care is seen, and its meaning gets tightened, loosened, distorted, I don't quite know how to describe it so well.

Thinker: It makes me wonder about what 'managing' means, how that stands with regard to care.

Therapist: Yes, you both raise the very concerns that I have too with regard to therapy. I see so much that appals me in the use and provision of therapy. One example has to do with the Employee Assistance Programme providers, or EAPs, that offer counselling and other services. The employer and the programme provider determine the degree of support that employees can have. But with regard to the number of sessions, it's all very short-term, with some – would you believe – offering only *three* meetings!

Carer: That, in a way, connects to what I was saying about caring work that has become so intensified in the need to divide my time between people who need my attention: it comes back to the idea of one carer attending to more people as being seen as 'better' care. It's a way in which time has become managed differently, and to everyone's detriment, except those who think in cost effective terms.

Therapist: It's based on a lack of understanding of care. Care, in their sense, is commoditised, and is a 'doing' something.

Thinker: And just picking up on what I heard you both saying about having time for others, being present to others in a certain way gets closer to an understanding of care?

Therapist: That care itself is time.

Thinker: It's so simple and obvious when phrased in that concise way.

Therapist: And yet it's the hardest thing for many people to see, especially in this age.

Thinker: That it's not loaded with lots of 'doing' to make it count as care. Of course, it involves doing, in a sense, or in certain expressions of care and caring, but if time is speeded up, accelerated, then care is compressed, compromised or even lost. We might even think of it as 'care-less-ness'.

Therapist: That was why I brought up the idea of short-term session work within an EAP setting. I don't care how many sessions they agree on, it's a silly approach. I know I'm pressing the same point here, but I feel we need to rehearse all this and bring it into the open, and loudly. If my dentist is working on a tooth that has a cavity and that requires a filling, I ask him how long it will take. He knows, he has the relevant experience to draw on. But if he says it is more complicated, because he needs to gather more of an understanding to see if the root canal is in need of attention, I trust him. He doesn't rush it, but rather, is receptive to what he uncovers as he investigates. He doesn't know what he might find, so he needs time.

Carer: I agree. The point is: do you *rush* care? Accelerate it, as you said?

Thinker: When I think of machinery, programs, streamlined processes, we have to treat everything, including ourselves, as parts of the system in which everything has to do only what it is there to do, and no more. If you try to question anything, you're not fulfilling your role in the smooth operation of the system. Woe betide you if you think, think differently or 'over-think'!

Therapist: What I heard in that is relevant to my work as a therapist. If I think of myself in that way, my background *experience* isn't taken into account, and it counts for very little. I suppose that was my main point about the dentist example, on whose experience we rely.

In fact, it gets dis-counted if it becomes managed, ordered and optimised. I can even see how our language is so saturated with terms of measurement and calculation, of 'count' and even being 'ac-countable'. Whatever we do also needs to have something 'complete' or a completeness about it: the end-goals that we need to achieve, the targets, the full-filment, even something reaching a fruit-*full* end, out-come. Something has to 'come out' of this, in other words. It has to be rounded off as quickly and as efficiently as possible.

Thinker: I understand what you're saying. All I would add to that is that we're all projecting towards some kind of 'telos', some kind of end that we're striving towards in all our endeavours, tasks, preoccupations. It's just that in therapy, I suppose it's staying more closely with the experience rather than being *solely* fixated on the end. The world, dare I say it, has become fixated with the result as the only thing of value.

Carer: Absolutely. If we just stay in the fixated, fixing mode, that's where the process is ignored. In other words, 'just get me there, I don't care how'.

Thinker: Care is more than many people assume it to be. Certainly, given your understanding of care.

Therapist: We don't need to be especially insightful to understand care. We just need to give ourselves a moment to dwell in it in order to then 'notice' it. And I think of my clients here, who have been through all kinds of traumas, experiential ruptures and deeply unsettling situations that have stayed with them for a long time. They remain unresolved for them. Memories and experiences have become embedded in their daily existence and this has shaped who they are, how they experience others, the world and themselves.

Thinker: And I suppose that you need to be caring, careful and sensitive to how they are being, and let things open up gradually.

Therapist: Yes, it has to let itself unfold of its own accord. No-one's pushing anything. There's no pressing, or pressuring going on. It's not 'three sessions' thinking here. We're not in a 'numbers' game.

Carer: Yes, absolutely. And when I hear you say 'unfold', that reiterates and underlines in bold the sense that time is central to care.

Thinker: I like to put it in the following way. We might talk of authentic time, letting the 'while-ing' of the client or person being cared for in their taking their own 'while', of not having to set the way that they 'while' along according to the clock.

Carer: Exactly. I see how people that I care for resist me in some way if they feel neglected, or if *I* take over their whiling away the time in the way that *they* want to. It's really basic. They cherish the one thing that we all covet: freedom. So, freedom and care are closely related to each other, I think. There is a kind of balance, and if you smother someone with care, or alternatively go in the opposite direction and give them a lot of freedom and space, they actually experience a form of neglect, so the balance of care is lost.

Therapist: I agree with what you say about care and freedom. It's central to therapy. But that's a whole other topic that's best left for us to discuss at another time.

Perspectives on Care

Various perspectives and studies have all approached care as the grounding question that is relevant to the various disciplines and domains from which they come. The diversity of backgrounds and interests from which attention is given to the issue of care and care ethics include education, politics, society, nursing, feminism, justice and law, as well as psychology and philosophy, to name just a selective few. Perhaps it is most important, however, to acknowledge the considerable influence of Carol Gilligan's *In a Different Voice*, which acted as a catalyst for establishing an ethics of care, or 'care ethics'. Many thinkers took this as a major contribution to a branch of philosophy that is commonly identified as 'ethics', though Gilligan spoke from the perspective of being a psychologist. A number of other theorists have also been responsible for developing an understanding of care ethics, including Nel Noddings, Joan Tronto and Annette Holba, but many ideas also come from the more philosophical writings of Milton Mayeroff, Maurice Hamington and Stan van Hooft. They approached the phenomenon of care from a phenomenological orientation, with some being informed by particular thinkers or approaches, as is the case with Maurice Merleau-Ponty's influence on Hamington, and virtue ethics in the case of van Hooft. However, Mayeroff's approach, to give one quick example, brought out eight major elements of caring in his study: knowledge, alternating rhythms, patience, honesty, trust, humility, hope and courage, as well as identifying what he claimed to be, 'illuminating aspects of caring', namely, the ability to care, the ability to be cared for, the constancy of the other, guilt in caring and reciprocation. It is only in van Hooft that we note a decidedly more Heideggerian approach, which merits a little further consideration here.

Van Hooft on Caring

Van Hooft's study, *Caring: An Essay in the Philosophy of Ethics*, presents 'deep caring as the ultimate foundation for being human', adding that it 'grounds ethics and must be included in any philosophical system of ethics' (1995:ix). It is 'deep caring', he says, that is our 'ontological being' (1995:48). In other words, humans exist caringly, and that is why they are inescapably caring beings. This, I take it, is the meaning of his use of the adjective, 'deep' in this phrase. This might all sound like a circular claim that doesn't really tell us anything, but van Hooft is using the ontological-ontic distinction here. That is, we are, to put it a little simply, 'stuffed' with *being* care – just as we are 'stuffed' with *being* mortal and with *being* a body, for example – which then 'seeps out' and manifests concretely as caring in various (ontic) ways. However, van Hooft goes on to claim that caring in the human being functions at the biological, perceptual, evaluative and proactive, and spiritual levels, which he feels justified to cover in his account because Aristotle similarly already posited a four-level picture of the human being, albeit with features that are different to his own. Although van Hooft's aim is to avoid Aristotle's 'reified and static' account, thereby offering one that is more sensitive to a more dynamic and temporal understanding, he is too invested in fitting this into a virtue ethics approach and an ethics of care. As well as this, although he draws cogently on philosophical ideas that speak to the ontological aspect, he succumbs significantly to a metaphysical way of thinking at various times, drawing on terms and concepts already located in theories, rather than staying close to the phenomena that are under exploration and elaboration. This is rather ironic, given that he is in pursuit of a dynamic and non-static account of caring.

Where van Hooft's study *does* become more illuminating is his reading of Heidegger, considering some of the implications of doing so that are also relevant to therapy. For example, he describes 'deep caring' as 'our "ownmost" being' (1995:76). Taking this term from Heidegger, he is arguing that, when we care deeply, we are 'most' our own; we stand out 'on our own', given that this care shows itself without being prompted by 'oughts' and 'shoulds', but rather as coming only from ourselves. Such care cannot somehow be dis-owned. Once we are caring in this way, we are authentic. That is, we are the author of our being true or 'proper' to ourselves, insofar as we are care.

Heidegger's Care

This now brings us directly on to Heidegger himself, who characterised our being as care. That is, care is the way of being that we *are*. He places it at the centre of his thinking about being human by describing it in terms of its 'care structure'. As a structure, it is reflected in our ontological constitution, that is, that which is most fundamental to us, rather than its being actualised or manifested in the various ways in which we, for example, worry about meeting a deadline, care for a relative or become preoccupied with the changes that are going on in the world at this moment in time. To put it as concisely as possible, the care structure is the condition for the possibility of these manifestations of care. Care is structured in terms of three basic elements: the futural, the past and the present. The futural element is existentiality, which is to say that we are always extending beyond ourselves, or 'ahead' of ourselves, as Heidegger describes it. That is, in the very way that we are, we are continually 'aheading' towards possible ways that we can be. Keeping in mind that this is temporal, we should not think of it as somehow static and stable, but always pointing ahead beyond ourselves in our 'now-ing'. Insofar as we are 'aheading', we are care, from this futural perspective. This 'aheading', in other words, does not come from a glib indifference to such 'aheading', but from the very fact that we are an issue for ourselves, and that our existence is at stake, not just at any one instant, but at all times, that is, throughout our lives, and for as long as we are alive. There is no rest or let-up on this; as Heidegger says, we repose in the weight of our being the basis of our existence (BT330). That is to say, nothing or no-one else is the basis of our existence, but ourselves.

As well as the futural element to the care structure, we always already find ourselves in a world, being thrown into it (BT236). In being thrown, we aren't ourselves *being* the active 'throwers' who are throwing ourselves into the world. Instead, we find ourselves absorbed in a world that is already suffused with significance and meaning, prior to our showing up *as* an existing being. This meaningfulness and significance that is the world was already 'there' before us, and how we embody and 'carry' this thrownness in our existence is our 'facticity'. This is a special term that Heidegger employs to convey the idea that our thrown circumstances are an 'existential fact' – that we *happen* to be born at this time, to this family, in this culture, in this body and so on – rather than a fact in the brute sense of, for example, a scientific fact. This facticity, then, is something that we constantly 'drag along' with us, certainly not out of choice, but because it constitutes us in terms of the care structure. We can only be, or exist, in terms of this element of what we always already find as meaningful and significant. If I was born in a remote settlement in the Amazonian forest, for example, instead of a Western European country, my thrownness would deliver to me a world that was wholly different to the actual one in which I exist. Pre-established customs, norms, ways of life, projects, identities and roles would all have been completely alien to me in that non-Western world were I to look at it from my currently-lived world. Care and mattering would nevertheless have been reflected in ways that accorded with the culture and norms in which I found myself.

The third and last element is the present. I am *already* absorbed in the world that is of my concern to me (BT237). I am alongside all the various 'entities', that is, whatever is 'presencing' in the world. Moreover, I 'fall into' the present, immersed in the moment of its showing up.

All three elements – the past, present and future, which Heidegger names in his own particular way, but which need not concern us here – constitute the care structure, which is a unity, rather than separate, individual parts. In other words, we should always think of it as a whole, and not as elements that *then* make up the whole.

Insofar as we are a care structure, care shows itself in our relation to the world, which Heidegger calls, 'concern' (BT157), and also towards others, which he calls, 'solicitude' (BT157). In being concerned, we are preoccupied with matters and entities in the world: for example, I need to complete some household chores, finish my tax returns, source various ingredients for a meal that I am preparing later on, and so on. I do this in a way that absorbs me in these tasks, relating to the various things that I use or pick up in a transparent way, much like my picking up a pen and writing with it, and using the table as a surface on which I can write. This, however, is not the way that I relate to others in my solicitude; I do not treat them as things to use, but rather, relate to them as other people. Were I, for some reason, to want to 'use' them for, say, exploitative advantage and gain, I would *still* encounter them most fundamentally as being human in order to *then* attempt to manipulate them. By contrast, the cup or the pen are used, but not exploited, so to speak. In the cases of clients who feel or have felt exploited, they are brought back and into what makes them human through the therapeutic relationship.

Care and Wholeheartedness

Heidegger uses the German term, 'Innigkeit' in some of his texts and lectures, a word that has been most popularly translated as 'intimacy' or 'inwardness'. It would be a mistake, however, to understand this as something internal to us, such as a feeling of closeness towards something or someone. It has nothing to do with feelings. In introducing this word, Heidegger is drawing on certain terms from the ancient Greek language, and in particular, the word, *suneches* (συνεχής), which means 'to hold together'. He is therefore rendering this in the German as an 'inwardness held to itself', that is, held together within itself. He wants to convey a unity or harmony that is in balance between those elements that are in a certain opposition and strife with each other, such as we might find in a family dynamic or in a relationship. An early Greek thinker, Empedocles, articulated this well when he talked about the forces that are innermost or intimate to each other, namely, strife and love, which we can take to really mean 'a loving harmony'.

A third possible translation of Innigkeit that I think offers us a much richer understanding of the term is provided by Daniel Dahlstrom, who renders it as 'wholeheartedness'. As he says, it is, quoting Heidegger, 'the supreme force of Dasein [being-there]' (2023:284). He adds that it is the 'capacity to be utterly open to, and engaged with, beings and the discord among them [...t]here is wholeheartedness only where conflicting powers are opened up in a way that is comparable to their "harmony"' (2023:284). Although Heidegger is using the term while addressing other issues in the course of his thinking, this seems to be very pertinent to the way in which therapists comport themselves towards their clients. In other words, care is not a disposition or feeling, but a dynamic sense of the wholeheartedness in which therapy happens in its essence. There is a unity, a holding together of the strife and love that the client is opening up in the conversations in which thinking and questioning take their course, a path-ing that itself is freeing in its true-ing, or disclose-ing.

Care as an Issue

Warren Reich has provided an informative account of the background tradition that has formed and shaped our current understandings of care. In his *History of the*

Notion of Care paper, he focuses on the Latin term for care, *Cura*, that is found in literature sources from ancient Rome. As he explains,

> [t]he term had two fundamental but conflicting meanings. On the one hand, it meant worries, troubles or anxieties, as when one says that a person is 'burdened with cares'. On the other hand, care meant providing for the welfare of another; aligned with this latter meaning was the positive connotation of care as attentive consciousness or devotion.
>
> (1995:349)

As he goes on to elaborate, the first meaning of care – the care that is so burdensome that it drags humans down – is contrasted with its second, as solicitude, a care that has the power to achieve the good (1995:350). This, he says, is something uplifting, since it attends to others in a 'positive' way. The sense of the 'positive' here, for him, is that care upholds, holds up or 'sees' the other in their being. As he puts it, it 'hold[s] the human together in wholeness while cherishing it' (1995:350). However, he also stresses that,

> [t]he word *care* is not without tension: The lifelong care of the human that would be undertaken by Cura entails both an earthly, bodily element that is pulled down to the ground (worry) and a spirit-element that strives upwards to the divine.
>
> (1995:350)

Care in Our Technological Age

As Hadjioannou articulates it (2019:65), both philosophy and science are driven by an ideal of certainty. He adds that modern science is an expression of what Heidegger calls a 'care for certainty', that is, the task to secure knowledge, in the sense of arriving at what is certain. In that way, it is a care for knowledge. In the care for knowledge, it secures both knowledge and 'existence and culture', as Heidegger puts it (1994/2005:44).

From the perspective of therapy, some phenomenologically-oriented practitioners apply Edmund Husserl's 'bracketing', which is the attempt to focus solely on the client's conscious experience and exclude, or put on hold, anything that is extraneous to this. In doing so, they are securing, keeping fixed in place, what they are attending to, which reflects a technological approach that is very much in keeping with what Heidegger describes as the essence of Ge-stell, as covered in an earlier chapter. Ge-stell is a regulating, ordering, im-positioning, securing and fixing in a way that fixates, or fixes its gaze on things by holding and grasping the situation in order to then control, manage or master it in some way.

In the process of applying bracketing, the therapist adverts to, perhaps without being so explicitly aware of it, a way of placing methodology above what it is addressing, and in this case, the phenomenon. Instead of staying with what shows itself from itself, and letting the phenomenon appear of its own accord, it takes a methodological approach by introducing a separation between the contents of consciousness and the world that is deemed external to it. Thus, its methodology conforms to the form and operation of consciousness, in terms of its care for applying secure knowledge rather than remaining open to what and how something presences, in its active, live sense. Such knowledge reflects a pedagogical orientation to enquiry, namely, one of following the guidelines of description, bracketing, horizontalization, equalisation and verification (Adams, 2013). By contrast, the practice of phenomenology is only possible in the very practical enactment of, and open engagement with it, rather than following any steps or procedures, which we might justifiably describe as a technological approach. Plunging into the experience itself opens one to seeing how it sharpens one's sensitivity towards the phenomenon, and the challenges that one faces as one tries to do so. If there is any source that provides a good illustration of phenomenological exploration, any one of Heidegger's published lectures over the course of his lifetime can be taken as outstanding examples.

In summary, taking a methodological approach reflects a certain concern for *attending* to the phenomenon, but not *caring* for it in the sense of letting it show itself of its own accord. In this sense, Heidegger is letting the phenomenon be, which is reflected in the term, *seinlassen*, that is, a 'letting be'.

An important question that now emerges is, how is care and caring in our contemporary age disclosing itself? Our technological understanding of being means that everything is being challenged forth to be revealed as a resource, so that it can be efficiently optimised and controlled. When anything is made into a resource, it shows a certain amenability, flexibility and availability. It can be stockpiled as inventory, that is, an immediately accessible resource, in order for it to be ready for use in as efficient and speedy manner as possible. In this sense, care is expressed inauthentically, because it takes a means-end calculative approach and attitude towards things when thinking of them as resources, rather than simply letting them 'be'. Taking everything as a resource reflects a way of relating to ourselves as wilful beings, that is, that our being human means that we exert our will on everything in order to bring it all under our control. The danger that this poses for us is that we then push out every other way of understanding ourselves. In fact, it conceals our basic sense of ourselves as being receptive to what we are already thrown into, and as that which already has 'authority' in claiming us in some way. This thrown character of how and where we find ourselves matters to us, even though the technological understanding effectively ignores this because any acknowledgement of our care-ing and things mattering to us takes us away from being efficient and reliable resources.

Business and technology care about a certain human activity and world in which certain relevant and meaningful activities are pursued towards some end, namely, to generate ever-increasing revenues, progress and growth, as a certain 'gigantism', as Heidegger calls it; the central concern is more instrumental and calculative in nature, rather than an attunement to the issue of being human, that is, its being an issue for itself. In fact, everything found in a business or corporate environment is viewed as a resource of one kind or another, such that it serves as a means oriented towards an overarching end or goal.

Care and Therapy

It perhaps repays us if we finally turn towards the fundamental question that is relevant here, namely, what is therapy? We can lay out all the various elements before us that describe or define therapy, as we would find in many introductory books on the matter. But, at its core, therapy is *care*. Although it is correct to say that every human activity, world and discipline is grounded in care, therapy itself brings care to a more central place in relation to ourselves. Care-ing in therapy manifests itself both in the minutiae and the overall relational character of the encounter. Put more emphatically, it founds therapy, and is what is essential to it. In other words, it forms the very basis of therapy, rather than being a more concrete practical expression of concern, preoccupation or worry.

In the therapeutic encounter, clients initially engage with the therapist in the hope that something will be resolved or overcome, so that they can feel more whole, or integrated as a person. Care, in its structural form, is being addressed in the issues that are being brought to the fore, whether the client is experiencing a form of distancing and alienation, or isolation and disconnection, to the point that they feel untethered, disaggregated or atomised in relation to others and the world. To put it in another way, their world has changed, diminished or become shrunken in some way, and given that care in its structural sense is temporal, or a happening, it has lost, or undergone a diminution of, its sense of movement. In fact, sense-making itself has been disrupted. Therapy attends to the structural sense of care, through relation, but most fundamentally, in and through *temporality* itself.

Here we begin to come to an understanding of the *essence* of care. Care is the mattering of temporality and its being temporalized, and therapeutic care-ing is caring for the client's temporality. Putting it in this way is very abstract and perhaps even somewhat incoherent. However, where we encounter clients as temporal beings, we recognise their care, just as we too, as therapists, care for and about our own temporality. More explicitly, we care about the way in which we temporalise our temporality: we ensure that our weekly schedule allows for ways for us to take care of ourselves, for example, by resting and not being over-stretched. In being disposed towards the client, the therapist tries to understand their way of temporalising their temporality, that in their temporality, they are mortals whose preoccupation with issues can be understood from a different perspective when they see themselves as a whole. By contrast, our everyday preoccupations lose us in a sequential 'nowing', as a connection of moments that are preoccupied with particular details as well as entities, rather than in their being constituted as a whole.

The core attunement that reflects a disturbance or disruption in the client's temporalizing of their temporality is anxiety. However, in contrast to its everyday sense, it reflects a disposition that discloses and reveals a worldlessness, or nothing, as we might say. To attempt to clarify this a little, I offer an example that comes from my own experience at a Virtual Reality (VR) art installation ('WHIST', Coronet Theatre, 2022). A Virtual Reality scenario placed me in a room with walls arranged around me in an octagonal shape. The walls were bright, though there were no objects or items in the room to focus on except the enclosed space. As time passed, each of the eight sections of the wall began to show a very feint glimmer of a black gap separating them, almost pencil-thin in width. Very slowly and gradually, these gaps widened a little more, which allowed me to adjust comfortably to this small change. However, as soon as I was given a little time to feel more settled, the gaps began to widen a little more. Again, I eventually absorbed the widths of the gaps. And once again, the gaps widened a little more. Over a period of time, the gaps had widened to the point where the walls had vanished, and all that was left was what I can only describe as a black emptiness, with absolutely nothing around me that I could relate to, or orient myself towards. I was, I imagined, experiencing outer space itself. I was worldless, so to speak; I had no anchor, no individual things to relate to, and nothing to support me, in every possible sense of that expression (ground, foundation, norms and practices, a shared world). I was deeply anxious, disoriented, even a little nauseous.

The overwhelming anxiety that we undergo reveals the fact that we are the kinds of beings that *are* care. This cannot similarly be said of the pencil sharpener, the table or the hammer. Care is possible only on the basis that the kinds of beings that we are necessitates a 'there', which the above articulates in terms of a world, and, to repeat, is absent in a thing or object (the pen, or pencil sharpener, since it is not constituted by a 'there' in its lying on my desk, for example; it simply 'is' in other ways).

Therapy offers the space to gradually come to an understanding about our way of being, namely, as care, through both the experience of being in a therapeutic relationship and also through the in-sights that come with continued attendance to the phenomena that arise in the course of conversations in sessions.

As Heidegger says in a lecture on the German poet, Friedrich Hölderlin (1992/2018:59), care is the 'obedience to the preservation of a belonging to what is essential in all beings – that is, to what is authentic, which is always the inhabitual'. By contrast, a nihilistic thinker sees nothing, death, and annihilation. Care, on that account, is being excluded from the picture, even though it is the very idea of 'nothing' towards which the nihilist *shows* care. What care means is safekeeping our own being, caring for it and therefore caring about what we are experiencing in the world and in being with others.

Note

1 I borrow this phrase from the philosopher, Immanuel Kant, in his characterisation of the good will.

Bibliography

Adams, M. (2013). *A Concise Introduction to Existential Counselling*. London: Sage.
Coronet Theatre. (2022). WHIST: Virtual Reality installation piece.

Dahlstrom, D.O. (2023). *The Heidegger Dictionary*. 2nd Edition. London: Bloomsbury Academic.
Gilligan, C. (1982). *In a Different Voice: Psychological Theory and Women's Development*. Cambridge: Harvard University Press.
Hadjioannou, C. (2019). Heidegger's Critique of Techno-Science as a Critique of Husserl's Reductive Method. In A.J. Wendland, C. Merwin & C. Hadjioannou (eds.). *Heidegger on Technology*. London: Routledge. pp.57–73.
Hamington, M. (2004). *Embodied Care: Jane Addams, Maurice Merleau-Ponty, and Feminist Ethics*. Chicago: University of Illinois Press.
Heidegger, M. (1982/1998). *Parmenides*. Trans. A. Schuwer & R. Rojcewicz. Indianapolis: Indiana University Press.
Heidegger, M. (1992/2018). *Hölderlin's Hymn "Remembrance"*. Trans. W. McNeill & J. Ireland. Indianapolis: Indiana University Press.
Heidegger, M. (1994/2005). *Introduction to Phenomenological Research*. Trans. D.O. Dahlstrom. Indianapolis: Indiana University Press.
Mayeroff, M. (1971). *On Caring*. New York: HarperPerennial.
Reich, W.T. (1995). History of the Notion of Care. In W.T. Reich (ed.). *Encyclopedia of Bioethics*. New York: Simon & Schuster Macmillan. pp.319–331.
Van Hooft, S. (1995). *Caring: An Essay in the Philosophy of Ethics*. Niwot: University Press of Colorado.

Chapter 10

Play-ing

Introduction

In the course of working with clients, the very mood that envelops the therapeutic space becomes a centrally important way in which conversations can become more open and take a certain poignant turn and direction. One element that features in such openness is play. I imagine that the term might possibly raise a measure of concern for some therapists, as it suggests an association with sports, jest and a general lightness of attitude. However, the sense of play in the therapeutic space is one that opens itself to exploration, considers alternatives, entertains possibilities and engages in a degree of letting go of one's accustomed ways of understanding the world, oneself and others. Therapy involves, and relies on, a certain predisposition to hear and engage with the conversation in a way that addresses the client's more sedimented stance and even degrees of over-conformity in relation to the world, themselves and others. My intention in this chapter is to provide a little background to the importance of play, whilst also introducing some thinkers' contributions along the way, and then reflecting on its relevance to therapy.

The idea of play is expressed in different ways. We can already see this in the domain of language, for example. When in the play of language, we are already in a 'language game' (Gadamer, 1960/1989:490), that is, we are caught and enmeshed in it, as opposed to having a choice as to whether or not we step into 'language'. We use language, but, at the same time, language uses *us*. Language uses us in the sense that our world and the things that we encounter are always already intelligible to us in our experiencing them through language in the first place. But as well as this, we have the ability to play with words and meanings, and to play around with ideas only because language already has a primordial hold on us. On the occasions that we play on words in our conversations, we sometimes introduce metaphors and similes that play with language in order to get at what we are trying to adequately express. We also talk in terms of an inter-play, being play-ful, or that something or someone is 'playing me'. This can even be extended to the expressions, 'dis-play', 'power play', 'overplay' and so on. The nervous poker player can underplay their hand, for example, whilst the loser of the game might be poor in bluffing the other participants because they too obviously overplay, playact or play up their hand.

DOI: 10.4324/9781003638698-11

In a sense, this reflects the dynamic character of language when it is open to its own intrinsic playfulness. That language plays with words is also illustrated in many forms of poetry, but is also well-represented in literature, as we see in James Joyce's two monumental classics, *Ulysses*, but more strikingly in his ingenious play on words taken to its uttermost extremes in *Finnegans Wake*.

When we are experiencing distress, unease, disorientation, dis-location from others and the world, we are not at play, as such. Instead, we experience its lack or absence, as we become paralysed, frozen and feel stuck in the circumstances in which we find ourselves. In such cases, the sense of play, that is, a way of moving in a more malleable and adaptable way in one's daily affairs, does not show itself as even a possibility, partly because the mood of the situation is wholly at odds with this even arising. Instead, we act and move to only meet certain basic needs or fulfil particular tasks. The experience lacks any sense of ease and investment of oneself in situations. Play, in the sense meant here, is an openness and receptivity to what the world presents to us at any time, and the feeling of choice in how we respond. A certain mood envelopes the experience of play, which embraces a measure of freedom and immersion in the moments in which we find ourselves. Where we lack this, we might be inclined to seek therapy as a possible way of opening ourselves to the issue that concerns us.

Conversational Play-ing

Errol is a 56-year-old man who is married to his wife, Deirdre. They have two grown-up children who have left home and are now in settled relationships. He works in an insurance firm, and after many years' service, is finding it increasingly difficult to continue in his job. He finds it meaningless and repetitive. However, he is looking to continue in his work for a few more years, then reassess the state of his private pension savings in order to decide on whether to take an early retirement. In the meantime, he is constantly feeling fed up. Deirdre is resistant to any change whatsoever, whilst at the same time wanting to support her husband. She works two days a week in a Chemist's shop as an assistant. Errol is, as he puts it, bored with his life, and himself, because he feels that he can't see how he can move beyond his current circumstances. He says that he remains wholly dependent on everything staying as it is.

Errol: I'm wondering how going into early retirement would change anything. OK, so I get to the stage where I can retire earlier: but then what? Lavish spending? That everything magically changes? I don't think so ...

Therapist: What would it change *from*?

Errol: What is happening now. I feel I'm in a rut, I've been working in the same company since I came out of school, I got a few promotions, more money, more responsibility, more worries, and now I'm thinking, what's it all about?

Therapist: Life?

Errol: Yes, life, *my* life. Where I am now. Where have I got to?

Therapist: What's it like asking that?

Errol: Frustration, I'm irritated, angry that time just went by and that I'm asking this question now. If I knew all those years ago to ask the question that I'm asking now …

Therapist: What if you were to ask yourself the question as a much younger man – how old would you be at that age? – what might the response be?

Errol: I'd be 25, no, maybe 35, to be fair. I'd ask myself, is this going to be what you want to do for the rest of your life? What would it be like to be doing this at 55, or 56? (he allows himself a brief, wry smile that then vanishes almost instantly). (Long pause). I was building something. I had a structure, a platform on which to stand as I was raising a family with my wife. We had a reasonably comfortable life. Friends, family. I'd spend Sundays taking the kids out and watch them get all excited and … naughty at times.

Therapist: What was that like, being with them?

Errol: Great. It was hard work sometimes, but the time I spent with them was irreplaceable.

Therapist: Irreplaceable?

Errol: Yes, you were *there*, in the moment, and there'd be a comment, or a situation, like the time … (he chortles) … when both of them saw a dog, and they just chased and chased it. Of course, they weren't fast enough to catch up with it, and the dog knew how to tease them, but their loud, ecstatic rings of laughter as they were chasing – pure joy – just let me see how full of life they were.

Therapist: And if you were you, as you are now, being there then, at that moment from the past, what would it be like?

Errol: I'd … feel … full, yes, full …

Therapist: In what way?

Errol: There wouldn't be anything to think about, nothing missing, I wouldn't be questioning anything.

Therapist: And coming back to you now, here again, how are you now compared to how you experienced you back then?

Errol: (Takes some time to engage with this. He looks up for a few moments, as if searching, and then gradually looks downwards. He speaks slowly, but with a kind of weightiness to it). There's a difference, sure. I can see how things are now that are more routine-like, set in place, predictable, nothing of the busyness that I experienced back then. Although I always have something to do, get through, like going to the local recycling centre to get rid of clutter in the house, fixing the guttering …

Therapist: What were you doing then that you aren't now?

Errol: Well, I was preoccupied with the same things, really, you know, practical things, but there was … something of an atmosphere then … yes, that's a difference … there's a certain atmosphere or mood now that surrounds me that was different back then. Back then, there was a kind of direction, movement towards something, the kids changing as they grew, I was changing too, I guess…

Therapist: How would you say you were changing?

Errol: I guess I was learning more about how to be a father. As I think of it now, I was changing as the kids were changing. I suppose I was a different father when they were in their teens to how I was a father when they were 5, 6 or 7, say.

Therapist: So, as time went on, you went through different experiences?

Errol: Yes, I had to make it up as I went along on how to how to deal with whatever it was that I faced at the time. (Pause). I remember once my son coming home from school with an envelope containing his school report. When I looked at it, all I could see were really poor grades in almost all the subjects, which was new. I couldn't understand it: he was bright, doing really well and then … (he raises his hands upwards in a gesture that conveys mystery and inexplicability). It took time to just be with it, and to go against a more direct and rigid approach, as my Dad took with me when I was a kid. It was the first time I felt we opened up to each other and bonded more closely.

Therapist: What was that like?

Errol: Scary! I came away afterwards and thought, was that what I should be doing? Am I being soft and a walkover?

Therapist: Is that you now thinking about you then, or are you seeing yourself as you were then?

Errol: I … think it's … both … I guess I'm expressing what I feel now about how I was feeling back then in that situation. Oh … (he wells up) … oh … I remember crying when I left his bedroom and went to make a cup of coffee in the kitchen. I was alone, so no-one could see me. I feel emotional now just thinking about it.

Therapist: (After a little pause) What comes up for you?

Errol: How much it meant to me, still means a lot to me. It was like a moment of not wanting to be the stereotypical father, you know, giving him a talking to about his poor grades, telling him to study more, trying to pull him into shape.

Therapist: Not following a script?

Errol: Yes, in the sense of being like my father, who acted as if he was following a rule, just saying what he thought a father should say and do. We weren't close in that regard, because he probably felt he had to be a disciplinarian: the principled father, you know?

Therapist: What did you see that was different about you, then?

Errol: Human, being receptive, listening, open, not hiding. Dare I say it, sensitive?

Therapist: And how similar or different is that to how you are now, here?

Errol: Oh … mmm … (something touches him in a way that is leaving him a little tense) … I … I'm … yes, I know I can be really attentive to others, have time for them, but I can be quite harsh towards myself. I berate myself for things nowadays, get irritated quite quickly, or get into a mood that comes back to the impatience that I have towards myself.

Therapist: You say 'impatience'. How so?

Errol: (Long pause and reflection) Not having patience. Not having … no, not *giving* time to myself, not *allowing* time for myself.

Therapist: (a little playfully, but in earnest) As if you're in a hurry?

Errol: Yes, I can't stop, I keep going, no slowing down.

Therapist: And if you did? Slow down?

Errol: I don't know. I'd lose time, waste it, indulge in wasteful squandering of time.

Therapist: So what would 'not-squandered' time look like?

Errol: Obviously well-used time, time used productively.

Therapist: It has to be 'productive'?

Errol: Well, it has to count.

Therapist: Count?

Errol: Yes, that it means something. That something has been worthwhile, you know? (Long pause). It comes back to how I'm feeling now about this particular stage of my life, thinking about the right time to make changes and what might follow from that.

Therapist: I hear that. But there is something about efficiency that I hear in the way that you talk about time.

Errol: What? Because I don't want to waste the time I have? I think it's sensible.

Therapist: Yes, it is sensible. So, what does being sensible give you?

Errol: I feel safe, or safer, when I'm doing what's sensible. I don't like to make mistakes. They have a way of deflating me, as I'm sure we all feel when something doesn't go as we expect it to. I'm not a risk-taker, I suppose.

Therapist: And being a risk-taker for you is?

Errol: Well, when I receive my annual questionnaire from my pensions adviser about me and the degree to which I'm willing to take risks or play it safe in my investment portfolio, my score comes out very much on the safe side. I don't want big swings in the value of my pension pot.

Therapist: Otherwise, any substantial swing would …?

Errol: Make me worry, I'd feel anxious. If the value dropped, I wouldn't know if it would ever come back to its original levels. I'm interested in just having enough, and not looking to make a fortune.

Therapist: And it being stable, not fluctuating, that's playing safe, not disrupting that?

Errol: Yes, that would make me feel more in control of things.

Therapist: OK, so that's how you might deal with savings and investments, and you decide the level of risk that you want to take. That's clear. So, once you have that safety, I'm wondering whether it excludes anything that you might want in some way?

Errol: (Long pause). I don't know, but what comes to mind is that when things are stable, they don't move. (Long pause). So, when they don't move, I feel stuck, I suppose. Then I get irritated, because nothing's changing.

Therapist: And you said earlier that felt you were in a rut?

Errol: Yes.

Therapist: So, let's just stay with that. You stay in the rut.

Errol: You mean in my work?

Therapist: Yes, work.

Errol: Well, I'm not moving, I'm fixed in position, nailed to the floor … not free to move.

Therapist: And if you were able to move, what would you notice?

Errol: (Extended pause). If I'm moving, I'd be free. I could move closer towards what draws me.

Therapist: What draws you if you're free?

Errol: I don't know … having more slack?

Therapist: Something loosening?

Errol: Yes, less tied up, tight, knotted. (Pause). I'm tied to my workplace. I feel uptight being there.

Therapist: So, the workplace is a place where it's tight, tied up.

Errol: I need to untie it. The question is, how? (Pause). I need to come back to how it was when I got into it and it was new and challenging. Learning again, or learning anew. Changing something about my role at work.

Therapist: What would changing allow?

Errol: Well, it would let something new in, something that opens things more. (Pause). I have this sense of things expanding, like blowing up a balloon. It takes up a bigger space.

Therapist: A bigger space?

Errol: Yes, a bigger world to play in. Maybe it doesn't need to be a bigger role, in terms of the position in the company, but a bigger sense of *myself*. New things that challenge me feel like they'd 'extend' me.

Therapist: I'm intrigued by you mentioning a bigger world, but I'm hearing that it's *within* the company world.

Errol: (Long pause). Rather than?

Therapist: Well, I was thinking of something like the world of insurance, for example.

Errol: What comes up is a bigger space, and that the company is just part of that bigger space. (Pause). I've thought about going freelance in my work actually, which would be very appealing. Some contacts and customers have pressed me on this at times, saying that they would give me some of their business if I were to decide to make a go of it on my own. This may be the time to look at this more seriously, or at least play more with the idea.

Therapist: Well, we can play with that, imagining yourself having made a change and working freelance. What begins to come up for you?

The session continues with Errol taking himself into another imagined world, projecting himself futurally and staying with his feelings as he does so.

The Play of Being at Play

In the notion of play, we are never at the starting point of a situation; we never 'enter' it, so to speak, from behind a screen, walking into it as if being an actor on a stage. Rather, we already understand something, or the situation, *as* something, which Heidegger and Gadamer think of as the hermeneutical 'as'. We are always already in an orientation towards something, or, something is already in play, or at play. It is the dialogue itself that plays, as therapist and client explore something brought before them. If we say that someone is 'in a playful mood', this is not to claim that the mood is subjectively 'in' them, but rather that the situation already presents itself as playful. In other words, there is no play unless the world and the situation itself reflects any playfulness. When we consider the case of the client and therapist, however, they are immersed in the play of the search for understanding. In this search, they lose themselves, that is, they are played in the conversation that ensues, meanders, questions and perhaps introduces imaginary hypotheticals. The play itself does not in any way suggest triviality and levity, but a seriousness towards the topic of the conversation. Such seriousness, moreover, is not itself something observable by us, as if we take a detached third-person position on ourselves. This is because we are lost in the play (Gadamer, 1960/1989:102). If we weren't being held in play, we would be experiencing something else, something quite different to this. There is nothing that we know explicitly about it when in play, even though we are engaged and participate in it, in a 'playing with', 'playing along' and 'playing-forth', which are ways in which we are already caught in the experience.

When we are drawn into a conversation, we experience it as something that is meaningful for us. Along with this, a certain sense of the futural comes into play. The conversation moves along, and we feel either drawn towards a possible end-point in the discussion or enquiry, or we simply continue to be led by the experience because we are captivated by its movement and openness. In certain instances, something is revealed as the conversation develops, and we feel sheltered and moved by its very mood and atmosphere. In the revealing, something is being illuminated such that the way in which the conversation is unfolding takes on an utmost significance. At other times, a conversation might include a narrative, or anecdote, for example, in which case the listener anticipates a certain message, significant realisation or meaning that will eventually come to light. In other words, we are inclined towards meaningful endings when stories, accounts, reports, parables, tales, chronicles or sketches of human beings who encounter each other in challenging situations and scenarios are presented to us. In this sense, there is a playfulness in and with the temporal aspect of the conversation. As well as this, it plays with our own way of *grounding* such meaning in one way or another. But there is also a freedom in the way in which our imagination is being played and is playing (with) us as we listen to the narrative presented.

Understandings of Play

Some philosophers have acknowledged play as an essential feature or aspect of being human. Briefly sketching a few of the ideas here might offer us possible further reflections on the relevance of play to therapy.

Hans-Georg Gadamer

Gadamer's account of play draws on both the work of Immanuel Kant, an 18th century German philosopher, and also the German playwright and poet, Friedrich Schiller. For Kant, play relates to the idea of aesthetic pleasure, which is based on the play of the faculties of the imagination and the understanding. For him, this is a purely subjective, internal play in our own cognitive abilities, which is, then, the basis of the pleasure that we take in the beautiful.[1] On this basis, we might well suppose that the idea of play suggests pleasure, fun, non-seriousness. Gadamer, however, argues that this is wrong, and that there are different ways of considering the idea of play. He goes into some detail on this in his work, *Truth and Method* (1960/1989), developing his own account of this phenomenon. For Gadamer, rather than trying to see play as something that happens in our experience of, say, the work of art, that is, in our consciousness, or internal to us, it is instead the artwork *itself* that is the play, or in play, and puts us into play, or plays with us. We are, as mentioned earlier, being played.

Gadamer also takes the position already previously outlined that play is not frivolous, or trivial, but serious play. To take an example from the world of sport for a moment, a tennis player is completely absorbed in the game and takes it seriously. Were they to remark, at some point during the match, 'we're only playing, it's not *that* serious', this would be to miss the point entirely (forgive the pun). In fact, the seriousness is discernible when observing and experiencing the intensity of the passion and commitment that goes into playing a game, and being 'in' the (play of the) game. Perhaps considered more as a form of posturing or as a goading piece of rhetoric directed towards rival teams, a past revered football Premiership club manager once quipped, 'some people think [the game of] football is a matter of life and death. I assure you, it's much, much more serious than that'.[2]

Friedrich Nietzsche

The German thinker, Friedrich Nietzsche, who lived quite some time after Kant but also a little before Gadamer, also brought the idea of play to a level of importance that had barely been appreciated since the 6th century BC Greek thinker, Heraclitus. He thought of the world, Nietzsche writes, as a 'playing child that places stones here and there and builds sand hills only to overthrow them again' (1886/1967:142). In a later work, *Beyond Good and Evil*, Nietzsche further emphasises in a very brief aphorism that, '[human] maturity – consists in having found again the seriousness one had as a child, at play' (1886/1989, §94:83). It is Nietzsche's reflections that Gadamer draws on, in terms of the need to retrieve or reappropriate the seriousness that we all had as the playful child.

Even Nietzsche's style of writing is playful, engaging with ideas by presenting them in various ways, whether through imagery, symbolism, allegory or allusion. At the same time, he is also playing with and along with the reader, by taking one position and then, in some cases, undermining it by presenting another that appears even more compelling. What this suggests for therapy, then, is that any attempt on the therapist's part to adhere to ideas or theories that correspond to the client's narrative and reflections obstructs and limits the possibility for a playful engagement in the conversation between them. Such attempts miss the fact that meaning comes to the fore for the client only when they invest themselves in the play of *alighting* upon meaning through understanding. That is, the conversation is an opening up and broadening of the issue so that further understanding takes hold and meaning is dis-covered.

Martin Heidegger

Part of Heidegger's project was to address the essence of metaphysics, and ultimately to understand it so that another 'beginning' or, better, 'inception', could come into being, rather than attempt to overthrow or 'step over' it. Today, many thinkers and practitioners assume that we can simply abandon metaphysics, and embrace a realm of 'post-metaphysics', or 'post-Cartesianism'. For Heidegger, this shows a lack of understanding of metaphysics and the age in which we live. The main oversight that such a position ignores, or does not appreciate, is that we are *already* captured, caught and immersed in metaphysical language. In fact, the terms mentioned above actually express this through the 'post-' prefix that claims a dependency on the very idea and presence of metaphysics for its own articulation. As well as this, the 'post-' here offers very little in terms of a different understanding of our age other than presenting yet *another* metaphysical position.

Heidegger is arguing that we should relate to metaphysics in a freer way. We do this by being more playful with language and words, so that, when they are freed up by looking more at their etymological origins, a polysemic understanding opens us to a richness and openness to deeper meaning. In this way, words themselves reveal their more verbal, dynamic character. This offers a way of playing-forth, as he puts it, towards the other beginning or inception.

Eugen Fink

Eugen Fink was particularly devoted to understanding play in his philosophical work. We show a certain care for our lives in how it plays out, he says, as conveyed in the following passage:

> The human being cannot rest content with simply existing on the earth, without questions like the animal; he seeks a sense, asks why and wherefore. His earthly sojourn is unsettled by the perpetual concern to find the right and valid sense of life and thereby true happiness. In everything that he does and leaves undone, he assesses, he evaluates his life circumstances according to a pre-projected ideal. He does not simply live out his life; he comports himself to his life by continuously taking a position with respect to it – and in doing so he is by no means certain and assured of the measure according to which he assesses. This tension of the uncertain search for happiness overshadows all the works and days of the human being and at a deeper level of understanding constitutes that which one calls the 'seriousness of life'.
>
> (2010/2016:86)

This 'seriousness of life', as Fink articulates it, is reflected in the very basis of our being as care. As the quote above intimates, we are temporal beings, given that we concern ourselves with the direction and meaning that our life course takes over time. Care itself is the structure of our being-there, which is grounded in temporality. The way that life plays out is that we immerse ourselves in worlds – the work-world, the student world and the academic world, for example – and then find ourselves absorbed in cultivating meaningful identities as we take on projects and challenges that further enlarge the scope of those worlds for us. We gain promotions, are accorded a certain status and standing amongst our peers and colleagues, attain more elaborate levels of understanding of these worlds and become very skilled in anticipating and addressing possible breakdowns that might arise. In other words, we become ever more playful and at the same time show an intense seriousness in this playfulness.

Fink places play at the centre of our thinking about human living, as reflected in the following passage:

> Play is affirmed and cultivated as a vital impulse of independent worth with its own status. It is thought to be a remedy for the harms of a contemporary technocratic civilization. And it is extolled as a rejuvenating, life-renewing power – like a plunge back into a morning-fresh primordiality and plastic creativity.
>
> (2010/2016:14)

Given that we are mortal beings, we are essentially players. As he says, 'Death, work, ruling, love, and play form the elementary structure of tension and the outline of the puzzling and polysemous character of human existence' (2010/2016:18). In fact, 'play is existence that is moved in itself' (2010/2016:19).

The Movement of Play

Given that play is not something 'subjective', it relates to the 'between' or, more accurately, the 'withness' of being with one another. Even though we commonly refer to two people who are immersed in the experience of play, the play-ing in its movement does not distinguish or differentiate between one person and the other. Self-awareness of any kind slips away, in other words. It is *because* it is a movement that such differentiation does not occur. As Monica Vilhauer puts it, play

> is fundamentally something larger than the individual player or his mental state; it is a pattern of movement that surpasses the players, and is something to which both players *belong* [...b]ecause it is the occurrence of this movement that constitutes play, it is not even necessary for there to be what we would properly call playing "subjects" – purposive human beings – for play to take place.
>
> (2010:32)

As she also adds, it is a process, which is to say that it is dynamic. She makes clear that, 'Gadamer perceives that what is essential to the definition of "play" [...]

is the spontaneous back and forth movement (*Bewegung*) that continually renews itself' (2010:32).

When we are in the play of an experience, we undergo change. In a therapeutic context, when the conversation opens itself to the exploration of an issue or feeling, both therapist and client lose themselves in it. The client loses, rather than holds onto, herself, in the sense that the world, as she is accustomed to engaging in and with it, slips away. The sense of formality or earnest seriousness that she adopts in dealing with the daily challenges and routines that she faces in her life is now replaced by a seriousness of a different kind. The questions, reflections and explorations are taken seriously in the space that itself allows for flexibility, movement, uncertainty, possibility and errancy.

Play and Errancy

As humans, we are essentially beings who are characterised by errancy. But what is errancy? We might hear this in the more practical everyday sense of reckoning with situations in the face of numerous limitations and constraints that lie outside our sphere of control and even understanding. We err insofar as we apply ourselves in the attempt to resolve what we face within the limitations of our facticity, such as our knowledge, skills, coordination, decisions and assessments in the moment, but in a way that can never deliver up a perfect outcome that escapes possible alternatives or further questioning and understanding. In this sense, we *are* fundamentally errant in our being. In being temporal beings, our situation continually changes, whilst we 'lag behind' the moment or situation into which we are thrown. In being interpretive beings, we apprehend the situation *as* something or other, rather than in having direct, unmediated access to it. The fact that we are beings who are free, we can veer from a chosen path, or take a stance that strays from what we hoped, planned or intended. It is not just we who can go astray, however; a historical epoch, or even a history of different epochal understandings of ourselves can take an errant path, as is the case with metaphysics, according to Heidegger.

Perhaps the challenge for us all is to embrace errancy as being constitutive of human existence. From a therapeutic perspective, this might mean that the client no longer feels a pressure to pursue certainty, to get things 'right', but rather to understand their way of being in a world that has grounded them in certain respects. Their fear of erring, making mistakes, might come to be seen as a technological way of relating to themselves, namely, as an efficient resource, which means existing within certain constraints. This is perhaps most pertinent in any sports activity, where play and errancy come together, as participants strive to make the most of the moments in which they manoeuvre themselves as skilfully as they can, but always also being vulnerable to 'missing the target' in one way or another.

Play in Therapy

Two therapists who have explicitly embraced the relevance of play in therapy will be briefly covered below, namely, the psychoanalyst, Donald Winnicott, and the family therapist, Carl Whitaker. Whilst each takes a significantly different approach in relation to play, they hold a similar stance in bringing play to the front and centre of therapy.

Winnicott

In his essay, *Playing: A Theoretical Statement*, Winnicott says the following:

> Psychotherapy takes place in the overlap of two areas of playing, that of the patient and that of the therapist. Psychotherapy has to do with two people playing together. The corollary of this is that where playing is not possible then the work done by the therapist is directed towards bringing the patient from a state of not being able to play into a state of being able to play.
>
> (2005:51)

He then goes on to say that too little attention is given to the distinction between 'the meanings of the noun "play" and the verbal noun "playing"' (2005:54). He, too, recognises that playing is neither 'outside' nor 'inside', insofar as it happens in a place, and that it also takes time. For Winnicott, 'playing is doing' (2005:55). At this point, it becomes more difficult to align oneself with his own account of play, as he is fundamentally Cartesian and metaphysical in his approach. Nevertheless, when he allows himself to be more descriptive than theoretically-driven in his analyses of play, he sheds valuable light on the way in which play in therapy can in no way be treated as something peripheral and incidental. In fact, even though his focus is almost exclusively on the child, he says that 'playing is itself a therapy' (2005:67).

In a case study that illustrates his therapeutic approach with a female client, he emphasises the fact that he withheld any interpretations in the course of sessions with her, which gave the client space to experience her own insights and interpretations some time afterwards. The point I think he makes is that the therapist needs to hold the client as being *able* to play, and in doing so to being creative in making such interpretations, which requires a certain forbearance and trust on the part of the therapist. It is in the sessions that the therapist's presence and their listening offer the client a sense that care is being re-introduced into their world. When care is less tangible for the client, it touches on the feeling of indifference, of nothing mattering, which in turn perhaps brings one to a certain nihilistic outlook. Care-ing, in its verbal sense, plants the seeds of the possibility of play, moving from a prior rigidity to a spontaneity in which play plays.

Whitaker

As a trained psychiatrist and family therapist, Carl Whitaker similarly took play as being of central importance to therapy. Although some aspects of his approach are arguably somewhat directive in his way of working, his overall intentions were to support the client to confront aspects of themselves whilst experiencing Whitaker in his playfulness, whether through his use of language, the nature of the dialogue or the dialectics of taking different positions and perspectives as the interactions unfolded. In fact, he took the movement of the dialectical process from one position to its opposite as a stimulant for further thinking about the very experience of being with each other, as well as the issue at hand. This, he thought, brought about a momentary confusion for the client, which then offered the possibility for them to see something that was previously unseen. Part of the way in which he used a dialectical approach was to allow himself to stretch the limits of good manners and behaviour, but at the same time leave himself open to being challenged by the client at any point. Overall, a sense of liveliness in the dialogue developed, with Whitaker introducing humour as and when this arose in a spontaneous way.

Perhaps Whitaker's attitude to play could be linked to a certain humanistic outlook taking hold from the 1970s and onwards, which was also embraced by other family therapists, including Virginia Satir, in her use of 'sculpting', as well Fritz Perls and Milton H. Erickson. It was Erickson in particular who had impacted considerably on many of those involved in the human potential movement of that time, based on his ability to masterfully craft words and narratives to bring about moods that supported a 'healing' process. In the main, he drew considerably on this ability to play *with* words and especially to play *on* their multiple meanings. Experiencing changes in meanings loosened the singular, overly-rigid stance that clients had previously embraced, to the extent that they eventually became open to playing with different ways of being. The ambiguous and ambivalent use of words meant that clients were faced with the need to make some kind of meaning of what they were hearing, which called on them to exercise a degree of imagination and creativity.

Final Thoughts

Therapy provides a space to play, and to be played. Without any space, such playing cannot show itself as play. As well as this, the therapeutic space needs to be experienced as a *free* space. Where the therapeutic space becomes managed and 'bureaucratised', it loses its sense of being free. This is well-illustrated, for example, in short-term therapy arrangements that are organised and offered in certain settings. In the main, such frameworks in which therapy sessions are made available constrain the space, which in turn impacts on the freedom to play and let play. What is ignored, or misunderstood, in such cases, is that therapy sessions take time to unfold and move hermeneutically towards greater understanding and possibility for the client. In other words, in taking time, a process emerges. This process is not one that can be managed, controlled, expedited and assessed in terms of its cost-effectiveness, and least of all in terms of its predictability.

Notes

1 As a purely parenthetical note, aesthetics since the 18th century has been influential in its use and study of certain terms that then became incorporated into the field of psychology, and then later in psychotherapy and counselling, as we see with the notion of empathy, for example.

2 The manager in question is the then Liverpool FC manager, Bill Shankly, in a quote from 1973.

Bibliography

Fink, E. (2010/2016). *Play as Symbol of the World and Other Writings*. Indianapolis: Indiana University Press.

Gadamer, H.-G. (1960/1989). *Truth and Method*. 2nd Edition. Trans. and Revd. J. Weinsheimer & D.G. Marshall. London: Sheed & Ward.

Nietzsche, F. (1886/1967). *The Birth of Tragedy and the Case of Wagner* (BoT). Trans. W. Kaufmann. New York: Vintage.

Nietzsche, F. (1886/1989). *Beyond Good and Evil*. Trans. W. Kaufmann. New York: Vintage.

Vilhauer, M. (2010). *Gadamer's Ethics of Play: Hermeneutics and the Other*. Plymouth: Lexington Books.

Winnicott, D. (2005). *Playing and Reality*. London: Routledge.

Chapter 11

Ungrounded Ground-ing

Introduction

In our everyday experience, we engage in tasks, routines, projects and worlds that are meaningful for us. They provide us with a role and identity through our involvement in activities that matter to us. In being engaged in meaningful worlds, we experience what we might describe as a sense of groundedness, which itself tends to be left unquestioned, or simply taken for granted. However, at times when we feel a certain disorientation, or a being out of place, we might be inclined to describe it in terms of feeling 'ungrounded'. This chapter looks to explore this experience, in the attempt to understand whether and how therapy can offer a space in which this might be addressed.

Conversation on Ungrounded Ground-ing

Client: I'm not sure how these sessions are actually working!

Therapist: How do you feel that they are going?

Client: I do feel more connected and involved with others. I'm not so overawed by how others might see me. I used to feel a bit fragile and distant around them, deferring to them even before talking to them. I think I was afraid of not being how I thought they expected me to be, or that I wasn't accepted by them.

Therapist: And there's something different now?

Client: Yes. I'm intrigued about what it is that has been happening here in our sessions and that has made things change for me.

Therapist: I suppose we've been looking at the very thing that you just said about being with other people, and some of the assumptions around that.

Client: Well, I notice that something's different, but I can't put my finger on it

Therapist: Uh-huh

DOI: 10.4324/9781003638698-12

Client: I'm not sure what you're doing that makes it different

Therapist: That would give you knowledge of how to be the way you are now?

Client: Yes, I guess it would. It must have something to do with technique or theory or knowledge of some kind, information that I don't have access to. If I did, or I had it before coming here, I would have been able to change long ago and by *myself*, I presume!

Therapist: But what if I were to say to you that I *don't* know?

Client: What do you mean?

Therapist: Well, I hear you saying that it has to do with knowing?

Client: Yes, that's right

Therapist: So, how would 'knowing' look to you?

Client: Pieces of information, details that string together into a clearer picture for me that I can absorb and make sense of.

Therapist: But if we think about how you happen to be with other people now, is it based on some kind of knowledge that you can draw on when you're with them?

Client: No. I just find myself with them and I feel I'm on firmer ground.

Therapist: Firmer ground?

Client: Yes, I'm not feeling 'off-centre', or on shaky ground. I can stand on it differently, more reliably.

Therapist: As opposed to before?

Client: It was as if I could fall through it more easily, if I said the wrong thing, or took what others said too much to heart, or didn't want to open myself too much in case I received strange comments.

Therapist: So, would 'knowing' something help? Maybe it has more to do with 'understanding'?

Client: Maybe, but I don't know if that's true.

Therapist: OK, *knowing* what is true?

Client: Yes. I know things, and I know what's true and what isn't.

Therapist: Yes. And you are looking for truths that you can know?

Client: I want to get to the bottom of things, the basic truth of who I really am, and not just go about my daily routines and chores, as if on auto-pilot. That's just a kind of dealing with the surface practicalities of living.

Therapist: But what if it's through looking at the everyday experience that you get to understand more about who you are?

Client: I'm not sure I see that.

Therapist: As I see it, it's in all the daily things that you get absorbed in that you find the questions. For example, when you talked about your job, when you visit customers at their offices, you engage in conversations with them. You go through those experiences, and then you come away with certain feelings about them.

Client: Yes, sure, that all happens. And sometimes, I really question myself. After a full day, I get home, and I feel flat and mope around. Sometimes, I dread going back to work the next day.

Therapist: Dread?

Client: Yes, a kind of bracing myself in advance.

Therapist: Because of the people that you'd see? Or something else?

Client: It's the whole thing. Driving to a customer's premises, having the meeting, seeing a manager who I either get on well with, or else someone I just get by with, where there doesn't seem to be much rapport between us. So, I'm trying to dig deeper and get to more of an understanding of what makes me feel like this.

Therapist: The 'digging deeper' will get you there?

Client: Well, there must be some core explanation that I can reach for what makes me the person I am; what makes me tick, so to say.

Therapist: The 'what makes you tick': something mechanical?

Client: Mechanical?

Therapist: Yes. Maybe I'm taking this a bit too far, but it's like the old clock that has wheels, gears, springs that make everything work? The wheels and gears themselves would then give you knowledge or an understanding of yourself?

Client: Something like that. I want to know it so that I then know myself.

Therapist: I see. But it may be that, in the times when you're least aware of yourself, you're *most* yourself, if you see what I mean.

Client: (Long pause). Yes, I get that. It's not so much like that for me in the situations that I've talked about, but it's when I'm playing football, or watching a film, or preparing some food, that I lose myself in it. But I don't think that helps me in the situations that I've just mentioned.

Therapist: OK.

Moments of extended silence follow. At this point, there is a certain 'hermeneutic turn' in the conversation, an interpretative shift or movement that opens another path of thinking.

Client: Maybe it has to do with the way that I'm seeing life, *my* life, like it's on two layers. One is the way I go about being with other people, having dealings with them, keeping the flow going, I suppose. And then there is the deeper feeling of, who am I *being* when I'm involved in all these things? What's drawing me to live in the way that I do, and live in *this* way and not some other way?

Therapist: I hear something about *being*, or being yourself, that underlies what and how you engage in things.

Client: Or just being me, full stop.

Therapist: 'Being me' – that sounds like it's pointing to something important.

Client: Yes, and I'm taken with the way you say that. It sounds really mysterious and ineffable.

Therapist: Well, I was thinking that we've moved from wanting to know yourself to 'being me'. So, the thing that I hear you mention is 'being'. 'Being who I am' and 'who I am being' sound just a little different to 'who I am'. And different to 'what I am'.

Client: And even 'what I am *doing*'. Or my knowing what I'm doing.

Therapist: Yes, exactly.

Client: Yes, so why is being so important here?

Therapist: Well, I'm just wondering what comes up for you when you hear 'being' as it is being said.

Client: (Long pause). There's a few things. But the main thing is, when I refer to being – *my* being – I'm identifying something that I can't see, or point to (laughs). Also, it's what other people can't see. Or maybe I *think* they *can*, somehow? I'm not sure. And yet … it's there, or, it's there and it's not there. That's the ineffability.

Therapist: It's like it's there, but not visible, as such?

Client: No, not even that. It's not even 'behind' anything, as if it's hiding there. It's more like it's deeply woven into myself in my simply showing up as me. Just thinking about it, if I try and think of it as something, a thing that I can point to, as I can when I'm identifying an object that I see before me, then I lose the very sense of it. It's like talking about living, or that I exist; I can't see my existence in its brute, thing-like objectivity.

Therapist: So, it's being, and 'being me'.

Client: Being me, yes.

Therapist: And you can't see being, from what you say, and yet you are being? Is that right?

Client: Yes. (Long pause). Have I been looking to nail my being down by 'thingifying' it? Getting a handle on it so that I can be its master by knowing it?

Therapist: So that you can then control and steer it?

Client: (Pause). Yes. I can then steer the direction I'm going in and know what I'm doing all along.

Therapist: But does life work like that? Is that how you really live?

Client: Yes. Or, no. Things just happen most of the time. But I guess I see others, and the way that they seem to have it all figured out. They're steering themselves in directions and making a success of their lives. As if they know what they're doing.

Therapist: But what if it's the other way round?

Client: How do you mean?

Therapist: I mean that you get pulled into situations and circumstances, and not any old situations, but ones that kind of 'speak' to you, they call you, or are calling on you, because there's something in the situation that is relevant and important and meaningful to you that, say, some other situations aren't.

Client: What, like a magnetic pull that draws me in?

Therapist: Yes, something like that, but you have no way of knowing what will pull you in and how strongly or weakly, but it's happening in a certain moment, or over a stretch of time.

Client: Yes. It's a bit like the way that I can be in social situations with others. It pulls me into behaving like one of the crowd, just like everyone else, so that I fit in and belong to the group, am accepted and not making any *faux pas*.

Therapist: Not standing out?

Client: Yes. (Pause). Don't think you're above others, know your place, stay under the radar.

Long pause. The conversation now takes another 'hermeneutic turn'.

Client: OK, when I think about what I'm experiencing here, I'm 'pulled' into what we're talking about, but I'm not steering it, as such. It's like it has a life of its own. Sure, I have something that I've brought in as a question, but it's just moved along someplace else from where we first started.

Therapist: So, we were being 'pulled in' all along?

Client: Yes! In this conversation, and my life too: it's a living in which I'm pulled into certain things as well.

Therapist: So, even if you had the feeling that you were in complete control, you'd <u>still</u> be pulled into situations?

Client: Yes, that seems to be what being me, being anybody, involves. It's like being attracted to someone you first meet.

Therapist: It sort of just happens? Like, it's not a rational process?

Client: That's right. But then, once I have already had certain experiences on more than one occasion, maybe very similar ones, I draw on them and try to understand what I was saying about myself in being drawn to those experiences.

Therapist: You bring them under something that captures what is going on that's *true* about you?

Client: That seems to be how it works. I have certain insights that speak to me.

Therapist: And I suppose you have to be open to *hearing* them.

Client: How do you mean?

Therapist: Well, there may be certain insights that you have that might just pass you by because you're not somehow attuned to them. Maybe there is another time where you go through something similar and you're differently attuned to it, and you hear it.

Client: Yes, I can see that. (Pause).

Therapist: What comes up for you now?

Client: There *is* a safety and predictability that I think I want, and I rely on. I think of the artist or the creative person who has a very different way of living their life. You mentioned experiencing a call or having a calling. They open themselves to it and then jump into that space.

Therapist: What does that evoke for you if you saw *yourself* as the artist in that way?

Client: (Long pause). I imagine it being like plunging into something without coming to its end, no bedrock. Like a void.

Therapist: And what would that be like if you were going through that?

Client: Scary! (Long pause). But, actually, I get mini-versions of that when I think about moments in my life where I had certain 'wobbly' moments.

Therapist: Wobbly? In what way?

Client: Well, there was one very intense time where I felt the ground had just opened up beneath me and I felt like I was in free-fall. I'd been in an intense relationship with a woman around my age. Things developed really quickly and we fell in love. I felt like I had finally 'found' myself. Everything shone brightly around me, life was great. Previous relationships hadn't been as intense and overpowering as what I was experiencing with her. It lasted six months. I was completely broken when it ended. (Long pause). I won't go into why we broke up. (Pause). Weeks after it ended, I remember going to Oxford for a meeting, and having some time to myself beforehand. I had no enthusiasm or energy for anything, so I just walked around, aimlessly, in the town centre. Everything looked grey and meaningless, bland and empty. Nothing mattered. And I just remember wandering around, looking intently into all the shop windows, just staring, staring at nothing, so that no one would notice me crying. I had no sense of time at all, it was all a blur. But I eventually came out of it and made my way to the meeting so that I was there on time. It was like a temporary jumping back onto the everyday treadmill, just to get through it and then eventually escape again.

Therapist: Maybe we can just stay a little longer with the experience of walking around the shops. How would you describe it if you slowed it down more?

Client: It was like the world had caved in and there was nothing to support me. I had absolutely nothing to stand on.

Therapist: To hold you up?

Client: Yes. I didn't feel I could stand upright. I folded. That void that I mentioned was what I was looking in to. There was nothing.

Therapist: And the relationship that you mentioned was the opposite to that 'nothing'?

Client: Yes. It was *something*, now that you say that. There was an intensity to it.

Therapist: The intensity – is that like a 'meaning'?

Client: Yes, the meaning.

Therapist: Meaning as something that is making sense, or shows a deep intelligibility to it? The world is making sense to you?

Client: Yes, it all hangs together. I knew how each of the many days would go when we were together. Walking in the countryside, eating at restaurants, being away on holiday, meeting friends – being together was when I felt most alive, and was more important than *what* we were doing, if you see what I mean, because it was more about sharing that time of being together.

Therapist: And then as your relationship ended, that 'hanging together' experience was absent?

Client: Then I could see how important all those things were to me. Whilst I was in the relationship, they were there, but I couldn't step back far enough to see how it all worked for me, as I can now.

Therapist: You can't just step out of an experience and observe yourself being in it?

Client: How do you mean?

Therapist: You surrender to the experience and really feel it rather than being a bystander?

Client: Yes. (Pause). And related to that, I remember telling my brother how upset I was feeling after the break-up. All he said was, 'better to have loved and lost than never to have loved at all'. And it made me so angry. I thought, you have absolutely no idea what it's like for me. In a way, I wouldn't have expected him to understand, as he was seeing it all from a far-off distance, rather than being in it, as I was.

Therapist: So much more is happening in the experience than a person listening to what you tell them about it could ever really understand.

Client: That's very true. What this has brought up is the way in which that experience of being in a void might be pointing to something that I might understand about myself more.

Therapist: It may do.

Client: When something important collapses in my life, like this relationship.

Therapist: It comes back to the experience of there being nothing to support you?

Client: That's right. In a void. There's nothing to grab on to. No ground.

Therapist: What comes up as you say that?

Client: That any ground could fall through. That scares me. But it might be that it's not like the floor in my kitchen that is a physical ground.

Therapist: So, if it isn't that, how would you describe it?

Client: (Long pause). It's a living ground, maybe?

Therapist: So, it lives ... and, if it lives, it can die?

Client: Yes. But then what's the point of having *any* ground, if it can die?

Therapist: A little like asking, what's the point of living, if we know *we* are going to die?

Client: Well, what *is* the point?

Therapist: Maybe it's you who *gives* it a point. You care about living to even *ask* that question.

Client: The relationship lost the ground that was there, and that we had cherished, but not something we did in an explicit and concrete way.

Therapist: Cherished?

Client: Yes, as if we were safeguarding it, protecting it.

Therapist: Being grateful for it?

Client: Yes. But that void is also something that changed me.

Therapist: How so?

Client: Well, there's no magic formula for how to go through that experience without the anxiety and pain. Eventually, I came through it and saw something different about being in relationships.

Therapist: Different?

Client: That I took it for granted that we would be together forever. What you just said a few moments ago has made me think about the way in which there is a ground but it's one that holds itself up for as long as we keep it going, nurturing it and seeing it as something that falls on us to nourish, without willing it, making it happen.

Therapist: Would willing it make it work better? Or is willing something possibly to get in the way of it?

Client: It would be something like planting seeds in the garden and then expecting plants to grow as quickly as I want them to. Using some kind of fertiliser to speed up growth and maturity, bringing to fruition, bearing fruit. Control, effectiveness, efficiency, I suppose. That then makes me think of the farmer who respects the times and the changing seasons in which she cultivates her crops; she doesn't push things.

Therapist: Which is a 'not willing', then?

Client: I think so, even though the farmer's life is one of being committed to making a living.

Therapist: Being committed, yes. And there's still a ground in that will-less way of being a farmer?

Client: Yes, and maybe it's better described as a 'groundless ground'.

Therapist: What comes up when you say that? A groundless ground?

Client: (Lengthy pause). It's scary, not easy, but feels true to being in relation to another person. Being with someone, and being close to them, and not trying to follow some kind of role or expectation of being a certain way. It's a shedding of ways that we all might find ourselves presenting, as an image of who we would like to be seen to be in the public sphere.

Therapist: What would be important about shedding that image if it presented itself?

Client: Well, I think of people showing off, or trying to be right, being clever or trying to control and dominate. It's too performative.

Therapist: And what would that convey to you?

Client: An ungroundedness, in the sense of believing that they are so grounded, but are actually deeply *ungrounded*.

Therapist: As opposed to the groundless groundedness that you mention?

Client: Yes, a groundless groundedness.

Therapist: So it's not just a groundedness?

Client: No. That would be to go around pressing out into the world and getting a glimpse of our ability to im-press others, press onto them how significant we are, so that we enter a kind of self-conviction that we are gods. We press ourselves into that god-like shape and more often than not stay that way. In the end, that would be to press down into the ground and claim a permanence in that.

Therapist: Mmm.

Client: It's not so much of a problem, as such. That's maybe how we have become and who we are. But this all just blinds itself to the truth of our way of being. (Long pause). That we are not grounded, all the way down. Rather, as you pointed to a moment ago, we *give* ourselves a ground, and that's a ground that supports us, but exists only for as long as we look after it, guard it with a certain feeling of being grateful, because it is finite.

Ground

As humans, we take ourselves to be living a grounded existence. But what is it to speak of such a 'ground', or 'groundedness'? Past thinkers have addressed 'ground' in terms of 'reason', or 'sense'. Such thinking frames the question in terms of 'what is that legitimates, or provides the reason for being human at all? On what grounds do we exist?' A rather more direct and commonplace understanding speaks of a physical ground, the floor upon which we walk in our moving around, and on which we build structures for the purposes of providing shelter, protection, privacy and our place of dwelling. Such a ground refers to an actual bodily standing on the earth, soil, firmament. However, this is not so much of interest to us when we consider ground in terms of our existence. Instead, the question that we are asking concerns a fundamental existential, or experiential ground that is so basic to being human. In this way of thinking, we are looking to identify the kind of supportive structure that foundationally 'upholds' existence, just in the way that we tend to think of the foundation that supports and bears a building structure. These are all important and relevant ways of thinking about ground. But in order to make some kind of headway on this, we need to first take seriously the question of what it means to be a human being.

If we follow a traditional path of thinking about ourselves, namely, a metaphysical path, then we understand our being in terms of an ultimate and basic ground that *causally* explains *what* we are. God as the first cause, for example, has for many centuries been the fundamental or metaphysical ground that explains the fact that we *are* at all. Or, in more recent times, the metaphysical ground for our existence is that we are fundamentally substance, which has a dual nature. One substance, or more accurately, 'stuff', is mental, as exemplified in thinking, dreaming, imagination, hallucinations and so on, and the other is material, physical, has extension and takes up space (that is, as Newtonian space) in the world.

Another way to think about this is to say that we live in various meaningful relations with others, whether this be in the form of smaller groups, wider communities, various activities and preoccupations, such as work, or the various recreational interests, projects and responsibilities that we bear over the course of our lives. In all our encounters and relations with others, we take up certain social and cultural identities that furnish us with a way of being in a world with others. The world is a social and cultural space of possibilities in which we take up meaningful roles that afford us a way of experiencing a grounded sense of ourselves as existing beings. Typically, such roles are expressed in the form of professions, careers and vocations of various kinds. As such, they offer us the opportunity to cultivate certain skills and experiences that extend our understanding, or know-how, as we engage in projects that allow us to express ourselves in that world. For example, the life of the musician is one of expressing a certain talent through music: skills broaden with experience, as does a knowledge of the music industry and the various ways in which self-promotion is possible. Such a life is intelligible to the musician, insofar as this is the identity that they embrace, and the many interrelated features of the world of music that sustain it. They express themselves creatively, and are open to ways of saying something that is important to them. In this sense, they can be said to be living a grounded existence.

Kierkegaard and Living a Grounded Existence

Perhaps an example of thinking in terms of ground comes from Søren Kierkegaard's short book, *The Sickness Unto Death*, which begins with a striking series of statements, that 'a human being is a synthesis of the infinite and the finite, of the temporal and the eternal, of freedom and necessity. In short a synthesis. A synthesis is a relation between two terms' (1849/2004:43). His particular preoccupation here is to find a way of becoming a 'self', or 'individual', rather than a 'particular'. What he means by this latter term is that we can exist in 'lower immediacy', holding certain wishes, obsessions and desires that demand immediate satisfaction and resolution. This is akin to the very small child who only understands the immediacy of wanting something in the moment and, moreover, must have it given to them without delay, there and then. In living in lower immediacy, we just follow our noses without questioning ourselves and the way that we are living our lives. To live as a 'particular', says Kierkegaard, means that we are only concerned about our own subjective needs and desires, that is, the finite, with no sense of the universal and infinite, to use Kierkegaard's terms.

We fall into a certain kind of abyss of despair when we realise that this way of living does not satisfy us at all, since we are continually chasing the next thing that will feel exciting and rewarding in the moment but which does not provide anything more enduring, i.e., infinite. We therefore eventually come to embrace the universal, which is to live according to the rules, norms and social and cultural practices that provide us with such a sense of the infinite, that is, something that gives meaning to us for as long as we are alive. When living in this way, we live in necessity, given the rules and conventions that we follow, but also in a kind of objectivity, in terms of our embracing what we see as their universal truth. In this, we claim to be living a grounded existence. Such a life takes it that the universal is higher than the individual, that is, the 'particular'. This means that we do what everyone else would do in any situations in which we might find ourselves. In other words, we should never make an exception of ourselves, because in this sphere of existence we live according to the abstract and eternal. By living in the eternal, we, in effect, take ourselves out of time and the temporal, just as past philosophers proposed, such as Plato, by not being alive to the moment and to our temporal existence, so to speak. By doing so, nothing of significance really happens in time; we simply *bide* our time, living a life expressed in terms of duty and good reputation within our community. Since this does not really amount to being most alive to the situation and moments in which we find ourselves, we eventually succumb to a certain feeling of despair.

In the light of this, Kierkegaard proposes a third sphere of existence. In living in the first sphere as particulars, and then in the infinite, eternal and universal in the second sphere, he says that we can open ourselves to a synthesis of the two – and *not* a combination – namely, of the finite and infinite, accidental and necessary, temporal and eternal. When we do so, we 'venture', as Kierkegaard puts it, or we embrace a 'defining commitment', as Dreyfus expresses it, which is unconditional and defines us in terms of being an individual, rather than as a particular, or as someone whose way of existing is reflected in the universal. We now live in a way that has now radically restructured time. The commitment that we have taken up is necessary; it is non-negotiable and also not reversible. Such an unconditional commitment is one that we are even willing to die for, as we find exemplified in various public figures, such as Ernesto 'Che' Guevara, Salvador Allende, Jean Vanier, Sophie and Hans Scholl, Martin Luther King Jr., Mahatma Gandhi and Nelson Mandela. Each of these individuals lived in worlds that called for certain actions and projects to be pursued without compromise. In their unconditional commitments, they understood the need to address social justice and equality, and to uphold a basic sense of fairness and dignity for all humanity. This meant that they each had a clear vision of how to live their lives, in *both* the finite and the infinite, the accidental and necessary and the temporal and eternal. To put it more concretely, their first waking moments at the start of each day were already directed towards pursuing schedules and appointments that related to the overall projects that they embraced in the infinite, the moments that were imbued with significance and meaning in the light of the eternal, that is, the lifelong projects that they embraced, and the sense of having serendipitously found themselves in their causes that had now become necessary. This is to live in the sphere of faith, according to Kierkegaard, because we have left ourselves no safety nets, so to speak, were our commitments to fall apart for whatever reason. For example, Martin Luther King might have lived to see the day when social justice and racial equality had finally been realised, but then his existing world would have become meaningless, with the ensuing collapse of his identity as a human rights campaigner. In that sense, to have a defining commitment is to also understand and accept the considerable risk that this brings, since much is at stake. At the same time, to live under a defining commitment is to embrace it as if it is the surest thing of all. In that sense, it is a *ground* that defines us.

In moving from one sphere of existence to another, we face abysses; we glance into the void. These are abysses that evoke despair, since the familiarity of our existing world collapses and leaves us with nothing that will break or even lighten our fall. As already covered earlier, in the finite and temporal sphere, we simply pursue immediate pleasures and moments that only last for as long as we are experiencing them. Eventually, we have an underlying sense of this being a very shallow and meaningless way to live if we continue to follow this path. But we lack the insight in that moment to see what we need to do to live in a more meaningful way. By contrast, when embracing our defining commitment, we are confronted with the abyss of freedom as well as the abyss of faith, a faith that comes only from ourselves and no one else.

Heidegger and Ground

Taking up a more Heideggerian, and altogether different way of thinking on this question, leads us to challenge metaphysical accounts that talk only of a ground or groundedness. Although he does not talk of a ground, Kierkegaard does address the self in metaphysical terms, as we see in the quotation given from *The Sickness Unto Death*. It is fundamentally shaped and guided by his question of *what* we are, which for Kierkegaard, is the sense of becoming grounded as a metaphysical self. However, he understands the self purely in relational terms, and not as a static Cartesian self. Even so, Kierkegaard's overall account remains metaphysical.

Instead of asking what we are, as Kierkegaard does, we need to ask *how* we are in our very way of being. In doing so, we address the way that we actually experience ourselves in our existing in the way that we do. We are no longer approached as an object, nor a subject, but instead understood in a distinctly different way of being that is uniquely our own and unlike any other kinds of beings in the world. First, where he speaks of a ground, Heidegger only means by it that which makes something the very thing that it is, that which is basic to that entity. What is basic to our existence, for example, is being-in-the-world. In other words, our existence is a being who is grounded in being-in-the-world. This is wholly at odds with Kierkegaard's account of finding and maintaining a ground in a *self*.

For Heidegger, we are our ground, but it is a 'thrown ground'. The 'ground' here is the basis, or that which rests with or 'in' us, as that which is nothing beyond or 'deeper' than ourselves. We are thrown into existence, and we are then faced with the issue of *giving* ourselves a ground by taking over our thrownness and making something of it. This fundamental ground of our existence is temporality. Given that, in our existence we are care, it is temporality that grounds care. That is, time is what gives sense to our way of being, namely, a being-there that is existence (see chapter 9 on Care-ing). Only when we understand ourselves as mortals, that is, as finite beings who face this with the anxiety that overtakes us, do we have a temporal sense of ground that would otherwise not be apparent to us in our everyday dealings in the world. In our usual, accustomed way of relating to time as a resource or something that is 'external' to us, the issue of ground is as far from our considerations as is our being mortal. In fact, we have no authentic sense of ground when absorbed in everyday living.

Grounding

This is a term that Heidegger uses in later texts, and is meant to convey a happening of a ground of its own accord, rather than there being something or other that furnishes, brings about or establishes a ground, as its basis or ultimate foundation. As human beings, we are always finding ourselves 'there'; we are worldly beings who are always already situated, absorbed and related to our surroundings. As such, we are continually grounding ourselves in the face of circumstances that we encounter, whilst being alongside things and with others. This grounding, however, is a dynamic, temporal phenomenon that never shows itself, as such, but is nevertheless present in its absence. Any claim that we establish an atemporal ground is a falling into metaphysical thinking, since grounding is a continual unfolding. A metaphysical ground, by contrast, is one that is certain, atemporal, ahistorical and enduring. Any collapse of such a ground, however, opens a chasm or abyss.

Nothing

We tend to think of the 'nothing' when we speak about things in a certain way. For example, we might say, 'Oh, it was nothing', when we simply want to negate the idea that 'it was something'. But what we mean by the 'something' in question here is shorthand for 'something meaningful'. In other words, there was nothing meaningful in 'it', whether it be a situation, another person's behaviour or something else. A person might ignore us, and if we make light of it, we attach no significance to it. There was 'nothing to it', we might say. In that sense, we maintain ourselves in our world in a way that dismisses this encounter as one that has no bearing on us. This way of speaking reflects a thinking of the nothing in terms of negation, and as an expression of the 'not' in the situation.

Nietzsche on the Nothing

Nietzsche thinks of the nothing in terms of nihilism. Nihilism is simply the 'highest values devaluing themselves', as he puts it. Our Judeo-Christian understanding of anything *as* anything has now collapsed as a whole way of encountering the world in terms of what is true and false, of what is of value and empty of value, what is important and what is trivial, and so on. In other words, it has been the lens through which we understand and perceive everything, and through which the world is intelligible to us. But Nietzsche thinks about the nothing as a being that must be overcome, surmounted and transcended. In this sense, he does not think his way *through* the nothing itself but instead pulls himself back from the brink of doing so.

Heidegger and the Nothing

Contrary to Nietzsche, Heidegger stares into the nothing and faces it, by thinking (through) it. He thinks of it as being present to the way that everything as a whole disappears into the nothing, as we typically experience when overcome by anxiety.

This is different to losing an item or thing that then presents itself in its absence. In other words, in the anxiety, it is not that individual entities themselves disappear, but, rather, that entities *in their totality* slip away. We can think of this in terms of experiencing a tragic loss, or undergoing a calamitous collapse in our accustomed daily routines that leave us without a world, as we might say. It is a nihilation of entities as a whole, but in experiencing the nothing of this nihilation, we are nevertheless brought before the *being* of entities. Prior to this, we only experienced entities as individual, particular beings, treating them as objects or things either for us to simply observe or as tools or instruments to use.

For Heidegger, metaphysics has no sense of the nothing, since it understands it as the negation or denial of being. Interestingly, Heidegger counters this by saying that, 'what purely and simply is not nothing is a being [i.e. an entity]. Nothingness itself, however, is being' (2009/2013:103). Elsewhere he similarly says, 'the nihilation of the nothing "is" being' (1977/2012:57). Both being and nothing are therefore in a necessary relation to each other, because, for one, we cannot, so to speak, make being present, otherwise we fall into metaphysics once again. Rather, stating that the nothing is being is to say that it 'noths', as Heidegger himself expressed in a lecture.

Abyss

The very idea of an abyss conjures up the image of our approaching the very edge of a mountain-top and looking down. As we do so, we search for a ground, a bottom that shows itself to us, but that we experience as non-existent. In the moment, we experience dread. The experience is one of something fathomless, unreachable, something that we can't transcend in any way by 'exceeding' it, getting it into our grasp, so to speak. In examples of this kind, we might be aware that there *is* a bottom or ground, since that is from where we have started in our climb upwards towards the mountain peak, for instance. But from the very top, we nevertheless still encounter the abyss.

Kierkegaard considers the abyss as something that we peer into and experience when we undergo the despair of not bringing our self into a synthesis of opposing elements, as mentioned earlier. Such despair comes when we misuse the freedom we have to engage and embrace the possibilities that come in relating ourselves to ourselves, i.e., being self-reflexive. However, when we *do* acknowledge our possibilities, we experience 'the dizziness of freedom' in the face of the abyss.

Friedrich Nietzsche also refers to the abyss in an aphorism from *Beyond Good and Evil*: 'whoever fights monsters should see to it that in the process he does not become a monster. And when you look long into an abyss, the abyss also looks into you' (1886/1989, §146 :89). There are many possible ways to read this, but one, perhaps more Heideggerian interpretation, is that, given that we take monsters to be evil and destructive, our battles and defences against those who stand on metaphysical grounds that are different to our own further harden, ossify and entrench us in our *own* metaphysics. We vehemently defend our ground, claiming to be in sole possession of the truth and try to show that it is the *only* possible way to think. This is precisely what it means to have or stand (on) a ground that is unshakeable. In the process, however, we might open our eyes to the fact that we have previously been blinded by metaphysics. In other words, it is the question of metaphysics itself that we need to address, which then means that we look into the abyss, which is the complete absence of any solid ground. The abyss returns our gaze, and in its doing so, challenges us to think, and think non-metaphysically, rather than re-engage in a search for another permanent ground, that is, as one that is metaphysical.

Heidegger's sense of the abyss is the unfathomable and endless depth that escapes our ability to surmount or transcend it. We see this in terms of whatever is unintelligible to humans, that exceeds our ability to somehow ground it for ourselves. From this, Heidegger asks if language is an abyss, by which I think he means that, however much we search for a ground for language, we fail, because 'language speaks us', and 'language itself is language', as he says in his essay, 'Language' (1971c:190). If we attempt to transcend, or go beyond it in order to make it intelligible, but at the same time avoid taking the metaphysical route, we are left in a 'dim confusion'. Similarly, death, freedom and even being human, are all describable in terms of an abyss, because we peer into each of these and cannot make them at all completely intelligible to ourselves by getting at what is 'behind' them.

Groundless Ground

When we think of ourselves standing at the abyss, there is no sense of there being a ground. But as Heidegger writes in his essay, 'Language',

> [i]f we let ourselves fall into the abyss [...] we do not go tumbling into emptiness. We fall upward, to a height. Its loftiness opens up a depth. The two span a realm in which we would like to become at home, so as to find a residence, a dwelling place for the life of [the human being].
>
> (1971c: 191–192)

That is, in *staying* with this experience, rather than fleeing from it, 'we fall upward'. In falling upward, we are not turning away, but rather, facing the experience of the nothing. This is not a nothing that we might think of as actual, however, but as possibility. Were we to experience it as actual, it would be to take it as something final, just as we do when thinking of our biological death. As possibility, we think of it in terms of the possibility of further impossibility, just as we think of our being-towards-death, which is our existing with the constantly present possibility of always approaching an end. In a similar way, our worlds can 'die', and when they do, we can raise ourselves up to a 'height' as we go through such unnerving experiences. We can either turn away from this nothing, in which case we 'lose' ourselves, or we turn towards it, in which case we 'find' ourselves. We find ourselves in realising that everything, including our world, and others, has fallen away, but that *we* nevertheless persist in our existence. We get a world back, so to speak, by now relating to ourselves in our 'mineness', which is our existence in its being our very own. Put simply, we exist, even though worlds can fall way and collapse.

Ungrounded Ground and Therapy

When we undergo particularly distressing experiences, which we might call 'breakdowns', we peer into an abyss that lies before us. The world that was previously held together, or 'collected' in its 'worlding' character, has now fallen apart. We no longer have a sense of ourselves in terms of who we are in that world, which, in our experience, now seems lost. The ending of a relationship, for example, leaves us groundless, and since no ground is available to support us, we look into the abyss, so to speak. We might feel so caught in this that we freeze, close down, lose a sense of direction of any kind and withdraw from our everyday world by secluding ourselves in some form of safe refuge. In the course of exploring such an experience in a therapy setting, however, we gradually put words to the feelings and moods, which 'fill out' what we had so far been experiencing as a void of sorts.

Speaking about our circumstances in therapy becomes a way of unveiling and disclosing what had been 'hiding' itself from view. From experiencing a sense of the abyss, we tentatively approach it, come to hover over it and gradually glare into it, facing it in the conversations that open themselves in therapy sessions. In doing so, we come to make some kind of sense of it, even though it always outstrips our ability to fully ground it by giving it any semblance of certainty. With time and continued reflection, we return to a world in which the previously unsettling, world-collapsing experience maintains itself, but only in the form of a memory and possible insight about ourselves in relation to the issue that originally led to the rupture. We are no longer 'in' the breakdown experience, but rather, oriented *towards* it, relating to it in a wholly different way. Therapeutic conversations 're-ground' the client through a gradual process of grounding, or ungrounded grounding, by disclosing a new world in which the client is 'reborn' with a new or reconfigured role or identity that sustains itself in its meaning and possibility.

Bibliography

Dreyfus, H.L. (1991). *Being-in-the-World: A Commentary on Heidegger's* Being and Time, *Division I.* Cambridge: MIT Press.
Heidegger, M. (1971c). Language. In A. Hofstadter (trans.). *Poetry, Language, Thought.* New York: Harper Row. pp.189–210.
Heidegger, M. (1977/2012). *Four Seminars.* Trans. A. Mitchell & F. Raffoul. Indianapolis: Indiana University Press.
Heidegger, M. (2009/2013). *The Event.* Trans. R. Rojcewicz. Indianapolis: Indiana University Press.
Kierkegaard, S. (1849/2004). *The Sickness Unto Death.* Trans. A. Hannay. London: Penguin Books.
Nietzsche, F. (1886/1989). *Beyond Good and Evil.* Trans. and Ed. W. Kaufmann. New York: Vintage Books.

Chapter 12

Free-ing

Introduction

In reflecting on the question of being human, freedom stands at the very centre of its concerns. It also speaks to the very heart of our considerations in relation to therapy. Whilst many clients tend to present issues in certain concrete and explicit ways, the sense of human freedom is very much the background context of the difficulties that confront them, or in which they happen to find themselves. Clients, in one way or another, face a real challenge when confronted with difficult circumstances where their freedom feels compromised or suppressed. In other situations, where this is not so pronounced, they deflect away from the responsibility to take a stand of some kind towards others and the various issues that preoccupy them. Instead, they look for ways and means to effectively run away from expressing themselves as free beings, as if it is burdensome, which then unavoidably leaves them with an experience, ironically, that is demanding in its own way, in presenting continuing tensions and feelings of unease. Facing up to, rather than running from, freedom then becomes a gradual process that the client, over time, might increasingly embrace as they return to a world that engages them with others and the difficulties and challenges that had previously overwhelmed them.

Conversation on Free-ing

Therapist: One way or another, clients that I have seen over the years have been really addressing one basic and underlying issue: freedom.

Thinker: Freedom is an important concept, yes. Human freedom.

Therapist: Yes, we have all the ways in which we construe and understand freedom as a concept. But I was thinking of it in a more pre-conceptual or 'un-conceptual' way.

Thinker: Unfolding it so that you get to the way that it shows up in the very way that it does for us?

DOI: 10.4324/9781003638698-13

Therapist: Yes. I think that staying at the level of freedom as a concept is a very detached way of looking at it. It's like talking about democracy without asking, how does that play out in the real world, as I live and breathe it? When I think of it in terms of participatory democracy, or a more direct form of democracy, as happens in the Swiss political system, I get just a little closer to its meaning.

Thinker: Yes. I'm sure that example is more relevant to an understanding of what it means to be free, why it's so central to being human.

Therapist: A significant element of what it means to be free relates to our own time now, the age that we are all living through.

Thinker: You mean the technological age that we're in? I think you're right. We get so distracted by social media, mobile phones, laptops, smart TVs, the internet, cloud storage and on and on …

Therapist: Yes, that's all correct. I agree that all of these various devices and instruments are how we experience our age and how day-to-day life shows up, but I was thinking about the deeper, more fundamental question of how our age reveals something about how we now understand our way of being and what it is for anything to *be*, just *be*.

Thinker: That's a much deeper question. It relates to what it means to be free, or how we think of free-ing. What I think you're talking about is how our age unfolds temporally, how it moves and sways, rather than talking about it in static and abstract ways. That's an abstract, third-person concept of freedom, which doesn't really get us to see how freedom happens, if I can put it like that.

Therapist: That's right. We could just call it the 'essence' of technology, and the 'essence' of freedom.

Thinker: So long as you don't mean by that the old or traditional way of thinking of 'essence' in terms of providing a definition of something and then listing its attributes and properties. That would be to talk about the essence of being human as being a thinking animal, or a creature made in God's image, or substance, and then laying out all the various qualities, aspects, elements that make up that essence, such as the brain, nervous system, organs, perception, memory and so on.

Therapist: Yes, that clarifies how I'm using the term 'essence'. I think it's important to get clear on this, as it is very different to asking, what is freedom, or what is technology. Some of the major thinkers tend to stay at that level, which is the theoretical, and miss the deeper question of the essence.

Thinker: We can certainly come on to the essence of freedom and the essence of technology, but perhaps we can just stay with the question of freedom, or the free, when we think of our way of being, of existing.

Therapist: That would be a way in, I agree.

Thinker: I think there are several ways of thinking of freedom. One is the freedom to choose to be myself. There are two parts to this, though. One is the freedom to choose one thing over another in my everyday life: to become a therapist, or to choose to study philosophy. I choose among various possibilities that are there for me to choose from.

Therapist: Which itself can be a problem, a real difficulty for many. For example, choosing to stay in a marriage or to make a decision to end it. Or to make a decision on how to deal with a very difficult relationship with a family member. These are very concrete examples of the dilemmas and tensions that we might face in our lives, and that clients tend to want to address when they come to see me.

Thinker: That's what makes us essentially human, that our world is very different to any other kind of being, living or non-living, because they either don't have worlds in which they 'live' – they are just things out there – or they are 'poor' in world, and don't have all the various ingredients that make up *our* world, such as the projects, skills, relationships, various roles and identities and so on.

Therapist: Yes, we have an understanding of what it is to be in the world, it's an issue for us in terms of the way that we decide to live our lives 'worldily'. I work with my clients in a way that tries to free them from the binds that they say entrap them in some way. It involves both addressing the issues, but it's so much more. As they open up, they open themselves up to me, they open themselves up to possibilities that were either unpalatable to them, or new, previously unseen possibilities, and *they* open themselves *to* themselves, which is the really important part. That itself is freeing.

Thinker: Here I hear you saying something about the open, which is very much the free. We can come onto that later. But for the time being, staying with the sense of the client seeing possibilities, they surely also feel the weight and the burden of having to shut off possibilities as well, which is the second part of choosing to be myself. If I make a decision to stay with my partner, I shut off all the various other possibilities that are available to me. Whichever choice I make – and once they feel like life-changing decisions – I tremble before them, because they place a burden on me to choose, and I'm invested so much in wanting to make the 'best', the 'right' and the most prudent choice. The sense of possible regret, or the guilt, anger, resentment, resignation that I might feel is a way of trying to anticipate the future without knowing how it will turn out. The future is uncertain, after all, and usually we just ride along with things as they unravel from the future into the present. But where we are so intensely futurally-focused to the extent that our usually settled and balanced way of being temporal becomes distended and distorted, we typically can't sleep, our eating patterns can change, and we keep thinking about possible scenarios. We worry that our world can break down if we make the 'wrong' decision.

Therapist: That's a really good account of living in the dilemmas and tensions that we face as human beings. It usually involves the issue of having a ground, feeling grounded, so that we don't come to feel ungrounded, or that we lose our ground.

Thinker: Yes, we certainly are the kinds of beings who are predisposed to ground ourselves, and to then tell ourselves that this ground really exists and is independent of us. But that might get us onto another and different path of thinking that would take us away from what you were saying.

Therapist: No, I think it's part of it, but it is a whole topic of its own, so I'll carry on from what I was saying a few moments ago. The therapy session lets the client express – I think of it as *ex*-pressing, pressing out – into the space, and talk about what has been held in, *in*-pressed, pressed in, withdrawn, hidden, as if a kind of secret, to speak loosely. We have to know what we are holding in, which is precisely what we mean by a secret. It's an interesting way in which we hold in what is difficult, either because we want to come across as copers, competent, as managing things, lest we feel we would be met with reactions that would unsettle us, or that people would change the way that they see us, and then presume that we would be left with more hassle than we needed anyway. So, the space in which I meet clients feels different, it's a freeing space.

Thinker: Is that what therapy is, then, a freeing space?

Therapist: Yes, but that's too narrow or inadequate a description of therapy in terms of its being freeing.

Thinker: What more is there to say about therapy that relates to the freeing, then?

Therapist: I think that what happens for many clients is that they run up against these lines and limits and rules and norms that are essential features of daily life. So much of it has to do with our relations to others. We are brought close to certain other people, such as our parents, our siblings, friends and so on. We participate in all kinds of activities and projects with other people. And our relations matter deeply to us, which we each express in our very own ways. We're not indifferent to others. If we *do* treat them as if they are indifferent to us, they have to first matter *in order* for us to *then* treat them as if they *didn't* matter, or that they didn't even exist. So, we can't get out of the mattering of being with others. It is given to us. I think of it as being *gifted* to us. But it's sometimes hard for clients to feel a sense of gratitude for the giving of that gift of being with others when others are the issue for them.

Thinker: So, what happens when we run up against the norms and rules in relation to others that you mention?

Therapist: It's the sense of trying to have the space to be yourself whilst also maintaining relations with those who matter to you, and also conducting yourself in ways that are not unacceptable, not violating everything that you hold as mattering. What matters to you is that you can be yourself, that you can maintain good and close relations, and that you can do this by not stepping outside accepted norms at the same time. It's a real balance that we all just deal with in our own individual ways. Some people tend to place more weight and emphasis on one and not so much on the other. For example, one person might be so concerned to please others, and to be what others would find acceptable, rather than being more attentive to their own life as an issue in a way that is not so much dependent on others' opinions, beliefs, admonitions and attitudes. Doing their own thing, as we say.

Thinker: It does bear further thinking about the impact that cultural and social norms can have on the ways that people live.

Therapist: My sense is that it comes down to the idea that freedom is about us in terms of being a 'self' in the world. Not just a self, but a *free* self. I have seen clients who feel lost when they come to therapy. They don't have a sense of who they are, and might even say that they *did* have the sense of being in touch with this, but no longer have it.

Thinker: Is it something that relates to the way that something might have happened in their lives, possibly something about situations, or relationships with others, or something *really* significant that has happened, which then left them relating to themselves differently?

Therapist: I think it's a certain change, yes, and because so much works in the background – and it has to in order for things to work on an everyday level – it isn't discernible or obvious to the client what's going on for them.

Thinker: Background? What are you thinking of here?

Therapist: Well, how we relate to others and our world, and how it just happens is a background phenomenon. Trust is another background phenomenon. If we show trust and foreground it all the time, we lose the sense of how trust actually 'works', how trust unfolds in its happening. In fact, some people who have been betrayed, or have been through something really distressing in relation to others, start to live in a more *intentionally* distrusting way. They come up against various situations, and they are already *wary* of others. So they pull away, even if they're not so *aware* of it.

Thinker: Yes, I see. And I suppose that relates to their way of being free, or not so free, in the way that they are leaning into the world.

Therapist: I think it helps to appreciate how we can't just perceive and lay out everything before us. We have to accept that so much is in the background of our experience.

Thinker: I'm not sure that 'background' is a good word to use here. I'd rather say it's veiled and withdrawn, hidden, absent. But let's get straight back to what you just said. Give me some more examples of what you mean.

Therapist: Well, understanding, meaning, mood, truth, and, of course, freedom itself.

Thinker: And I suppose that the idea here is for the client to gradually put into words what may be concealed and that presents itself as a kind of tension for them. In the course of working with them, my sense is that clients feel freer, but as they do so, they encounter *other* challenges that then come to the fore for them. So, they're more present, more in the space or spotlight, which then means that they bring some of the issues that they face with this feeling of greater freedom that they carry around in their daily interactions with others and the world at large.

Therapist: Yes, I agree.

Thinker: But there is a second sense of the freedom to choose to be oneself that I mentioned quite a while ago. The first was the fact that we have the freedom to choose one thing over another in our everyday life. The second is to *be* free, existentially speaking.

Therapist: Right. So what's the difference?

Thinker: Well, it's really picking up on what you mentioned a moment ago about the self and the free self. It's when we are free for our own existence *per se*, rather than the freedom in relation to others, to the rules and regulations, the norms and the everyday practices that have an effect on how free we feel.

Therapist: OK, so this 'existence *per se*': say more.

Thinker: It's the moment in which we confront our mortality. That evokes anxiety, of course. It's the anxiety in the face of the nothing. The nothing that we peer into says nothing back to us! It's an empty nothing, as we experience it. But then we take heed of the finitude of our own lived time in which we exist, and we face the choice of how we relate to the norms and rules that we live by in a way that doesn't leave us cowed and subjugated by them. We understand them as necessary for our being able to live structured lives, but we don't feel stuck in them, overwhelmed by them.

Therapist: Why not?

Thinker: Because we live more freely in relation to them. We see them for what they are. And what has brought us to this is the fact that we are temporal, and moving towards an end that is our very own death. We realise that we have a stake in our time and how we can either live reactively and passively according to the norms and practices, or we can see them in terms of the ways that conventions are *always* in place, and they change according to the gradual or dramatic cultural changes that happen over time. So, in this second stance, we understand and see them in a different way, rather than in being more authoritarian, absolute standards that we are regimented to live by. We see them as having a positive purpose, but also that when we take them overly seriously, we are completely gripped by them.

Therapist: Yes. And we hand over our time to them, rather than living in a way that embraces our time.

Thinker: The clock is a good example. We tend to live by clock time. Time, for us, becomes the clock. And we don't see that *we* are time. To understand what it means to exist is to see that we are temporal.

Therapist: And that difference in the way that we see things is freeing. We loosen the hold on doing the 'right' thing, or the thing that is 'expected' of us. But we don't completely ignore it, we pay attention to it, because it matters.

Thinker: Yes. But it also comes with a certain anxiety. And the anxiety is not this overwhelming, stultifying sense of being frozen. Rather, it's telling us that that we're free, in the sense that we're facing the fact that we're existing temporally, and not existing according to clock time, as we've already mentioned.

Therapist: This is really showing us the inauthentic and authentic way of existing, isn't it?

Thinker: Yes. Being mortal and facing that opens me to my temporality. I own my 'self', I see myself in my individuality, rather than being lost in the amorphous mass of being with others. I prefer to put it that way, rather than the 'authentic' and 'inauthentic', because these terms get so badly misconstrued and abused that they end up becoming ready-made ways of thinking in terms of morality, moral behaviour and so on.

Therapist: There are many people who would think that thinking about our mortality is life-denying, as if it's negating life and running towards death. That would feel un-freeing, surely?

Thinker: We are certainly running headlong towards death, but as I've described it, we're not waiting for death to happen. That's not a freedom, because it's simply killing time, *our* time.

Conceptual Freedom

For the most part, freedom is usually grasped in conceptual terms rather than elucidated and understood in a more dynamic and existential sense. What we might mean by the word has been subject to various interpretations, and is usually fleshed out in terms of its opposite or contrary. For example, a well-established philosophical distinction is made between freedom, or free will, and determinism, the latter taking the position that everything is pre-determined or pre-ordained to happen in the way that it does, that all events, behaviours and outcomes have already been ordered and structured in advance, according to 'the laws of the universe'. Freedom, by contrast, is then articulated in the claim that we can and do exercise our will to enact choices and inclinations in whatever ways we choose, being unfettered and unhindered by 'external forces' of any kind. Presenting these positions in this way might well come across as overly simplistic or incorrect, mostly because such a dualistic way of putting it lacks a more nuanced understanding, and so a third stance is taken that expresses a *compatibilist* position between free will and determinism.

Others, and most notably Isaiah Berlin, understand freedom in two distinct ways: 'negative' and 'positive' freedom. Negative freedom is the absence of any constraints being placed by others on one's own ability to act in ways that one chooses, whilst its positive sense is the ability to act in ways that fulfil one's desires, needs, goals and wishes. In short, the difference is expressed in terms of a 'freedom from', whilst the latter is a 'freedom to'. This distinction has been important to thinkers who are more engaged in the realm of political philosophy, but it also bears significantly on the ways in which we each understand ourselves in terms of our freedom to act and engage in the world today.

The idea of freedom is also related to other phenomena, such as safety and security, as well as personal responsibility and the degree to which we also consider the consequences of our actions and choices. These are all relevant to our everyday understanding of freedom, and the stance that we happen to take on it in terms of its meaning for us.

Typically, we encounter talk of 'freedom of the will', and the expression of freedom as an abstract social, political and economic value and aim that we aspire to follow in one way or another. In a more concrete way, we live our lives by embracing projects and activities that provide a source of meaning for us, shaped by the decisions and choices that we make for ourselves, rather than by the dictates of the state, community or culture. We 'empower' ourselves by exercising our autonomy in choosing paths that are of our own making, in other words.

Heidegger's Freedom

Heidegger takes a very different approach to more traditional ideas and understandings of freedom. For him, talk of free will and of determinism has not disentangled them from their metaphysical moorings and trappings, and so he addresses freedom in a different register, whether in terms of bringing-forth, presencing or letting be. However, he makes clear his position in relation to a conceptual understanding of freedom, as the following passage shows:

> Freedom is not merely what common sense is content to let pass under this name: the caprice, turning up occasionally in our choosing, of inclining in this or that direction. Freedom is not mere absence of constraint with respect to what we can or cannot do. Nor is it on the other hand mere readiness for what is required and necessary (and so somehow a being). Prior to all this ("negative" and "positive" freedom), freedom is engagement in the disclosure of beings as such. Disclosedness itself is conserved in ek-sistent engagement, through which the openness of the open region, i.e., the "there" ["*Da*"], is what it is.
>
> (1976/1998:145)

Where Heidegger talks of the 'ek-sistent', he means by it that which stands out in the truth of being, that is in the disclosedness of the 'there'. Our kind of being, which Heidegger calls Dasein, or Da-sein, is ek-sistent. He continues to clarify how he understands freedom: 'The human being does not "possess" freedom as a property. At best, the converse holds: freedom, ek-sistent, disclosive Da-sein, possess the human being' (1976/1998:145).

Following Dahlstrom's (2023) presentation of Heidegger's account of freedom, I draw on three senses that we can identify in his thinking.

1 Existential freedom – this is the freedom to choose to be oneself. As Heidegger puts it, it is '*being-free for* the freedom of choosing [oneself] and taking hold of [oneself]' (BT232), being-free for one's ability-to-be (in some way or other) (BT236), that is, being-free for actualising one's own possibilities for oneself (BT331). He adds that, '[f]reedom, however, *is* only in the choice of <u>one</u> possibility – that is, in tolerating one's not having chosen the others and one's not being able to choose them' (BT331).

Freedom, for Heidegger in his earlier work, is associated with the choice that we make either to remain in the everyday norms and social practices which bind us to live according to what is good and bad, right and wrong, acceptable and unacceptable and so on, or to take heed of our conscience and realise that it is our existence that we need to address and own up to. In the case of the latter, we are authentically free when we face up to our finitude, and the inescapable fact that we are mortal beings whose being we can otherwise describe as 'deathly', rather than being secluded in the norms that maintain us in a fixed, present way of living. When we challenge ourselves to recognise the way in which everyday norms fail to address our temporal character, but instead draw us into a way of just 'coasting along', such that we take time as only the clock time by which we live from day to day, we open ourselves to the freedom to choose to either be authentic or inauthentic.

In the everyday, inauthentic mode of existing, we, at times, encounter the nothing, or nothingness, but quickly turn ourselves away from it, because we consider it to be 'outside' what we might call our 'normal' human experience. Life, we take it, and living well, is to exist in a way that has everything running smoothly, seamlessly and 'unworthy' of questioning. Anything that hinders this is a 'problem' that must be overcome or removed as quickly and as painlessly as possible. But this 'nothing' is, in fact, what is presupposed in freedom (Dahlstrom, 2023:186). In the everyday, inauthentic mode of existence, we shun the nothing, and preoccupy ourselves with something, or particular entities, or objects, as we typically render them. In doing so, our everyday world and the totality of all the things that we find in it, all 'hang together' as a whole. We avoid this nothing because it evokes anxiety. This is not an everyday anxiety, as we might think of it, in the sense of being anxious that I will arrive at the concert on time. Such an understanding of anxiety remains directed at things and entities, namely, the concert. The anxiety described here, or perhaps more accurately, existential anxiety, is not directed at anything at all, because the anxiety comes face to face with the fact that the totality of things or entities as a *whole* – not just one single entity – falls away, thus exposing, or pulling us into, the nothing, or nothingness. At such times, we stand out against the nothing, but we also see that beings, or entities as a whole, *are*, and are not nothing. The nothing that we encounter in the experience of the dropping away of entities as a whole is a moment in which we can transcend beings as a whole, but also one where we encounter our *being*. When we are anxious, it is the world that is disclosed to us *as* world (BT232). Insofar as the world is disclosed to us, we are free to engage with our world in a way that now recognises its finite intelligibility. My world of being a therapist, for example, might collapse at some point, whether it be because it no longer holds sufficient or any meaning for me in my life, or due to an incapacity or infirmity that no longer enables me to sustain that world in its viable 'ongoingness'. But the very way in which I relate to the temporal character of my world frees me in the face of the nothing that I face when worlds collapse. In my inauthentic way of being, I see the nothing as something to oppose and even deny, by fleeing in the face of it. I hold on tenaciously to my world as the sole basis to my existence. As it subsides, and sinks away, I try to hold on to what there is left of it, or insist that it still persists in some way, thus making attempts to maintain it as if it is still buoyant and salvageable. In an authentic mode of existence, however, I live with the awareness that worlds can die and that my identity or role, possibilities, meaning and being with certain others, also die, along with it. But how I *hold* that world collapse authentically is to be free for how I choose myself to be in the face of this. I am not caught in a 'this is not normal' attitude, which reaches for norms to ground me, but rather accept the nothing that brings me back to seeing entities as a whole. I now relate to entities differently than as simply particular things that I separate one from another. To see this reflects an important aspect of our existential freedom.

An example might offer further clarification. When we think of death as an event, convincing ourselves that it is only something that happens to others, we distance ourselves from ourselves and our own existence. We avoid or deny our mortality, that is, that we exist headlong towards our own death. When we face this authentically, that is, we own our existence as uniquely our own issue and we thereby 'face the facts' about us, to put it in more common terms, we face the nothing of our existence. This is disclosed to us in anxiety. This is what Heidegger means when he says, '[i]n this [disposition of anxiety], [the human being] finds itself *face to face* with the "nothing" of the possible impossibility of its existence' (BT310). He then goes on to say that our facing this existing towards our death actually

> brings [us] face to face with the possibility of being [oneself] [...] in an impassioned ***freedom towards death*** – a freedom which has been released from the illusions of the [everyday social and cultural norms that keep us in a compliant and conforming inauthenticity].
>
> (BT311)

In other words, when we see ourselves as a *whole*, that is, as existing not as a sequence of 'nows' that run from one moment to the next, but as being temporal, which means that we are finite and not 'infinite', so to speak, we relate to ourselves authentically, because we have now come to own our being the way we are, insofar as we are human. To embrace this, however anxiety-provoking, is freedom, because we now release ourselves from the binds of living in a conformist way. We loosen the unquestioning attitude that we had previously taken all the while, and now see that we can choose to choose, which is to embrace our freedom by deciding when, how or to what degree we go along with such norms and rules that conventions carry within them.

2 Transcendental freedom – freedom has a most basic and fundamental relation to groundedness. Groundedness has three senses. This freedom, we can say, grounds us, but not in the sense of feeling grounded when taking an inauthentic stance by blindly following the everyday norms and practices to the letter. We do continue to behave and conduct ourselves according to such norms and customs, but we can also orient ourselves towards them in a different, that is, authentic, way. What grounds us in the authentic mode of existence is that we relate to ourselves as an 'utter nullity' (BT354), that is, a nullity through and through. To expand, we are the 'null basis of a nullity', which means that in making choices and decisions, I am responsible for closing off (that is, nullifying) other unpursued choices, options and possibilities. Only I can live with that fact and decide whether to take responsibility for it. As well as this, I have no *basis* that I can provide as a ground for opting for one choice and pursuing it rather than others. That is because I am my own ground, which is not something that is independent of me, but rather is what I have been thrown to *be*, i.e. my ground. To put it differently, I am always the basis for my existence – the buck always stops with me, as the saying goes – but that is different to being a *foundational* ground, much like the foundations that builders and architects put in place when building a house. I am my own basis, my own ground, but I can't get behind my being thrown, i.e., befallen by my body, my birth, the family that I was born into, the age and culture in which I found myself and so on. My freedom is expressed in accepting this thrown aspect of my existence, and making various choices in the light of it.

When we consider freedom in terms of ground, we can *project* a ground for ourselves, and thereby express our freedom, by 'establishing' or 'founding' a world, as Dahlstrom puts it (2023:124). To illustrate this, a doctor might decide to completely change her career and take up farming, after moving to a rural part of the country. Her world has now become meaningful insofar as she is a farmer, which is the identity that she embraces wholeheartedly. She exercises a different set of skills, talent and abilities, as well as knowledge of being a farmer, and is committed to the project of growing and tending to the crops and the farmland each year. Her world is one that she founded, thus expressing a freedom in making this transition on her own terms, or her own basis.

In a similar way, freedom is reflected in our ability to surmount, surpass or go beyond the world by addressing things in using them, transforming them, handling them, and generally relating to them in ways that we choose. In a sense, we also express a freedom in being with others. In cases where we fall deeply in love, for example, we experience an overwhelming freedom even though the feeling of love is something that befalls us, but is also, at the same time and for the most part, welcoming. Clients come to therapy with the possible feeling that their freedom to address issues with certain others, whether it be with a parent, sibling or partner, is severely constrained, and the sessions offer the possibility for them to express themselves freely and to transcend this stance. They also free themselves from the assumption that certain background norms cannot be challenged and loosened, or seen for their rigid grip on matters. Where a client is of a certain age that is incumbent on them to make autonomous choices, whether it be related to marriage, lifestyle, career or education, this might go against the family and community's wishes or, more emphatically, their rules. In such a case, we see a clear illustration of freedom running up against expectations that are expressed as strict, non-negotiable norms that have been framed as 'the right and necessary thing to do'.

3 Liberating freedom – freedom is also expressed in a 'letting be'. This is countenanced in the way that we orient ourselves towards things, others and ourselves. Most importantly, when we understand ourselves in our existence – how we essentially are, in other words – then we are liberated by dint of this understanding. As Heidegger says (2012/2015:70–71),

> existence as understanding of being is letting be: freedom. The transition to freedom leads to lack of shelter, thus to a liberation from something to something. But what does liberation from shelter mean? Into what are humans placed? Liberation to existence, understanding of being, *be-ing* [my modification]. That occurs only in a stance and in self-comportment to oneself [...] [t]here is freedom only out of and as liberation.

We free ourselves when we let things be, which means not relating to them merely as tools and objects for our use and control. We think of them as *being* the things that they are, and in doing so, we are free towards them, as well as from them. Put otherwise, we are free in their 'presencing', i.e., their being before us. In this relation towards things, we are not bound to them in any way.

Freedom and Our Technological Age

In our daily lives, we adapt ourselves to technology and its advances, taking for granted the ways in which it enables us to engage in situations so that we can reach satisfying outcomes more quickly and efficiently. We manage our finances online, order meals, find information through search engines, entertain ourselves with films and plays without having to travel beyond the confines of our own homes to do so, whilst able to also accelerate the decision-making process of booking holidays. However, the question that lurks behind this is the extent to which such technology impacts on us in our very existence. As Daniel Dahlstrom points out: 'Part of the danger of the essence of modern technology is precisely the threat to fail to let beings be – to fail to be released (*gelassen*) to them' (Dahlstrom, 2020:43). But, as Heidegger makes clear, letting be, and being released to whatever is present to us a being, 'does not refer to neglect and indifference but rather the opposite' (1976/1998:144). That is, we engage with beings in the 'openness into which every being comes to stand, bringing that openness, as it were, along with itself' (1976/1998:144). It does not mean that we lose ourselves in them, somehow feeling hostage or bound to them, but rather that we restrain and withdraw ourselves so that such beings can expose themselves. As Heidegger says,

> As this letting be it exposes itself to beings as such and transposes all comportment into the open region. Letting be i.e., freedom, is intrinsically exposing, ek-sistent. Considered in regard to the essence of truth, the essence of freedom manifests itself as exposure to the disclosedness of beings.
>
> (1976/1998:144–145)

For Heidegger, freedom is not a subjective phenomenon, but rather, the way in which the truth of what comes into presence, and presences, reveals its *being*, and not simply itself as a thing or object, which confines our understanding solely to the region of beings. To put this another way, when something is unveiled, it has emerged out of its hiddenness. What has emerged is the *being* of the thing that appears, albeit in terms of its being *a* being. But, in the unveiling, an open region, or openness, or clearing, is what makes possible such appearing to manifest.

Freedom and Therapy

When working with clients, they are in search of a resolution to the dilemma, problem or tension that preoccupies them, whether it be a particular issue or situation that has arisen in the more recent past and remains in the present, or whether it is something that that has carried itself as a deeper issue or question for much of their life. The conversation moves in, out and around what concerns them, and this itself can feel freeing: after all, where else, and with whom, can they talk about such things, and in this attentive, listening ambience? But as the exploration continues, the mood that envelopes them, as they look for some kind of illumination, leaves them increasingly open to what might 'fit' as the 'missing piece' of their understanding. They are sufficiently relaxed to receive possible alternative perspectives to their own, even if at times this feels odd or jars with their own stance. Clients are also receptive to something being presented in a way that is meaningful and that illuminates what has previously been hidden. What is offered might be an observation, or an intervention or reflection that is more philosophically-oriented in its approach.

Some clients who are unfamiliar with the therapeutic process tend to express a need for therapy to follow a straight and uncomplicated path towards the answer to their issues, assuming that thinking has already been done on the matter, and that certain ideas simply need to be 'implanted' into them. At the same time, they relate to the therapist as someone who is in possession of these ideas, and can therefore pass them onto them, as if carrying out a transmission or migration of data from one receptacle to another. From that point of view, the client is not, strictly speaking, 'free'. By the same token, some therapeutic approaches are simply pursued in a way that applies certain techniques or pieces of packaged knowledge that can then be introduced to account for the client's experience, with the intention of 'undoing' the difficulties and challenges that clients bring to the therapy session. Whilst I have no doubt that this may all somehow *feel* freeing for the client, it expresses something more fundamental about the subjection to theory and expertise as a standard for making sense of one's own existential struggles and life challenges. In the submission to theory and technique, therapy veers towards a 'technotherapy', as Louis Berger has called it, by which he means that therapy has become more technologically-minded, by drawing on technological thinking, and taking a more scientifically-oriented attitude in addressing human issues. The Canadian philosopher, Charles Taylor, sets out clearly the problem when thinking about the more general and pervasive way in which we relate to ourselves and our age:

> We might call this the primacy of instrumental reason. By "instrumental reason" I mean the kind of rationality we draw on when we calculate the most economical application of means to a given end. Maximum efficiency, the best cost-output ratio, is the measure of its success [...] In one way this [...] has been liberating. But there is also a widespread unease that instrumental reason not only has enlarged its scope but also threatens to take over our lives. The fear is that things that ought to be determined by other criteria will be decided in terms of efficiency or "cost-benefit" analysis, that the independent ends that ought to be guiding our lives will be eclipsed by the demand to maximize output.
>
> (1991:5)

How does this relate to therapy? Perhaps an example might illustrate something of the issue that we face when we embrace theory as the ground for therapy. A client expresses a common experience with friends, and they can't quite articulate the dynamic that is going on for them. The therapist suggests an impasse based on the Parent-Adult-Child model found in Eric Berne's Transactional Analysis, and draws the conclusion from this that the client is being the 'Adapted Child' to the 'Controlling Parent' of their friend, or that they remain in a mode of anxious attachment to others, or that they find themselves entangled in a Karpman drama triangle. Whilst something freeing for the client might emerge from this, it places theory as the overarching basis for understanding ourselves, that is, a representational way of thinking that looks for a correspondence between theory and experience. But theory is intrinsically flawed, since it reifies and ossifies a seemingly coherent understanding of the person, and then claims that this is how we *always* understand ourselves. Such theory is invulnerable to challenge, which means that not even Karl Popper's falsifiability principle can be employed to 'test' it. As therapy aligns itself more closely towards such an approach and understanding of itself, we no longer understand freedom, or it withdraws, in the sense that it remains 'hidden', and is thereby understood more in instrumentalised terms.

Bibliography

Berger, L.S. (2002). *Psychotherapy as Praxis: Abandoning Misapplied Science*. Victoria, B.C.: Trafford.

Dahlstrom, D.O. (2020). Im-Position: Heidegger's Analysis of the Essence of Modern Technology. In A.J. Wendland, C. Merwin & C. Hadjioannou (eds.). *Heidegger on Technology*. London: Routledge.

Dahlstrom, D.O. (2023). *The Heidegger Dictionary*. 2nd Edition. London: Bloomsbury Academic.

Heidegger, M. (1927/1962). *Being and Time*. Trans. J. Macquarrie & E. Robinson. Oxford: Blackwell.

Heidegger, M. (1976/1998). *Pathmarks*. Ed. W. McNeill. Cambridge: Cambridge University Press.

Heidegger, M. (2012/2015). *The Beginning of Western Philosophy: Interpretation of Anaximander and Parmenides*. Trans. R. Rojcewicz. Indianapolis: Indiana University Press.

Taylor, C. (1991). *The Ethics of Authenticity*. London: Harvard University Press.

Chapter 13

Intuit-ing

Introduction

This chapter attends to the essence of intuit-ing, as opposed to intuition, which we take to be a particular kind of state that the therapist embodies at a certain time whilst with the client. When considered in terms of the verbal, ongoing sense of its 'presencing' in the moment or situation, therefore, we address it as intuit-ing in its essential movement. However, for the purposes of convenience, I use the term, 'intuition', in what follows, as a mere convenience to point to the phenomenon under discussion here.

A rarely acknowledged and under-appreciated experience in our living encounters and dealings with each other as human beings is our capacity and predisposition to be intuitive. Whilst we acknowledge its prevalence at certain times, it is nevertheless a difficult phenomenon for us to articulate, because it sits so opaquely before us when we try to characterise it as the thing that it is. At first blush, we take it to be something that emerges as we immerse ourselves in thinking about something, listening intently and not being concerned more practically with problem-solving or being fully engaged in rational, logical reasoning that looks to arrive at a conclusion that is valid, consistent and sound. In its intuit-ing or intuitioning, it lets what is heard suffuse the hearer with something that resonates in some underlying way, murmuring, but also resisting being put explicitly into words.

A Hermeneutic Unfolding of Intuition

Intuiting is not a claim to know something, at least not in the usual sense of knowing. In other words, it is neither a 'knowing that', nor a 'knowing how'. I know, for example, that the square root of 9 is 3, that our planet Earth revolves around the Sun, that the Sun provides light and heat, and that turbochargers run at about 100,000 rpm when a car undergoes full acceleration. But I also know how to tie my shoelaces, begin a therapy session with a client, and use my mobile phone in order to make payment transfers. Intuiting lies outside the sphere of such knowing.

Insofar as I intuit something, I might describe it as that which goes beyond, or underneath, what is being conveyed, uttered or spoken about, and which intimates some kind of awakening realisation in me. It is something experienced and

DOI: 10.4324/9781003638698-14

undergone in the course of a dialogue with either oneself or others. Nothing can prepare us for such a moment in advance. It is not quite as strong and resonant as a flash of insight, like an epiphanic 'Aha!' that comes to us when we suddenly feel we know the answer or solution to a problem or issue. Nor is it something that is based on instinct, which draws on the idea of this being something like a natural predisposition. Talk of instincts follows a more biologically-oriented explanation of ourselves as beings who, for example, instinctively withdraw from extreme heat and cold, or danger and harm, and are drawn towards comfort and safety. We respond instinctively to threats made towards our family members, by protecting them from potential or actual harm, and similarly act without delay when we are in need of sustenance. Instinct reflects, in other words, something very definite and immediate about it. By contrast, an intuition seems to come out of nowhere, but also from somewhere, and somehow. It comes from both an explicable 'nothing' that has no real origin of its own, other than an intense listening and attentiveness towards the other, and being wholly immersed in what they are expressing in their speaking about something.

If we are attentive to the other's speaking, both in terms of what we are hearing and the manner in which they are speaking, then how does intuiting happen in that context? To address this question, imagine that we focus solely on the assertoric understanding of truth, namely, that truth is 'packaged' in assertions or propositions, then we might say that intuition happens whenever something is spoken in a truth-bearing way. So, if I utter the proposition that 'it is raining outside', for example, the person hearing this does not intuit that it *is indeed* true that it is raining outside. However, they can plausibly intuit whether I am being honest or deceitful in making a true statement about the weather. For a statement to be true, it is confirmed either way by going out into the world to see whether something is in agreement with the statement or not, or by simply subjecting it to straightforward analysis, as is the case with the sentence, 'all bachelors are unmarried men'. Intuition, however, discerns *more* than simply checking and analysing the statement, since it attends to *how* the speaker is *being* in the act of speaking. It reaches beyond purely assertive claims.

Intuition is also at play when the hearer hears words spoken that gradually, and with time, culminate in an unfolding of the whole, the 'big picture', as we might say, or the outer horizon that reaches beyond the speaker's spoken words. Since we speak in a linear fashion, words that follow one another and form a series of sentences, rather than in a way that says everything all at once, it takes some time for the hearer to experience a sense of the whole, which is realisable only when the speaker has managed to put into words, or speak at length, what they had the intention to say or express. A clear example of this is the experience of listening to someone relating an anecdote to us.

To proceed a little further, we find terms that might be deemed interchangeable with intuition, such as 'premonition' and 'hunch'. On closer inspection, however, they each rely on slightly different intended meanings to intuition. Premonition suggests the sense of a foreboding event or outcome, of something impending that will usually be unwelcome or unpleasant, for example. One might also have a more exact premonition of how something will eventually materialise, that, say, a friendship will come to an end. It has at least two elements to it: it is, firstly, directed towards a future moment or state of affairs, and secondly, the future event places one under a certain disposition of alertness towards it. When we consider the idea of having a hunch, however, this comes closer to the idea of an intuition. Where it differs is in the way in which it narrows its focus towards something more specific and concrete. In this case, then, I might well say that I have a *hunch* that Novak Djokovic will win the point in his rally with Carlos Alcaraz, as I think that he shows an air of confidence in returning difficult shots, thereby putting pressure on his opponent to avoid making unforced errors. By contrast, it is only over the course of several sets that I might *intuit* that Djokovic is going to win because he has been reading and apprehending the tactical changes that Alcaraz is making in his approach, and adapting himself accordingly. Intuition therefore takes in the wider and more general sense of the situation and what it lays before us, as opposed to the more instant assessment of what presents itself, and is expressed as a hunch.

Another possible way of thinking about intuition is that it is a hinting. We usually think of a hint as an indirect intimation of something that is either conveyed in the form of an utterance, or is a way of pointing us towards something that is at the same time unclear as to what it is pointing *at*. For example, 'something is brewing at the meeting being held at the town hall today'. The hint here reflects the idea that something is rising to a point of eventual exposure and disturbing or surprising revelation. In the scenario of a game, however, we think of the hint as a clue that aids us in some way towards a resolution or gain that contributes to winning. In another context, the private investigator looks for hints when trying to follow a trail that will decipher a puzzle about a suspect's movements.

A client might be hinting *at* something, though unintentionally, through their disclosures. For example, they talk about the heated arguments and disagreements that they frequently fall into with their partner. Such difficulties in the relationship might be hinting at any one or more things. As the client elaborates further, issues of space, time, identity, the challenges of being receptive and open whilst maintaining a sense of themselves, and the conflictual nature of worlds colliding and becoming incompatible or non-malleable, all seem to emerge as possible meanings or sources of conflict. With time, it becomes more apparent that they both experience a tension between the increasing sense of heaviness in maintaining everyday routines, on the one hand, and the experience of aliveness when more adventurous paths are occasionally pursued, on the other. This can then be related back to time and space, as well as identity, which were originally opaque whisperings that the therapist was hearing in their listening.

Intuition is a larger and more embracing sense of what the client is relating, whilst hinting offers glimmers of light that alight upon what might be an *aspect* of the more holistic meaning of the client's experience. Intuition, however, listens for possible hints that beckon the therapist towards and beyond what is presented in the session to the *meaning* of what the client is expressing and articulating. In its deepest sense, such beckoning is drawing the therapist to listen to the client's *being*. The client's being, or 'is-ing', is reflected in the way in which they have constituted, that is, concretely actualised their existence.

Our capacity to intuit develops in a more pronounced way as we become more trusting of its tendency to illuminate something that requires close listening and that we heed in its significance. As we allow it an increasingly more prominent place in our way of being with a client, for example, it opens certain paths that lead to a possible understanding of what presents itself for them in their world. In this sense, we listen to ourselves as much as to the client's words, gestures and the overall way that they comport themselves. Typically, we experience this in terms of our embodied presencing as we try to understand what is being expressed by the client. A gut feeling, as we might say, or a dissonance, consonance or resonance of our being present to what we hear is to intuit through the bodily feelings that befall us.

So far, our attempts to understand intuition and intuiting have taken us along a thinking path that has made attempts to allow the phenomenon to unveil itself. However, there are two possible challenges or criticisms that we might now face in response to what has been uncovered so far. One is based on the idea that the human body prevents us from intuiting the truth directly, because its desires and passions, urges and inclinations simply corrupt and waylay this as a possibility. This position suggests instead that intuition is something more like an intellectual capacity to discern a situation or experience, rather than being based on gut feelings. Another, more general, and broader criticism of intuition, is that it is inherently biased and should not be trusted. This resonates with a stance that many people might take, and that might be reflected in their overriding reliance on logic and rationality over intuition.

Intuit-ing in Conversation

This short dialogue attempts to bring out the way in which intuition plays a key role in the therapeutic experience. Since intuition itself is not something that is easy to convey in such a format, I have added some comments and reflections in the attempt to make more accessible what I am trying to present here.

Much of what I have introduced in terms of my experience of intuition in therapy sessions has been adapted in a way that is reflected in the movement of the dialogue with the client. With regard to the themes that are presented here, what follows in the dialogue itself is completely fictionalised. At the same time, the issues that are discussed are real and actual insofar as they reflect some of the deep tensions and anxieties that clients can and do bring in their recollections of earlier experiences in their lives.

Here we imagine a 52-year-old female client who initially comes to therapy because she is experiencing difficulties at work with other staff members and also with her supervisor. Her account of some challenges that she faces in the work setting have led her to eventually take paid leave of absence, but this has left her with the prospect of returning at some point soon, which is fast approaching. From the first session, I was never sure that her work issues expressed everything that was of concern to her, as she presented a certain tentativeness in sessions at times, as if holding something back. At the same time, when she spoke about her experience at work, she was voluble and quite expressive in articulating some of the tensions that she faced, so there wasn't a particular reluctance on her part to engage with me in the sessions. In fact, she seemed to settle into them quite well.

Client: I just want to get on with my job. But I find people just too much. I'm on the check-out tills, so it happens that sometimes it gets busy. It's when I get some comments from the supervisor which aren't very nice ....

(Pause).

Therapist: Not nice? In what way?

Client: Well, I'm told I'm not working hard enough, that I'm too slow in checking out the items, and moving the customer queue along. It's like a criticism ... and I don't like it. And the way it is said, it sounds so authoritative and ... nasty.

Therapist: What happens when you're there, hearing it?

Client: Well, I just keep quiet. But I'm upset inside. I don't want to be there.

Therapist: You want to withdraw from being there?

Client: I feel like I'm being invaded ... I know that sounds a bit dramatic, but that's how I feel ...

Therapist: Invaded. Let's stay with that for just a bit longer.

Client: It's like someone has come into my space ...

Therapist: In this case, the supervisor has come into your space?

Client: Yes ... I was doing the job, I do it at my pace, and that feels comfortable for me. I don't waste time like some of the others do on the tills.

Therapist: So, doing things at your own pace, not wasting time ...

Client: Yes, and then it's this invasive thing that I mentioned. The supervisor cuts into the space and she violates it. She picks out something about me that then stops me from continuing ... at my pace.

Therapist: And as that happens?

Client: I get very self-conscious and don't know how to respond.

Therapist: Let's say that you felt able to say something in response. That your supervisor was quite different in her attitude and said exactly the same thing. What comes up for you?

Client: Oh, I don't know. I mean ... I find myself in situations like this more often where I just close up and don't know what to say. It all happens so quickly and suddenly. I don't have time to think.

Therapist: Would you want to say anything?

Client: Mm, I'm not sure. I mean, it feels like there's a lot at stake. There have been so many times where I just felt that I had no control over the situation, and I just froze.

Therapist: You say, 'a lot at stake'. What would be at stake?

Client: (Long pause). I ... it's hard to talk about certain things sometimes.

Therapist: Hard ... in terms of?

Client: Well, remembering some things, and also just talking about them.

Long silence.

Client: I feel like I've been picked out because I'm an easy target.

Therapist: Easy target?

Client: Yes. I don't complain, I'm quite quiet at work. (Looks down, and starts to cry.)

A silence ensues for a short while. The client looks across at me, and then looks back down again. This happens several times.

In the silences, I have a sense that something is on her mind. It doesn't seem like she is thinking about the scenario with the supervisor and her feelings around this, but about something else. I feel that something more is happening for the client, though I have no idea what it could be. My sense here is not to jump into the space and ask, 'what is going on for you now?', as this would potentially discourage her staying with what presents itself as it does so. This would, to put it a little differently, afford her a way of staying in the space, a 'clearing', opening, a 'space of possibilities', that would in turn illuminate what shows itself in the moment. I don't search for any linear thread of any kind here, but rather, am a little awash with something akin to an expanse that is in the room. Something vague comes to me about her tendency to be quiet in the face of others, and presumably certain others – strangers, possibly, or those from whom she feels estranged – that has shaped and moulded her way of being. Nothing more is there for me, other than a sense that my client has more to say, but that it hasn't yet been put into words.

We finish the session and then resume our meeting the following week. In the next session, after initially settling into our seats, we exchange brief glances and acknowledge each other, whereupon the client begins to speak, slowly and in a measured way.

Client: I remember when I was a child living at home with my parents. It was just myself and my two sisters. One is older and the other a little younger than me. I must have been about twelve. Mum and Dad used to go out drinking every night, down to the local pub. We'd stay home, as we were told.

I was anticipating something unravelling about the family home, something that might perhaps relate to her experience of being in the workplace. But I didn't have any inkling of whether this had any bearing on what the client was moving towards at this point. All that I could sense was the change in the client's subtly slower way of talking, as well as a certain change in her breathing, which intimated a tinge of raised anxiety or tension as she spoke.

The client continued.

Client: They'd be out for the whole evening, and then they'd get back quite late. They would usually get to know some people in the pub, and then have a good time drinking with them, so that when last orders came, and they had to leave, they'd invite these people to come round and carry on drinking in our house.

This all now felt quite serious and intense, and I could see that it was heading towards something that my client had been holding back, perhaps even from herself. There was something decisive about her demeanour, as if she wanted to release something from and out of herself.

Client: So, I was in bed, my sisters were in bed, it was so late, and we could hear the loud talking and laughing downstairs. It would get quite raucous sometimes. But there was this one occasion when we heard people were coming into the living room downstairs with Mum and Dad, and they were laughing and joking and making quite a racket. It was like they were having a party, a celebration.

Extended silence.

Client: And it went on for quite a long time. But then … I can't remember very much, it's so difficult to remember … but after a while, I'd hear someone walking up the stairs, there would be an opening of the bedroom door, and someone would walk in … I … I can't remember much … if anything happened, but it was terrifying. It happened several times, not just once. I haven't even spoken about it with my sisters, but I think they were scared as well.

Therapist: And your parents had no awareness of this?

Client: No, I could hear them downstairs, so they weren't able to notice what was going on.

The rest of the session continued with the client expressing her thoughts and feelings about this experience, without saying explicitly whether something had then happened, either towards herself or her sisters. Nevertheless, this was an experience that she had now remembered, or had been carrying with her for some time. The session, to summarise, had opened a space for her to disclose herself to a past experience that was now present for her, and that had left her with mixed feelings of anxiety, confusion, uncertainty and also wariness of others.

Intuition in this case intimates the sense that something is being withheld, which itself is a certain disclosing of oneself in the conversation. What is being withheld is, understandably, somewhat troubling for the client to put into words, that is, is unspoken, but also being said precisely by not being put into words. Part of the experience of intuition is also intimated through the pace and movement of the conversation, as well as the awareness of the relevance of *place* and *space* and *timeliness* for the client to disclose something that is more deeply unsettling and uncertain in its way of being revealed.

Intuition and Cognition

In terms of intuition being more like an intellectual capacity, this has been an issue that has been addressed by past philosophers, though perhaps based on a rather different understanding of this term. However, it suffices to say that they generally think of intuition as being completely *separate* from our 'cognitive' capacities. For example, the famous polymath and philosopher, René Descartes, talked of intuition as a very fundamental way of coming to know something, and that is wholly at odds with coming to know something through reason. To claim that Paris is in France does not involve the use of logical reasoning that then leads us to a conclusion. In other words, we do not follow a process of deductive reasoning in order to make this knowledge claim, but rather intuit it in its immediate and distinct clarity. It does not touch on our reasoning in any way. The German thinker, Immanuel

Kant, took a somewhat similar approach in claiming that intuition comes directly from the faculty of sensibility, and is the immediate way in which something presents itself to us through the forms of space and time. Out of such intuitions we can form concepts, and this comes from the faculty of understanding, which structures what comes through our sensibility. Later on, the phenomenologist Edmund Husserl took intuition to be an immediate awareness of something that comes through our sensations. It is not mediated or filtered in any way. Other thinkers have also contributed their own understandings of intuition, though the main implication of their positions is that intuition is not really something that falls within the realm of the cognitive, intellectual or rational.

Intuition and Bias

As for the charge of bias, this is a term that has its place in rationality, and more precisely, in statistics, science and mathematics. It starts from the central assumption that there is a true reality 'out there', and that the 'data' that we collect, or observations that we make of what is 'out there' are true and accurate reports or representations of the reality that is external to us. Given that such data and observations are possible only on the basis of the *method* that allows access to reality, such method is the 'mediating' tool through which we can access that reality. However, we are also vulnerable to inaccurate representations, or even misrepresentations, through the very use of such methods. Ways of calculating bias are then introduced to address certain possible deviations and distortions. Such an account of bias is one that I think is easy to dismiss when we consider its relevance to intuition in the sense that I have introduced it. As was mentioned earlier, intuition is not an empirical or analytic matter, nor does it fall under the operations of reason and logic. Moreover, when we talk of bias in relation to other human beings, we are not operating within the realm of science, experimentation and calculation.

In the context of therapy, were the therapist to be accused of a certain bias, it suggests a 'closedness', that is, of being closed off to what is being opened in the conversation. The conversation takes place, but the therapist, let's imagine, only approaches it as a means towards some end, whether this is expressed in the need to be in the right, or achieve a certain outcome, or to incline the client towards an explanation that favours and satisfies the therapist. Given this presentation of a biased therapist, any suggestion that a certain intuition is at play seems inaccurate and incorrect. Intuition necessarily relies on openness and uncertainty, not closedness and certainty, or an attitude that reflects a degree of rigidity in claiming to be in possession of the truth.

Intuition and Play

Does intuition require a mood of play, of being at play with what one is experiencing? In play, one experiences a freeing space in which one surrenders to what one is present to, without leaping into what emerges. It is a creative act, but not in the sense that one is an agent who produces something. Rather, it is a listening based on one's own practical experience of living, of a connection of things said that form into a whole, but without our making concerted attempts to do so. Intuition has no prior origin that can be identified as the ground or basis that underwrites the intuition, other than what has been conveyed over the course of a set of reflections by the client, for example. It emerges, rather than being measured and calculative.

Nietzsche himself valued intuition greatly. It is in his early work, particularly in *The Birth of Tragedy*, that we find him famously noting that 'it is only as an *aesthetic phenomenon* that existence and the world are eternally *justified*' (1886/1967:52). His central idea is that reason itself cannot become the dominant approach that we take to understanding ourselves, since that would suppress and even exclude our imagination, intuition and creativity. Doing so would see our existence as something to be 'corrected', optimised and made better (1886/1967:95). Instead, we should embrace both Apollonian reason and Dionysian spontaneity and intuition, seeing them not in an opposition to each other, but in terms of a tension or strife with one another, understood, however, only as a *harmonious* strife. We find today a battle that has ensued to suppress and submit one, the creative and intuitive Dionysian element, in favour of the rational and logical Apollonian. Some therapeutic approaches, too, it seems, have emphasised and oriented themselves more around this Apollonian element, whilst seeing intuition and imagination simply as helpful but ultimately more peripheral features of a therapeutic conversation.

It is in the character of Nietzsche's Zarathustra (1892/1978) that we see human intuition at play; in his discerning approach to situations with others, he shows insight and in-tuition, a kind of 'learning', we might say, that happens when we are deeply absorbed in something that draws us passionately towards it. For example, upon leaving his mountain home to begin his journey to engage with the world of others, Zarathustra enters a forest, where he meets an old saint. After some brief exchanges, Zarathustra very quickly intuits that the saint is only really listening to *himself* when speaking, thereby imprisoned in a world of his own making. His only relationship is with God, rejecting any contact with human beings, because they are 'too imperfect a thing' to be worthy of his attention or consideration. He implores Zarathustra not to go to the people, but to stay in the forest, which is presumably the natural world that God has designed in its perfection. Zarathustra intuits that the saint's actions and way of living are overly mechanical and rigid, attached to routine and an illusory stance of having finally arrived at the ultimate truth of things. With this, Zarathustra leaves him, as he draws on his intuition that there is no hope of being able to converse with him (1892/1978:10–12).

Throughout the whole of *Thus Spoke Zarathustra*, in fact, we see Nietzsche presenting the namesake of the book title as continually drawing on his intuition. As Lucy Huskinson, quoting Carl Jung from a seminar he gave on Nietzsche's *Zarathustra*, writes,

> Nietzsche [...] simply touches upon a thing and off he goes. He does not dwell upon the subject, though in the long run one can say he really does dwell upon

> it by amplification. But he doesn't deal with things in a logical way, going into the intellectual process of elucidation; he just catches such an intuition on the wing and leaves it, going round and round amplifying, so that in the end we get a complete picture but by intuitive means, not by logical means.
>
> (2004:115–116)

The Russian writer, Fyodor Dostoevsky, also recognised the importance of intuition, though he described it as a 'knowing with the heart', rather than through reason and intellect. Dostoevsky portrays this well through certain characters in his novels, notably in the figures of Father Zosima and young Alyosha Karamazov from *The Brothers Karamazov*, as well as Prince Lev Myshkin in *The Idiot*. The same line of thinking can be found in the philosopher and mathematician, Blaise Pascal, who reflected that intuitive thinking and knowing was different to mathematical, that is, logical thinking.

Husserl, Merleau-Ponty and Heidegger on Intuition

Husserl

A philosopher who made much of intuition, though in a way that was more relevant to his project in terms of describing the structure of consciousness, is Edmund Husserl. For him, intuition is the making present of an object. What he means by this is simply that we intuit the givenness of such objects in our experience, rather than their being manifested by our somehow actively constructing them. Such givenness, he adds, has to be freed from any accustomed ways of already seeing something in a certain socially or culturally-shaped way. He wants to be free of the everyday prejudices or assumptions that underlie what we take something to be, and to let what we experience come to us in a more descriptively-focused way. An example might be the experience of seeing someone crying, and already taking that to be the person's experience of despair and helplessness in reaction to a particularly overwhelming event. Instead, Husserl stays with what is present, and undertakes a careful elucidation of the experience as it is given to the person's consciousness, to use his language. In his sense, then, intuition is the very opposite of any pre-formed attitudes and beliefs that one might hold in response to what is given. To this extent, we might understand intuition in a similar way to that described so far, namely, its openness to let what is given come to the fore, rather than adopting a theory, belief or position in response to what we hear or see.

Merleau-Ponty

The French philosopher, Maurice Merleau-Ponty, took the stance that philosophy itself is a reaching towards intuitions through experience. For him, words themselves are only preliminary markers for the meaning of a certain experience, and don't actually offer us any insight just in virtue of using them. Instead, we are required to attune ourselves to our own experience of something in order to arrive at its meaning. This is well-illustrated in his own works, where he presents finely-nuanced descriptions of an experience in which meaning then emerges. Merleau-Ponty follows Husserl to the extent that they both attend closely to consciousness in the very experience of something. In that way, for him, we intuit the meaning itself.

Heidegger

For Heidegger, almost every approach takes intuition as falling within the domain of knowledge, even if some distinguish it from cognition and conceptual thinking. Heidegger's own approach rejects any association of intuition to 'knowing', and places it in the understanding. For him, we are already immersed in a way that understands how to go about our world and deal with things, others and ourselves. In other words, we already intuit what it is to be our kind of being; we have what he calls, a 'pre-ontological' understanding of our being, insofar as it is not an explicitly spelt out set of instructions for how to go about dealing with the world as we encounter it. That is to say, we are constantly intuiting by dint of our way of always being preoccupied with things in some way or other. To use an example, I follow my culture's background norms and social practices by way of intuiting the appropriate thing to do when I decide to dine at a restaurant, which, at bottom, is based on my *understanding* of the overall situation in which I find myself. I politely accept the waitress's greeting and welcome as I enter, and then follow her at a leisurely pace to my assigned table, having already intuited a whole series of movements that I made throughout in order to comport myself as the diner that I am being in this situation. Were a certain breakdown moment to happen, such as bumping into a table and knocking a glass of wine onto the floor, my immediate intuition is to apologise profusely, and offer to pay for the wine spilt as a way of atoning for my clumsiness.

Phenomenology as Intuition-ing

Phenomenology is a way of exploring what is given to us in our experience, through a rigorous process of describing what appears to us in its 'pristine innocence' (Spiegelberg, 1982:680). There are two main ways in which we can adopt a phenomenological attitude to enquiry. A first way is based on Edmund Husserl's prerequisite that we 'position' ourselves by holding back, or shutting off, our 'natural attitude', which is the usual and customary way in which we go about thinking about things. This involves and includes certain prejudices and assumptions, but also theories, beliefs and convictions that are ready-made interpretations of the world. The second, Heideggerian approach, involves attending to the customary way in which we already encounter and claim to know and understand our world. This allows a starting point from which to undertake a hermeneutic probing of the phenomenon in question. As we address the phenomenon, we let it appear to us, rather than adopting a logical approach. Nothing is being pushed or willed in the gradual unveiling of the phenomenon. Instead, we intuit what presents itself to us. It is, in other words, a letting be of what comes to us. It involves a hermeneutic process of listening and questioning ourselves in our way of being receptive to something that we are hearing or seeing, rather than taking it that such openness is free of various preunderstandings. In its hermeneutic openness, it conveys a readiness to question what has exposed itself as an obstruction to hearing and seeing something more closely. Our reflective attitude therefore becomes central in this process, which is itself intuitive in its essence. Intuition can also be associated with the old Greek term, *nous*, which is a discernment or *sense* that we have of something. It has nothing to do with logical thinking, but rather is a form of understanding towards which we are already predisposed in our way of being.

Intuition-ing and Therapy

Most thinkers approach intuition in a way that ultimately rests on a metaphysical stance. This is particularly evident in the world of psychotherapy, as we encounter in the work of Sigmund Freud, Carl Jung, the Humanistic movement, and even in the present-day clamour for an 'Integrative Psychotherapy', which is, to put it bluntly, based on a rather misguided and essentially flawed set of assumptions.

To take the example of Jung, we are already co-opted into his own use of terminology and theoretical constructions that effectively entrap us in an overarching system that then relies on intuition to convince us that he is on the right track with his 'discoveries'. Reading Jung's work can tend to leave us with the feeling that, whilst he had shown extraordinary imaginative powers in his writing and thinking, he had also succumbed to unwarranted leaps of explanation that were speculative in character and that came only from the product of his own imagination. For example, he took as his initial starting point the human psyche, which he then described in terms of its having 'rational functions', constituted by thinking and feeling, as well as 'irrational functions', in which we find sensation and intuition. Intuition, for him, plays a central role in balancing the conscious and unconscious, where the latter holds complexes, or archetypes, which themselves already find expression in myth and ancient narratives. This seems more a kind of Constructivist approach to understanding rather than one that attends closely to what shows itself and is given to us, without adorning and overlaying it with more speculative abstractions.

In short, in taking a metaphysical approach, such contributions to psychotherapy rely on a two-tier understanding that has, at its sensory, observable, manifest or 'surface level', various actions, behaviours, perceptions and experiences (and which requires an extensive explanatory account to ground it), and then the underlying, foundational, 'deep level' that provides the final explanation for the manifest, surface level. This foundational level, however, is theoretical in nature. Where intuition seems to come into this particular picture is when the therapist intuits some aspect of the client's narrative that accords, fits or corresponds with elements of the theory that the therapist holds in their therapeutic orientation.

Finally, we once again return to the question: how do we understand the *essence* of intuit-ing? It is a disclosing of that which withholds itself. The silence of the withholding discloses what might be being said without its being spoken. The client has spoken about many things, for example, but something is being withheld. What is being withheld is *said* in the silence. The therapist becomes attuned to, and hears what is being said in the light of what has already been spoken. Both client and therapist also intuit the mood in the session as reflecting something that is withheld but at the same time said. The more stilted and tentative way in which the session continues is saying something perhaps more than can simply be put into words.

Intuition is not a tool that we can use and apply wilfully. However much we feel that we are prone to being intuitive, we are always at the mercy of something speaking to us silently, but not knowing when or how it happens. In the case of the client, they might become more open to their own intuitions when engaging more openly in phenomenological explorations. This involves a contemplation and gradual unveiling of the more detailed elements of a troubling or difficult situation as it is presented over the course of the therapeutic conversation.

Bibliography

Huskinson, L. (2004). *Nietzsche and Jung: The Whole Self in the Union of Opposites*. Hove: Brunner-Routledge.

Nietzsche, F. (1886/1967). *The Birth of Tragedy and the Case of Wagner*. Trans. W. Kaufmann. New York: Vintage.

Nietzsche, F. (1892/1978). *Thus Spoke Zarathustra: A Book for None and All*. Trans. W. Kaufmann. London: Penguin Books.

Spiegelberg, H. (1982). *The Phenomenological Movement: A Historical Introduction*. London: Martinus Nijhoff.

Chapter 14

Clear-ing

Introduction

When speaking of a clearing, the term points to a very simple yet difficult to grasp phenomenon. It is key to understanding human existence, that is, the very basis of being human. A way of exploring this idea is to start from our usual way of understanding ourselves in order to then move towards a further possible understanding of the term under consideration.

Our current understanding of being human does not speak of the clearing at all. In fact, it has no sense of it, because of the way that it conceives of our way of being. We go about our everyday dealings in a world that we assume always already provides a ground, or foundation, for everything. This assumption, which has subsequently anchored and rooted us, has played itself out historically in different ways. Our current 'ground' is an understanding of ourselves as subjects set over against an external world of objects. As subjects, we employ reason to navigate our world. Reason, or rational thinking, is a fundamental feature of our kind of being, a thinking that originates in consciousness. Conscious thinking lies at the basis of our ability to know and grasp objects, from a conceptual point of view. The conscious, or consciousness, lies at the most fundamental, and most foundational level when we talk about a human being, or person. We are conscious, and conscious thought is directed towards the world of objects, about which we can claim knowledge. But how is this knowledge gained?

Consciousness, or the mental, is directed towards what is 'external' to it, which is an external material world. At this point, the overall picture is based on an internal-external distinction. From the internal perspective, a conscious subject has an internal representation of an external object, such that the internal representation corresponds correctly and adequately to the external object, whether it be a person, a thing or a state of affairs. So, in summary, we deal with ourselves as conscious subjects in the world of objects about which we have knowledge based on the representational way in which our mind operates, so to speak.

This has all seemed entirely persuasive to us for at least some 600 or so years, in fact. Prior to this, we embraced other fundamental 'grounds', which provided the basis for understanding ourselves in radically different and distinct ways.

DOI: 10.4324/9781003638698-15

Conversation on the Clear-ing

Therapist: I think of all the various therapeutic approaches as being based on a theory about the human being. But what intrigues me is whether a theory might have presuppositions about being human that we can open up and discuss here.

Thinker: Even what we make of what there *is* as anything at all.

Therapist: How so?

Thinker: Well, we can start from ourselves as the pivotal centre of any enquiry, or we can start from just what shows up.

Therapist: One that leaves us out of the picture?

Thinker: No, not at all. It just doesn't place us at the centre.

Therapist: If we do that, how will that inform therapy, if at all?

Thinker: I don't know, but we need to follow a path and see if it lights up something as we do so.

Therapist: That sounds intriguing. It's the opposite of any approach to enquiry that has a method or procedure ready to use in advance.

Thinker: It's what I consider to be a going back to what is most basic and most in need for us as human beings in our time.

Therapist: Which is?

Thinker: Thinking.

Therapist: We don't think? Is that what you're saying?

Thinker: We think, but we think with scaffolding already in place. We can walk around the timber planks and hold on to the scaffold tubes, we feel safe, but when we do that, we miss so much that comes before it.

Therapist: Like what?

Thinker: Let's start with the idea of therapy itself. Has it always been around?

Therapist: Not to my knowledge. We could go back into the past, when I think there was a sect that attended to people by walking with them and engaging in conversation. But, in terms of how we think of therapy today, it might be somewhat similar to people in past times seeking to confide in a priest, or the elder of the monastery.

Thinker: So, there was no therapy, or psychotherapy, as such, and certainly not in the way that we understand it today, in the early 1500s, for example. It just wasn't showing up at all.

Therapist: Yes, that's right.

Thinker: So there is something about the way in which something comes into being, and not <u>what</u> it is that comes into being, such as psychotherapy.

Therapist: If I understand you correctly, it's like asking, what enables psychotherapy to come into being?

Thinker: Yes, what makes it open into being therapy. I think this is important, as it also addresses the way that we can come to think of therapy.

Therapist: And that then fundamentally shapes our understanding in terms of being therapists, and what the essence of therapy is, its way of being?

Thinker: Yes. So, when you think of yourself as a therapist, how would you describe your way of being with the client?

Therapist: Being in a therapeutic conversation, engaged in a certain kind of listening, being with the client in a way that is a searching, looking together to clarify and bring into the light what was there but withdrawn in some way.

Thinker: Yes, and 'bringing into the light' is an interesting way to put it. Do *you* bring it into the light? Or the client? What is this 'bringing into the light', I wonder?

Therapist: It's brought into the light … or brings *itself* into the light.

Thinker: We're still circling around it, but that's fine. So what happens as you're engaged in conversation with the client?

Therapist: The client is talking about something that really concerns them in some way. It has some kind of bearing on where they happen to be in their lives, or something that has unbalanced them since our last session. The client enters into a certain account of the events, or a set of reflections. We then see how we can throw light on what they are presenting, by taking time to see how certain elements or aspects of the issue begin to emerge out of what the client had already put into words.

Thinker: But that reflects something about our way of being, doesn't it?

Therapist: Yes, but I think you're trying to get at something in saying that, right?

Thinker: Yes, I am. In all that you have said about the client, a world has to open up in the first place, there has to be that space in which a world can show up.

Therapist: Okay … and so what's significant about that?

Thinker: It goes back to what I was saying earlier. There was a time in the distant past where there was no space of intelligibility for psychotherapy to show up. There was no *clearing*, in other words. That's the meaning of the clearing. It's the very disclosedness of being-in, being-in-a-world. Come the late 1800s, say, and along comes Freud. He couldn't do what he did if there wasn't an openness there already, a light that makes being-there – the human being – open and bright for itself.

Therapist: So, it's the clearing that we're talking about here. But what happens in the clearing?

Thinker: It's language that sets up the clearing. It opens up worlds. Imagine a Roman Centurion trying to talk about AI! There's no way that his world has been set up through the language needed to open a clearing for that. It is only through language that he can disclose his world, and he can't open up anything like semiconductor chips, quantum computing and so on, because it hasn't been named or understood in any way.

Therapist: So that's what a clearing does. And that's not something that we can do? We're not at the centre of things, as you said early on.

Thinker: That's right. It takes a shift of perspective, and a considerable one, because we have to reconfigure the way that we understand the very way we understand anything at all, if you see what I mean.

Metaphysics

The different fundamental 'grounds' that have underpinned our understanding of what it is to be human at different times over the last 2500 years have been what is called, 'metaphysical'. This is a term that reflects an understanding of ourselves in terms of something else. For example, one expression of the current metaphysical epoch in which we live is that, at bottom, we are material bodies. It draws on the mind-body distinction, but modifies this in eliminating the mental in its approach. It is a position that is currently taken up by neuroscience, for instance. In taking a more biologically-oriented approach, it claims that the human being can be explained in full by recourse to the study of its neurons, fibres, patterns of brain activities, and so on. On this basis, neuroscience is metaphysical in its essence.

The Clearing

Heidegger introduces the idea of the clearing in his essay, *The Origin of the Work of Art*, though it is also mentioned in numerous other texts. Here he reflects on the way in which entities, or beings, are unconcealed, that is, come into presence. But, he says, 'it is not we who presuppose the unconcealment of beings; rather, the unconcealment of beings (being) puts us into such a condition of being that in our representation we always remain installed within and in attendance upon unconcealment' (2011:113). He continues: 'Things are, and human beings, gifts, and sacrifices are, animals and plants are, equipment and works are. The particular being stands in being' (2011:114). So far, then, Heidegger is saying that entities, beings, things unveil themselves, but this is not something over which we have agency or control. Rather, they manifest themselves, are opened in their unconcealment. They are particular things that *are*, that is, in their 'is-ing'. They 'stand' in being, he says, which is not to say that there is a dual layer that is composed of the entity itself and then being that somehow stands behind it. Rather, an entity, which we call a being, has woven into it its is-ing, much like the fact that I am a being, and, as this particular being, I am is-ing, being. We very rarely have a sense of our is-ing in the course of existing as the being that we are. When we do, it tends to 'show' itself more when we undergo breakdowns and collapses of the ungrounded ground that constitutes our world.

Heidegger then proceeds to ask, how does this unconcealment happen? If it is not we who bring about the unconcealment, since '[b]eings are never of our making', he says (2011:114), nor are they representations that we make, based on our correspondence theory of truth, then how is it that entities can show up in the first place? It is at this point that Heidegger introduces the clearing, as we see in the following passage:

> And yet – beyond beings, not away from them but before them, there is still something else that happens. In the midst of beings as a whole an open place occurs. There is a clearing. Thought of in reference to beings, this clearing is more in being than are beings. This open centre is therefore not surrounded by beings; rather, the clearing centre itself encircles all that is [...]
>
> (2011:114)

It is only because there is a clearing, an opening, that the being of entities, things, beings are manifest in their being. In his essay, *Letter on Humanism*, he says that, as entities, we are thrown open into the clearing, stand out in it. Only on that basis can we then go on to talk in terms of there being a 'subject' and an 'object', 'relation' and so on:

> [the human being] in [its] essence is ek-sistent into the openness of being, into the open region that clears the "between" within which a "relation" of subject to object can "be".
>
> (2011:172)

As 'ek-sistent' beings, we are 'ek-', that is, 'out of', 'stasis', which means, 'standing'. So, we are the kinds of beings who are taken or moved out of our place, unlike the table or statue, for example. In the clearing, we relate to beings, but the clearing is what makes this possible, because in their unconcealment, it is their *being* that is unconcealed.

We should note, however, that we can also think here in terms of a general clearing. It is language that sets up a whole clearing of a culture by naming the style, such that many things can show up and solicit us to say things about them. We can think, say, of a Medieval age where a particular style was prevalent, such that aspects of that culture were named, such as being 'pious', a 'creature of God' and so on. Alternatively, language can clear a 'regional' clearing – a world – which is what happens when many things in that world come into their own, such as the wine jug (see Gather-ing chapter), or when several or more things gather themselves into each other, so that a world is opened. For instance, we can think of the world of nature, and the leisurely walks in the countryside, where paths, fields, forests, streams, gates and companions all gather themselves into a onefold significance.

We can gain some further understanding of the clearing if we follow the thinking of the ancient Greeks on this. They introduced the idea of *phusis* (φύσις), which was their understanding of how things *are* as anything; in other words, the *being* of whatever shows up as something. Paul Colaizzi also addresses *phusis* based on the writings of the Greek thinker, Heraclitus, in order to distinguish between the notions of living and existing. He claims that all psychotherapy addresses life and 'problems with living', whilst existential therapy attends to human existence and existing. As Colaizzi says, *phusis* is 'the Way (*sic.*) of all beings' (2002:83). He explains that beings 'rise into being, they linger for awhile in being, and they pass away from being. *Rising lingering passing* is the Way of all beings' (2002:83). He adds that '[t]he Way of all beings thus is the Way of beings in their finitude' (2002:83). Since we are self-ratifying beings, as Colaizzi puts it, which is to say that our existence is self-revealing, we are the only kind of being that is aware of itself in its finitude. Our finite existence is revealed to us in terms of the 'rising lingering passing' that stretches across the temporal dimension of our way of being. However, in all this, Colaizzi fails to acknowledge, at least more explicitly, that *phusis* itself is possible only on the basis of the clearing.

Given that metaphysics was addressed earlier, it behoves us to return to it once again briefly, in the light of the foregoing explication of the clearing. Metaphysics ignores, or does not stay with the clearing, but 'fills' it with theory, or *a* being that provides the explanation for everything. In doing so, it really amounts to erasing the clearing, or pushing it into oblivion. In that way, we lose any sense of awareness of it. That means that we lose touch with the clearing.

Two Perspectives on the Clearing

Plato

Perhaps we can understand the idea of the clearing when we turn our attention to two figures whose arguments and ideas are presented in more literary and narrative terms: Plato in the form of an allegory, and Dostoevsky in the form of fictional characters who reflect on certain significant moments in their lives.

Plato's allegory of the cave, in brief, has a number of people living in a cave-like dwelling, chained in such a way that they can only see what is directly ahead of them, which is the wall of the cave that they face before them. Behind them, on a raised wall, a fire burns, so that some light illuminates the cave. Between the shackled individuals and the low wall behind them, a number of puppets and solid figures are moved around, so that the light of the fire projects images or shadows of these puppets and figures onto the wall in front of them. All that these people see are the images, and not the puppets themselves. They take these shadows as being actual and real.

After a time, the people are unchained. They move around and see that what they took to be real were actually the *shadows* or *images* of real things, namely, the puppets and figures that were illuminated by the fire. In other words, they come to gain knowledge about the world in which they exist. They walk further along the cave towards its opening. It is an ascent that brings them to the cave's exit, and they emerge, out into the light of the sun. Their eyes take time to adjust to what they are now seeing, but they no longer perceive reflections of what is real, only the things themselves, including other people. It is the light of the Sun that brings light to everything. As they gradually become more accustomed to this, the people are finally able to look at the Sun itself.

There are many possible interpretations that we can make of this allegory, including its reflections on knowledge, truth and education, but one that I think that is of particular interest to us is the introduction of light and the Sun. It is the Sun that makes everything intelligible to those outside the cave. The Sun is the source of the light that illuminates everything. For Plato, the Sun is the origin, cause and most supreme being from, and out of which, reality and understanding is possible. In other words, it is the 'first cause' that makes light possible. Translating this in terms of a clearing, then, Plato makes it into *a* being, *something*, namely, the Sun, because the light, according to his thinking, must have its origin.

Dostoevsky

Dostoevsky looks at this rather differently. In his classic novel, *The Brothers Karamazov*, he mentions three particular characters who undergo an experience that gives them insight into how it is possible that everything is present in the first place. A moment of transcendence opens them to understanding beings in terms of their being gathered as one, or a whole, rather than simply being particular things. What makes this possible is, in what has been rendered, with very slight differences in various translations, 'the slanting rays of the Sun' (1880/2005:21). Elsewhere, mention is made of the 'long slanting rays' (1880/2005:265). These are the oblique rays of the setting sun, a shaft of light that enables us to experience anything at all. Dostoevsky uses this as a metaphor, but, in the description, it is the *rays* rather than the Sun that he brings to the fore. Here he contrasts himself with Plato, who presents the Sun as the ultimate and first cause that we should then behold as the basis for making everything intelligible. For Dostoevsky, it is the 'slanting rays' themselves that is the light, or clearing, that gives intelligibility to a world. To bring the Sun into the picture, then, renders it *a* being, or object, that confers the intelligibility on our understanding of beings, things, particulars, which ultimately entraps us in metaphysics. This is one move too far, for Dostoevsky.

The Clearing and Therapy

In having a sense of there being a clearing, this places us in a position of preserving and nurturing it. Historically, since Plato and Aristotle, there has been no awareness or understanding of a clearing, or, in other words, that we are world-disclosers. To have no sense of a clearing means that metaphysics and theory effectively make it inaccessible, because it denies or overlooks the fact that there is a clearing to preserve in the first place. Truth, for example, becomes understood only in terms of correspondence, rather than unconcealment. What is lost in this is an attitude that excludes an understanding of ourselves as disclosers, and our being receptive, rather than simply willing beings. In other words, we move from originally understanding ourselves as being given, thrown and receptive, to being active subjects and agents. In fact, this is something that we can also attribute to such figures as Freud, who thought of ourselves as the kind of beings who strive for maturity.

To attempt to gather into a final summary, then, of what has already been said, the only way in which things can appear, and be manifest to us at all, is on the basis of there being a clearing in the first place. We can become focused solely on something showing up, being in the open, so to speak, but not understand that there has to be something that makes it *possible* for this to happen. In other words, the clearing is the condition for whatever it is that shows up as being intelligible to us, and that we already understand in their being present, and presently presenc*ing*. The clearing is not some-thing or other, and certainly not something that we can somehow perceive, which is mainly what makes it so difficult for us to understand and to even consider. Rather, it withdraws itself in clear-ing.

Bibliography

Colaizzi, P.F. (2002). Psychotherapy and Existential Therapy. *Journal of Phenomenological Psychology*. 33:1: 73–112.

Dostoevsky, F.M. (1880/2005). *The Brothers Karamazov*. Trans. C. Garnett. New York: Dover Publications.

Heidegger, M. (2011). *Basic Writings*. Ed. D.F. Krell. London: Routledge.

Plato. (375BC/2007). *The Republic*. Trans. D. Lee. London: Penguin Books.

Chapter 15

Final Comments

When we put to question the very idea of therapy, such questioning attempts to unveil its essence. The process itself can feel unpredictable and uncertain. This is not so surprising, since we are so accustomed to following a protocol and an established method or path that can carry us towards an outcome or conclusion. We feel vindicated in doing this, because we arrive at answers. But such answers might not be reaching deeper into the essence of things. Moreover, it is not our coming up with answers that is at issue here, since we have generated more than enough 'answers' for ourselves in the world of therapy. This is clear from the many hundreds of therapeutic approaches and orientations that have staked out their own place, with schools and institutes all clamouring for a claim that theirs provides the most pronounced meaning and understanding of therapy. Teachers teach, trainees learn, ideas are passed on and therapists are gathered into the world of therapy. But perhaps a point is reached where we can be sufficiently open to questioning the basis of our practices and our understandings of our own human way of being. In this regard, then, little or insufficient attention is currently being given to such basic questions that are in desperate need of just being heard, let alone addressed.

In the time that I have been privileged to practice as a therapist, I have increasingly felt that the therapeutic space offers a way of engaging with others that is so unlike any other form of caring, or care provision, that exists in our world today. Hopefully, this book has been able to convey this by pointing to those elements that constitute therapy, as I see it. Put plainly, therapists invite the opening of a continued path of thinking that is given little opportunity to otherwise express itself in our everyday practices and even, in many cases, with those closest to us. It is not only that true thinking can emerge in a therapeutic encounter, but that the client be given a space to think for *him*, *her* or *themself*. This is what I take to be what Aristotle calls, the 'highest good', in my attributing this to the realm of therapy. Such an endeavour might well reveal itself as a lonely experience as clients attempt to think past established structures, frameworks and supportive guardrails. However, many clients tend to reach a point where they take a leap from the safety of everyday thinking, as they become increasingly insightful about their way of being over time. It requires a measure of courage, since it relies on no other source for its thinking than on itself. In that sense, the client is their own ground, their

DOI: 10.4324/9781003638698-16

own source. That source is their *being*. As human beings, we are extraordinarily complex, and this is why a wealth of questions can arise and linger as we reflect on the particular way in which we have made our own existence, our way of being, meaningful to ourselves. In taking these questions as pointers, indications, we have the opportunity to think along with the questions and let them be. Just as a stream moves along a certain course, and finds obstacles that it then negotiates in order to continue on its way, thinking similarly moves and meanders as it journeys and sojourns.

In my own case, the work of Heidegger, but also other thinkers, including Nietzsche, has challenged me to think 'against' them, rather than following them to the letter, thus setting myself in a 'productive strife' when in conversation with them. This has mainly come from the very attitude that Heidegger held towards his own writings and thinking, which was to critique and, at times, abandon his stance on a view or path of thinking that he invested considerable time and effort in pursuing and thinking through. This reflected his understanding that we are always in the process of thinking, and that our thoughts can and do change, because this is imbued in the essence of thinking itself.

The increasingly worrying direction that the various professional bodies that regulate psychotherapy and counselling both in the UK and across the world are taking at this moment in time reflects an urgent need to return to the simple questions that seem to have been forgotten, rather than a preoccupation with increasing the levels and degrees of governance and systematisation of the practice of psychotherapy and counselling. At bottom, therapeutic practice cannot be reduced to an ethical rulebook or to codes of conduct; these are all applicable to other worlds, such as business, organisational life and legal and religious institutions. Sensitive and precarious conversations in the therapy room come with a measure of uncertainty and, at certain times, discomfort, but these are moments that evade any generalised and universal standard by which to assess the correctness and acceptability of the work between the therapist and client. Based on what has been brought out in each chapter of this book, therapists are particularly sensitive to openness, whether this be in relation to the conversation, thinking, unveiling what lies covered over, intuiting, caring or the sense and experience of being free. Where this openness, in all its various ways of being manifest in the therapeutic relationship, is not present, then the client senses, and is highly perspicacious in discerning that the setting is not one that is therapeutic.

Bibliography

Adams, M. (2013). *A Concise Introduction to Existential Counselling*. London: Sage.

Arendt, H. (1958). *The Human Condition*. Chicago: The University of Chicago Press.

Berger, L.S. (2002). *Psychotherapy as Praxis: Abandoning Misapplied Science*. Victoria, B.C.: Trafford.

Berlin, I. (1969). *Four Essays on Liberty*. Oxford: Oxford University Press.

Blanchot, M. (1969/1993). *The Infinite Conversation*. Trans. S. Hanson. Minneapolis: University of Minnesota Press.

Braver, L. (2024). *Heidegger on Thinking*. Cambridge: Cambridge University Press.

Capobianco, R. (2021). Lingering. In M.A. Wrathall (ed.). *The Cambridge Heidegger Lexicon*. Cambridge: Cambridge University Press. p.462.

Colaizzi, P.F. (2002). Psychotherapy and Existential Therapy. *Journal of Phenomenological Psychology*. 33:1:73–112.

Cooper, R.A. (1984). *Dwelling and Hospitality: A Phenomenological Inquiry into Therapeutic Community*. Unpublished PhD Dissertation; Open University.

Coronet Theatre. (2022). WHIST: Virtual Reality installation piece.

Crowell, S. (2020). The Challenge of Heidegger's Approach to Technology: A Phenomenological Reading. In A.J. Wendland, C. Merwin & C. Hadjioannou (eds.). *Heidegger on Technology*. London: Routledge. pp.74–95.

Dahlstrom, D.O. (2020). Im-Position: Heidegger's Analysis of the Essence of Modern Technology. In A.J. Wendland, C. Merwin & C. Hadjioannou (eds.). *Heidegger on Technology*. London: Routledge. pp.39–56.

Dahlstrom, D.O. (2023). *The Heidegger Dictionary*. 2nd Edition. London: Bloomsbury Academic.

Dalle Pezze, B. (2006). Heidegger on Gelassenheit. *Minerva*. 10: 94–122.

Davies, K. (2024). *Heidegger's Conversations: Toward a Poetic Pedagogy*. Albany, NY: Suny Press.

Dreyfus, H.L. (1991). *Being-in-the-World: A Commentary on Heidegger's* Being and Time, *Division I*. Cambridge: MIT Press.

Fink, E. (2010/2016). *Play as Symbol of the World and Other Writings*. Trans. I.A. Moore & C. Turner. Indianapolis: Indiana University Press.

Fiumara, G.C. (1990). *The Other Side of Language: A Philosophy of Listening*. Trans. C. Lambert. London: Routledge.

Flickinger, A.T. (1992). Therapeutic Listening. *Phenomenology + Pedagogy*. 10. 186–193.

Führ, E. (ed.). (2000). *Bauen und Wohnen/Building and Dwelling. Martin Heidegger's Foundation of a Phenomenology of Architecture*. Münster: Waxmann.

Gadamer, H.-G. (1960/1989). *Truth and Method*. 2nd Edition. Trans. and Revd. J. Weinsheimer & D.G. Marshall. London: Sheed & Ward.

Gadamer, H.-G. (1976). *Philosophical Hermeneutics*. Trans. and Ed. D.E. Linge. Berkeley: University of California Press.

Gans, S. & Redler, L. (2001). *Just Listening: Ethics and Therapy*. Bloomington, Indiana: Xlibris.
Gilligan, C. (1982). *In a Different Voice: Psychological Theory and Women's Development*. Cambridge: Harvard University Press.
Hadjioannou, C. (ed.). (2019). *Heidegger on Affect*. London: Palgrave Macmillan.
Hadjioannou, C. (2020). Heidegger's Critique of Techno-Science as a Critique of Husserl's Reductive Method. In A.J. Wendland, C. Merwin & C. Hadjioannou (eds.). *Heidegger on Technology*. London: Routledge. pp.57–73.
Hamington, M. (2004). *Embodied Care: Jane Addams, Maurice Merleau-Ponty, and Feminist Ethics*. Chicago: University of Illinois Press.
Harries, L. (1998). In Search of Home. In E. Führ (ed.). *Bauen und Wohnen/Building and Dwelling. Martin Heidegger's Foundation of a Phenomenology of Architecture*. Münster: Waxmann. pp.101–120.
Heidegger, M. (1927/1962). *Being and Time*. Trans. J. Macquarrie & E. Robinson. Oxford: Blackwell.
Heidegger, M. (1953/2014). *Introduction to Metaphysics*. 2nd Edition. Trans. G. Fried & R. Polt. London: Yale University Press.
Heidegger, M. (1954/1968). *What Is Called Thinking?* Trans. J.G. Gray. New York: Harper & Row.
Heidegger, M. (1954/1977). The Question Concerning Technology. In W. Lovitt (ed.). *The Question Concerning Technology and Other Essays*. New York: Harper & Row. pp.3–35.
Heidegger, M. (1971a). Building, Dwelling, Thinking. In A. Hofstadter (ed.). *Poetry, Language, Thought*. New York: Harper & Row. pp.145–161.
Heidegger, M. (1971b). Poetically Man Dwells. In A. Hofstadter (ed.). *Poetry, Language, Thought*. New York: Harper & Row. pp.213–229.
Heidegger, M. (1971c). Language. In A. Hofstadter (trans.). *Poetry, Language, Thought*. New York: Harper & Row. pp.189–210.
Heidegger, M. (1971d). What Are Poets For? In A. Hofstadter (trans.). *Poetry, Language, Thought*. New York: Harper & Row. pp. 91–142.
Heidegger, M. (1976/1998). *Pathmarks*. Ed. W. McNeill. Cambridge: Cambridge University Press.
Heidegger, M. (1977/2012). *Four Seminars*. Trans. A. Mitchell & F Raffoul. Indianapolis: Indiana University Press.
Heidegger, M. (1980/2014). *Hölderlin's Hymns "Germania" and "The Rhine"*. Trans. W. McNeill & J. Ireland. Indianapolis: Indiana University Press.
Heidegger, M. (1982/1998). *Parmenides*. Trans. A. Schuwer & R. Rojcewicz. Indianapolis: Indiana University Press.
Heidegger, M. (1983/1995). *The Fundamental Concepts of Metaphysics: World, Finitude, Solitude*. Trans. W. McNeill & N. Walker. Indianapolis: Indiana University Press.
Heidegger, M. (1992/2018). *Hölderlin's Poem "Remembrance"*. Trans. W. McNeill & J. Ireland. Indianapolis: Indiana University Press.
Heidegger, M. (1994/2005). *Introduction to Phenomenological Research*. Trans. D.O. Dahlstrom. Indianapolis: Indiana University Press.
Heidegger, M. (1994/2018). *Heraclitus: The Inception of Occidental Thinking; Logic: Heraclitus's Doctrine of the* Logos. Trans. J.G. Assaiante & S. Montgomery Ewegen. London: Bloomsbury Academic.
Heidegger, M. (2000). Remembrance. In K. Hoeller (ed.). *Elucidations of Hölderlin's Poetry*. Amherst, New York: Humanity Books. pp.102–173.
Heidegger, M. (2009/2013). *The Event*. Trans. R. Rojcewicz. Indianapolis: Indiana University Press.
Heidegger, M. (2011). *Martin Heidegger: Basic Writings*. Ed. D. F. Krell. London: Routledge.
Heidegger, M. (2011). Letter on Humanism. In D.F. Krell (ed.). *Martin Heidegger: Basic Writings*. London: Routledge. pp.147–181.

Heidegger, M. (2011). On the Essence of Truth. In D.F. Krell (ed.). *Martin Heidegger: Basic Writings*. London: Routledge. pp.65–82.
Heidegger, M. (2012/2015). *The Beginning of Western Philosophy: Interpretation of Anaximander and Parmenides*. Trans. R. Rojcewicz. Indianapolis: Indiana University Press.
Huskinson, L. (2004). *Nietzsche and Jung: The Whole Self in the Union of Opposites*. Hove: Brunner-Routledge.
Kahn, C.H. (1987). *The Art and Thought of Heraclitus*. Cambridge: Cambridge University Press.
Keiling, T. (2020). Letting Things Be for Themselves: *Gelassenheit* as Enabled Thinking. In A.J. Wendland, C. Merwin & C. Hadjioannou (eds.). *Heidegger on Technology*. London: Routledge. pp.96–114.
Kierkegaard, S. (1849/2004). *The Sickness unto Death*. Trans. A. Hannay. London: Penguin Books.
King, M. (2009). *Heidegger and Happiness: Dwelling on Fitting and Being*. London: Continuum.
Laing, R.D. (1967). *The Politics of Experience and the Bird of Paradise*. Harmondsworth: Penguin.
Lewis, C.T. & Short, C. (1879). *A Latin Dictionary*. Oxford: Clarendon Press.
Lovitt, W. & Brundage, H. (1995). *Modern Technology in the Heideggerian Perspective Volume II*. Lewiston: The Edwin Mellen Press.
Lykou, S. (2025). *Therapy: The Basics*. London: Routledge.
Maltz, M. (1960). *Psycho-Cybernetics*. London: Souvenir Press.
Mayeroff, M. (1971). *On Caring*. New York: HarperPerennial.
McLeod, J. (2025). *An Introduction to Counselling and Psychotherapy: Research, Theory and Practice*. 7th Edition. London: Open University Press.
Nietzsche, F. (1886/1967). *The Birth of Tragedy and the Case of Wagner*. Trans. W. Kaufmann. New York: Vintage.
Nietzsche, F. (1886/1989). *Beyond Good and Evil*. Trans. W. Kaufmann. New York: Vintage.
Nietzsche, F. (1892/1978). *Thus Spoke Zarathustra: A Book for None and All*. Trans. W. Kaufmann. London: Penguin Books.
Petropoulos, G. (2021). Heidegger's Reading of Plato: On Truth and Ideas. *The Journal of the British Society for Phenomenology*. 52:2: 118–136.
Pickering, A. (2010). *The Cybernetic Brain*. Chicago: University of Chicago Press.
Reich, W.T. (1995). History of the Notion of Care. In W.T. Reich (ed.). *Encyclopedia of Bioethics*. New York: Simon & Schuster Macmillan. pp.319–331.
Reich, W.T. (ed.). (1995). *Encyclopedia of Bioethics*. New York: Simon & Schuster Macmillan.
Rogers, B.W. (2025). *Heidegger on What It Means to Dwell*. www.planksip.org
Spiegelberg, H. (1982). *The Phenomenological Movement: A Historical Introduction*. The Hague: Martinus Nijhoff.
Taylor, C. (1991). *The Ethics of Authenticity*. London: Harvard University Press.
Van den Berg, J.H. (1953/2021). The Conversation [Het Gesprek]. In M. van Manen & M. van Manen (trans.). *Classic Writings for a Phenomenology of Practice*. London: Routledge. pp.31–46.
Van Hooft, S. (1995). *Caring: An Essay in the Philosophy of Ethics*. Niwot: University Press of Colorado.
Van Lennep, D.J. (1969/1987). The Hotel Room. [De Hotelkamer]. In J.J. Kockelmans (ed.). *Phenomenological Psychology: The Dutch School*. Dordrecht: Kluwer. pp.209–215.
Van Manen, M. & van Manen, M. (2021). *Classic Writings for a Phenomenology of Practice*. London: Routledge.
Vilhauer, M. (2010). *Gadamer's Ethics of Play: Hermeneutics and the Other*. Plymouth: Lexington Books.
Wendland, A.J., Merwin, C. & Hadjioannou, C. (eds.). (2020). *Heidegger on Technology*. London: Routledge.

Wiener, N. (1948). *Cybernetics: Or Control and Communication in the Animal and the Machine*. Cambridge: MIT Press.

Wiercinski, A. (ed.). (2011). *Gadamer 's Hermeneutics and the Art of Conversation*. London: Transaction Publishers.

Wilberg, P. (2004). *The Therapist as Listener*. Eastbourne: New Gnosis Publications.

Winnicott, D. (2005). *Playing and Reality*. London: Routledge.

Withy, K. (2019). Finding Oneself, Called. In C. Hadjioannou (ed.). *Heidegger on Affect*. London: Palgrave Macmillan. pp.153–176.

Withy, K. (2021). We Are a Conversation. In C. Engelland (ed.). *Language and Phenomenology*. London: Routledge. pp.132–148.

Withy, K. (2022). *Heidegger On Being Self-Concealing*. Oxford: Oxford University Press.

Wrathall, M.A. (2011). *Heidegger and Unconcealment*. Cambridge: Cambridge University Press.

Wrathall, M.A. (2020). The Task of Thinking in a Technological Age. In A.J. Wendland, C. Merwin, & C. Hadjioannou (eds.). (2020). *Heidegger on Technology*. London: Routledge. pp.13–38.

Wrathall, M.A. (ed.) (2021). *The Cambridge Heidegger Lexicon*. Cambridge: Cambridge University Press.

Xuereb, A. (2025). From Bayt to Baita: The Poetics of Dwelling. *The Wednesday*. Issue 203. Oxford: The Wednesday Group. https://www.thewednesdayoxford.com/2025/06/04/the-wednesday-issue-no-203/

Index

For Product Safety Concerns and Information please contact our EU representative GPSR@taylorandfrancis.com
Taylor & Francis Verlag GmbH, Kaufingerstraße 24, 80331 München, Germany

www.ingramcontent.com/pod-product-compliance
Ingram Content Group UK Ltd.
Pitfield, Milton Keynes, MK11 3LW, UK
UKHW022022211026
476876UK00010B/494
* 9 7 8 1 0 4 1 0 7 0 7 5 7 *